T0354924

We were created in a vacuum
Until our freedom allows our ego
To infuse it.

It's great to know
We have that same freedom
To challenge our ego
To defuse it.

Thus - it is presumptuous
to say - there is a vacuum when
we are detached from
Religion.

First published in June 2004
by Bodensee Logistics as:
Arab Conspiracies Against Islam

2nd Edition: June 2005
Cover designed by: Red Czar

Print information available on the last page.

ISBN: 978-1-4120-6541-2 (sc)
ISBN: 978-1-4120-8156-6 (e)

Trafford rev. 12/04/2019

Trafford
PUBLISHING   www.trafford.com
North America & international
toll-free: 1 888 232 4444 (USA & Canada)
fax: 812 355 4082

MENTAL BONDAGE

In the name of God

A Research Book on Religion

Revised and Expanded Edition

AIDID SAFAR

Trafford Publishing
Suite 6E - 2333 Government Street,
Victoria - British Columbia V8T 4P4,
Canada
http://www.trafford.com

TABLE OF CONTENTS

PART NINE

PART TEN

PART ELEVEN

PART TWELVE

Preface

A lady physician from Canada wrote to me and said, "*If we aim to understand our creator we are bound to commit error of personification*". I cannot agree with her more. And, in addition - '*the error is aggravated when we try to find the answer from organised religion*'.

With all that humans have been taught by their religions - by their priests and their rabbis and their mullahs and their monks - how is it that, in the collective experience of a huge portion of humanity, it has not done any good?

Collectively, humans - in spite of their religious beliefs, are unceasingly and increasingly violent with their own kind. They did very little in addressing oppression, prejudice, gender discrimination, child abuse, denying civil rights, exploitation, and injustice in their surroundings. Ignoring these sufferings is as much a form of violence as inducing it.

We need to pay attention to the fact that our aspiration for an orderly way of life is dying. We need to notice what the world has gone through, and what it has tried to give us, and we need to wake up to see what we, our parents and our neighbours are doing, collectively and individually.

How much more will mankind allow themselves to endure before they begin looking for the underlying reason that the world is the way it is? Those who say that they believe God is powerful enough to be the cure for the world's ill, have themselves failed to see that an inaccurate belief could be more powerful to be the real cause.

Let me get to the heart of the matter forthrightly devoid of rhetoric. The majority of people on earth regardless of their standing are slaves to earthly gods in the name of religion – consciously or not.

For example, people who enslave their mind who thought they knew what God wants called themselves the Chosen People hanged men and women in town squares, and burned others on the stake, holding up the Good Book and declaring them witches. They are the same people who passed laws making it illegal for humans of differing races to marry.

Approximately 1.5 billion people have shackled their mind to a bigoted idea that God needs their worship, animal sacrifice, ritual prayer, fasting, and homage to a rock hunk that symbolises God's Glory. Their earthly gods told armies of Muslims to send marauders far and wide to kill and conquer every land and culture and bring it under the Nation of Islam.

Almost two billion people are in bondage to the idea that suffering is to be used by them to better themselves, and to purify their souls. One whole religion is built upon this belief, asserting that all beings have been saved by the suffering of one being, who died for the sins of the rest.

After Abraham, a man called Moses committed himself to the Ten Commandments, a providence that could lead to an orderly way of life assuring *peacefulness*. Without his knowledge, his enemies wrote the Talmud, the Jews see as God's revelation. It became the tenets of Judaism, a religion unknown to him.

Jesus went to the same community calling them to restore the original law - and for that - the Talmudic rabbis decreed that he was guilty of blasphemy and ordered him to be crucified. A simple question comes to mind. Did he die because he sinned against the rabbis - or *for* the sins of the rest? The answer traumatises every dogmatic mind - including that of United States President. Nevertheless, a new religion was created after him.

Like Moses, Jesus never knew there would be a religion called 'Christianity'.

Out of mercy the Creator sanctioned the same providence to an Arab confirming previous scriptures, but his own people created a new religion and packed it with Arab myth and tribal cults. Like Moses and Jesus, Muhammad had no idea about any *religion* called Islam. This kind of news is obnoxious to the bigoted minds, including that of armed forces or police generals, Supreme Court judges, or scientists. Unfortunately, that is the truth.

Organised religion creates a system of one direction of power to control. Pharaoh enslaved people with religion. Today, Kings and Queens, Presidents and Prime Ministers and their officials knowingly or unknowingly are slaves of Pharaohs in different garbs of rabbis, priests, monks, and mullahs. Thus, Pharaoh's artifice is here to reign - unless we start to think!

So far, no organised religion has provided mankind with effective guidance in how to live as one nation, in peace and harmony. They have created dissent, disorder, and their doctrines are taking us from the light of life to the deepest abyss. People now live in mass hypnotism and mental bondage. Have we lost the courage to take the challenge to unload the burdens and remove the chains that binds us?

This book presents a comprehensive study of one of the three main religions from its original scriptural text. It exposes the manner of how the enemies of a prophet distorted the **'words'** to create a religion of *'Islam'* as we know and see it today. Like Judaism and Christianity, the religionists have invented the Arab religion. Obviously, this research shocks the Muslims around the world, yet it sovereigns the bondage of the critical minds among them – it is a revelation to humanity.

INTRODUCTION

The confrontation between logic and 'faith' has always provided man with food for thought.

Mental Bondage is the result of years of deep reflection about *Islam,*[1] and is written with the primary objective of understanding the reason for the failure of the Muslims and the widespread hostility among non-Muslims – including secular Westerners, Hindus and Jews – against *Islam.*

I have come to realise – and will prove by reference to the Qur'an itself – that such prejudice is not misplaced. It might surprise the reader that those who claim to be the 'Muslims' are professing what is, in fact, an invented Arab religion.[2] Perhaps they deserve the incessant suffering and humiliation, which they are subjected to, until and unless they return to the one true God. By presenting a more accurate picture of real *Islam*, this book exposes a great falsehood and reveals a greater truth - both of which may otherwise have remained hidden.

Islam, as we know and see it today, is not at all what is envisioned in the Qur'an. Whatever the reader's personal beliefs, he will find cited in this work many interesting facts that are commonly and flagrantly overlooked with regard to

---

[1] The word *Islam* is derived from the Arabic root *SLM* or *Salam* that means *'peace'*. *Aslama* means peaceful, *Muslim* means the one *at peace* and *Islam* means *'peacefulness'*. Being a Muslim does not make a person a true believer or mu'min - until faith enters his heart (by the will of God) 49:14.

[2] The term *Arab religion* is used throughout this book because the non-Arab 'Muslims' are forced to use Arabic terms in almost everything. Praising, magnifying and glorifying God must be done in Arabic. Even the greeting *Peace be upon you* must be uttered in Arabic. The Arabs insist all 'Muslims' – irrespective of their racial origin and language – follow the supposed personal habits of an Arab prophet in all things, including the way he dressed, stood, slept, ate and cared for his teeth, etc.

the subject of *Islam*. It is hoped that this book will better equip the reader to weigh the evidence of what is and is not *Islam* on the basis of the text of the Qur'an itself, free from any superstitious or religious bias.

What we find when we undertake such a task is that the Arabs are shown on the basis of the Qur'an itself to be guilty of conspiring against God and His messenger and of corrupting the *deen* (or the orderly way of life), and of reducing it to a ritualised pagan 'religion'. The result has been presented as 'the religion of *Islam*' and is, unfortunately, perceived as such throughout the world at present.

In a nutshell, the Qur'an is not about religion. *Islam* is not a religion in the ordinary sense of that word. *Islam* means *'peacefulness or bliss'* as a way of life *(deen)* sanctioned by the one God. The thesis that is established by this study is so detailed and far-reaching that its publication is for the benefit of those seeking to discover true *Islam*.

As a Muslim from birth, I was told from childhood that the Qur'an is the supreme source and guidance for my religious belief. In spite of that conviction, I was only taught to recite the Qur'an in Arabic without any instruction on the significance and meaning of the Book. At the age of ten I was the pride of my family since I could recite the Qur'an in Arabic fluently. There was a slight hitch however. I did not understand what I was reciting. It seemed to me then that reading the Qur'an was simply another religious ritual, akin to the singing of hymns without understanding.

I first examined the Qur'an seriously upon my return from a pilgrimage to Mecca in 1980. I supposed that I had fulfilled my obligation as a Muslim. However, upon study and reflection of the Qur'an, it dawned on me that I had not fulfilled anything ordained by God by my presence in Mecca. Moreover, neither has anyone else[3], as will become clear as we proceed.

Before I began this study, I asked myself some fundamental questions:

- Is it true that God has chosen to reside in a house built by humans on the Arab soil?

- Does He need a house to live in? And, if not, why do they call it God's house? Or is that expression merely a figure of speech?

- Why do I have to bow and prostrate to an empty square structure built from mountain rock, then circumambulate it and kiss a black stone embedded therein?

- Why do I have to pray ritually five times a day facing a rock structure even if I live thousands of miles away?

Questions like these perplexed me and prompted a study of the circumstances surrounding their origin and I looked for the answer within the Qur'anic texts in the hope of finding an explanation for what I had done in Mecca, and also as to why I had visited a grave in Medina.[4]

At the time, I knew from translations of the Qur'an that the Book contained passages about the lives of Noah, Abraham and his children Isaac and Ishmael, and Jacob and

---

[3] [3] The journey of a Muslim to Mecca within the Arab religion fulfils one of the five requirements touted by that religion as requisite for entry into Heaven.

[4] As readers acquainted with the rituals and obligations as propagated by the religion of '*Islam*' will appreciate, the actions outlined here are all part of what Muslims are taught they must do as part of their commitment to God.

his children Joseph and his brothers. I knew, too, that it gave details about David and his son Solomon, Zechariah and his son John, Moses and his brother Aaron, and Jesus and his mother Mary. However, very little information is to be found about Muhammad, the only gentile[5] prophet to received revelation. I looked earnestly inside the Qur'an for a detailed life history of the man idolised by millions, but there was nothing to be found but verses depicting his frustrations and disappointments during his tenure as a prophet of God. The picture which emerges is that of a prophet – like the prophets before him – who failed in his mission to convince the people about God's Scripture. This being the case, it comes as no surprise to find that in the Hereafter:

> The Messenger will say, my Lord, my people have deserted this Qur'an. (25:30)

Before I studied the passages of the Qur'an in the original Arabic text I placed much reliance upon translations all of which echoed the interpretations of the old scholars. I soon realised to my dismay that there were numerous discrepancies and contradictory statements in many of the interpretations and translations. The one that disturbed me most is the following illogical rendition of 2:125. A typical rendering of this passage reads:

> We then designated the house as a focal point for the people and a sacred sanctuary. You shall use the station of Abraham as a place of prayer. We directed Abraham and Ishmael to sanctify My house for

---

[5] Gentile or *ummy* – a person, race or people who had no prior knowledge of God's scripture (ref. Q 2:78) and they cannot be illiterate. Jews consider people as Gentiles because they were not chosen to receive the scripture.

those who encircle it, retreat in it, and bow and prostrate to it. (2:125)

All the 'traditional' scholars consistently maintain that God owns a house and that people must worship Him through this particular house. It struck me that something was amiss, but it was not until I had learnt to understand the Arabic and read the original text that I realised the precise meaning of certain verses in the Book and my suspicions were confirmed.

My basis for understanding and approaching the Qur'an is simple. The Qur'an places emphasise on words (*kalimaat*); the Qur'an is a reliable text and we are to approach it in seriousness for answers:

- God taught Adam His words (see 2:37)

- Abraham was tested with God's words (see 2:124)

- God revealed the message to Moses with His words (see 7:144)

- The Jews perverted the meaning of God's words (see 5:13)

- John the son of Zechariah confirms God's scripture by words (see 3:39)

- Mary upheld God's words and His scripture (see 66:12)

- Jesus the son of Mary was confirmed a messenger and he was God's words (see 4:171)

- Muhammad believed in God and His words (see 7:158)

- No man can change God's words (see 6:115 & 18:27)

- God wanted to establish the truth with His words (see 8:7 and 10:82)

- God is able to erase any falsehood and re-establish the truth with His words (see 42:24)

- The Qur'an was written by the hands of those who were assigned. They were honourable and righteous (see 80:15-16)

- God says He preserves His book (see 15:9)

- The Qur'an is a sign from God (see 29:51)

If we want to study the Book we have to focus on the words the way they are spelt and pronounced. In 7:204 it says when the Qur'an is recited we are to listen to it carefully. (*Reference for the above verses is annexed in this chapter*)

We are called upon to regard the Qur'an with care and to make sense of it. I have discovered that certain key words have had their meanings twisted. This perversion has the following catastrophic consequences:

- It has a huge impact on how people regard their transactions in this life with their Creator

- It puts a huge amount of power in the hands of the priests and scholars

- It reduces many peoples' opportunity to respond to their Lord by trivialising their perceptions in terms of tribal and pagan regalia

Non-Muslims judge the Qur'an by the benchmark of the (unacceptable) behaviour resulting from the so-called Muslim world's misunderstanding of these terms

This work seeks to reclaim the territory lost on the basis of the Book and its elucidation of its own terms, free from those ascribed to it by a ruling class of religion-mongers. There is nothing wrong with God's words. Rather, there has been a deliberate manipulation of the meaning of His words by men, and this has given rise to wildly inaccurate notions about God.

Moreover, the same discrepancies, contradictory statements and illogical interpretations of passages of the Qur'an have found their way into all the translations of the Qur'an. I could not find even a hint of the important matters I had uncovered in any one of the many translations available. For instance, the subject of wildlife conservation – which is discussed in a later chapter – was distorted in all cases to become pagan rituals. I was momentarily beset with doubt. Might I not be mistaken in my understanding? Had I not perhaps merely contrived a fanciful interpretation rather than uncovering, as I thought, a clear founding principle, provable on the basis of the meaning of the Arabic text? How could it be that I was right and the 'authorities' in the venerable seats of learning were wrong?

Nevertheless, I ploughed on. But it was only after in-depth study involving extensive cross-reference of the many verses on each subject spread throughout the Qur'an that I became convinced of the correctness of my suspicions. I observed the incompatibility of statements in the Qur'an and the myths and mysteries prevailing in the Arab religion – a cultic entity that systematically negates the idea of God. I assembled a list of these erroneous ideas and the contrary proofs from the Qur'an. In the end, I had to acknowledge the force of the evidence before me. Surprising as it will doubtless be to many, the Qur'an completely denounces religion, rituals, worship, animal sacrifices, rites, pilgrimages and the like, categorising such practices as idol-worship. This I was able to establish beyond any doubt.

Translators are basically men of letters. More often than not, they mistranslate or ignore the elementary purpose of the message when translating the Qur'an. Perhaps due to their personal religious convictions (prescribed for them by the aforementioned religious elite) the message is lost, resulting in a misconstrued, illogical and contradictory text. The truth is, in order to translate the Qur'an correctly one must first comprehend what one is reading. In fact, in order to approach it at all profitably, one must be clear of preconceived notions. We should come as critical explorers to discover its meaning, not as religious zealots to shore up our tribal and historical inclinations.

As has been indicated, popular translators are greatly influenced by the notes provided by earlier clerics and commentators whose personal views are often never verified or researched against the measure of the Qur'anic text. With the passage of time, such commentators have come to be regarded as authorities while – it must be stressed – they never committed themselves to a stringent study of their subject on Qur'anic terms and were thus unable, for example, to recognise the passages pointing to the seriousness of idolatry written in the Qur'an. They were more concerned with reading the text in terms that supported their own preference for an idolatrous Arab religion – a religion which, in fact, though not in name – they professed, and they misconstrued the Qur'an accordingly. The translators, then, make every possible effort to render the contents of the Qur'an via the legacy of such commentators and 'authorities'.

Muslims who rely on these 'translations' of the Qur'an (simply because they are incapable of understanding the Arabic language) fail to realise the essence of the Book's substance: that the Qur'an upholds individual rights and liberties, tolerance and freedom. It includes information about human relations, warnings against racial polarisation, the promise of happiness in this life and the Hereafter, how to achieve global peace, the need for compassion towards each other, and regulations for people's social orderliness. Its plan is applicable in any cultural setting and has nothing to do with 'religion' whatsoever.

Translators, as a rule, do not attend to specific subjects or compare verses with other related verses in the Qur'an – a process that would have provided the key to understanding the words and expressions in the Qur'an. As a result, they mistranslate both whole passages and the key concepts behind individual words. This result in translations riddled with ambiguity, inaccuracy and inconsistency, which are spoiled, on occasion, with completely nonsensical statements.

On starting this research some sixteen years ago, I was unable to draw on previous works about the true *deen* – or way of life – for there were none. All I could refer to was the few translations dealing with themes in the Qur'an of interest to 'men of religion'. There was no overall study of the Qur'an on the basis of the Qur'an alone.

Research of the type presented in this book requires free and critical thinking. It is not easy for those who are so-called scholars of 'religion' to appreciate such knowledge because they are rigidly biased toward their religious convictions. Indeed, the points raised in this study present a direct threat to the two largest sects of the 'Arab religion' – the Sunnis and the Shiite – fettered as they are by the Arabian culture and tribal laws, which essentially make up their religions. Only those with critical and open minds who are acquainted with (and able to engage with) the Arabic text in its literal form will truly appreciate this study. However, this book is written in an easy style, and it is hoped that the absence of specialised knowledge pertaining to the Qur'an or Arabic among some readers will not hinder from following the arguments outlined here.

My method has been to read critically each and every passage in the Scripture containing keywords on any one subject. In the majority of cases such verses are scattered throughout the Book. The Qur'an is indeed a concurrence of reflections on a wide variety of subjects referred to one after the other and taken up again in other places, often repeatedly. The entries on a precise theme like *idol-worship* or *way of life* must, therefore, be discerned and collated from throughout the Book and brought together under a single heading. As may be appreciated, many hours are spent tracking down verses. Thematic indexes already provided by translators, Arabic lexicons, and even the Concordia are incomplete or inaccurate in many instances after generations of 'religious' influence by corrupt scholarship as shall be demonstrated.

After a critical study of the Arabic text I was struck by the disparity between my religious practices and what I had been told as a child: that is, that the Qur'an was the supreme source of my guidance and belief. I was also struck by how so many words were translated incorrectly and often ludicrously from the Arabic text, and in the most inconsistent manner. According to the translators, a word would mean one thing in one place and yet mean something entirely different elsewhere in the Book, and all this despite tireless scrutiny of generations of 'scholars'. It is undeniable: contradictions, improbabilities and incompatibilities in the translated versions abound. When taken as a whole, one is at a loss as to why or how the scholars, commentators and translators pretend to be unaware of – or else try to camouflage – these fallacies.

The majority of the non-Arabs are unaware of the distortion in the translations of the Qur'an. This ignorance exerts an extremely damaging effect on their belief in God. Even if there are a few who are able to discern such discrepancies, the vast majority of non-Arabs never take an intellectual stand against these illogical interpretations and commentaries.

I was motivated to undertake this critical study in the light of the following verse:

> O mankind, you shall serve your Lord who created you and those people before you that you might be observant. He is the one who made the earth habitable for you. He is the one who constructed the sky. He sends down water from the sky to produce fruits for your sustenance. Therefore, you are not to set up any idol next to God when you understand. (2:21-22)

I realised the message in the Book was addressed to all mankind irrespective of racial origin or sectarian faith. It emphasises that people should be subservient to the one Master who created them. They should not set up any kind of idol next to the One God. However, men of all religions are teaching precisely the opposite. They either teach people to idolise God's servants or to devote themselves to something tangible. It came as a profound shock to me when, having read a few more chapters of the Qur'an, I discovered clear-cut statements like such as:

> If you follow the majority of the people on earth, they will divert you from the path of God. They only follow conjecture, and they only guess. (6:116)

> He has prescribed for you the same way of life enjoined upon Noah, and what is revealed herein, and what was decreed for Abraham, Moses and Jesus. You shall uphold the one way of life and not be divided. It is simply too difficult for the idol-worshippers to accept what you advocate. God is the one who brings towards Him whomever He wills. He guides towards Himself those who return. (42:13)

In the first, simple statement, God warns us not to follow the majority - and that was really an eye opener to anyone. The second verse says there is one God and He is common to all mankind and that all people need to be united in serving the one unseen God Who revealed the Scripture to the prophets and messengers.

He is the only one who can bring us and guide us towards Himself. The bearers of the message can not do so. Simply put, the message is more important than the messengers. There is no need for any prophets or messengers once they have delivered the message. Their duty is not to guide but to call the people to God. 42:13 also tells us in no uncertain terms that those who idolise humans or icons are considered idol-worshippers and that they will not respond to such a call.

How is it then that there are so many religions each claiming to profess and practice the right way to God? The Qur'an gives the answer to this predicament:

> You shall all submit to God, observe Him, and uphold your commitments[6] and never fall into idol-worship; and do not be among those who change the way of life into '**religion**', each sectarian is happy with what they have. (30:31-32)

> Follow those who do not ask from you any wage, they are guided. (36:21)

Religion is a false creation of men. Religion's devotees are happy with what they practice. There are so many religions today but only one Creator. The fact is these religious institutions survive through various forms of income. The Qur'an is against such a system.

Now to some examples:

- Those who specialise in the Arab religion will tell you that one of the 'pillars'[7] of their faith is to visit and to worship a rock structure in Mecca, walk around it a number of times and then kiss a black stone embedded at one corner of this rock structure. Then they are to go to another location and throw some stones (and

---

[6] Collins Co-build Dictionary defines *commitment* as 'a strong belief in an idea or system, especially when it is shown by your action and behaviour. If you commit yourself to a course of action you decide that you will do it and you let people know about your decision'. In the context of the Qur'an, man is required to uphold his commitments all the time when serving his Lord. Thus, it is a way of life. He serves God by disciplining himself to observe the *sanctions* within God's system or the *bayt al-muHarami* as espoused by Abraham. This is discussed in detail below.

[7] The 'religion' of so-called *Islam* based on hearsay and extra-Qur'anic sources claims are five 'pillars' of faith, that is, five things a person must do to be sure of obtaining good in the next life.

sometimes slippers) at some stone pillars whilst imagining these stones represent the Devil. At the same time, one must also believe the 'reverse osmosis'[8] water supplied in Mecca to be very holy.

- Specialists in another religion who technically subscribe to the Gospel as found in the Bible will tell you that the pillar of their faith is to believe that the Supreme God has begotten a son who ate food with the people; they also believe that a high priest from the synagogue had the power to issue a decree ordering the crucifixion of God's son.

- The same religious specialists (who supposedly subscribed to the Torah) accused God's prophet of blasphemy and ordered his crucifixion. Their counterparts today will tell you that a righteous man wears a skullcap and does not cut the hair at the sides of the head or trim the edges of his beard.

These 'specialists' all get paid handsomely for promoting such ridiculous ideologies – and more than half of the world's population is paying money to these jesters in the form of 'Zakaat'[9] and various other systems of tithes. The Qur'an says, *'Follow those who do not ask from you any wage'*.

The Qur'an constantly reminds people to use their common sense. People know it is wrong to defy reason, but they still do not make the effort needed to understand:

---

[8] The Muslims believe the water supplied at the mosque is miraculously supplied by God and they call it zam-zam water. This kind of absurdity is not found in the Qur'an. The Meccan Arabs will not drink this water even during an emergency. They drink only the imported mineral water.

[9] This word will be dealt with later.

We have assigned to Hell multitudes of *jinn* and humans, those who have hearts that do not understand, eyes that do not see and ears that do not hear. They are like animals, No! They are worse than animals, but they are not aware. (7:179)

In my study, I have based my observation on facts from the Qur'an alone and have presented the logical deductions necessary to be drawn from them. If I had not carried out this research, sooner or later, others would have performed it in my place.

The study represents an innovation in the method of examination of revelation, especially as far as non-Muslim readers are concerned. In the eyes of many 'Muslims', a critical study of the Text does not immediately suggest the need to draw lessons from it for a meaningful way of life meant for all human races. As far as they are concerned, the Qur'an deals purely with 'religion'. This approach is totally contrary to the facts for the Qur'an opposes 'religion', and until the Muslims grasp this essential point they will continue to be ignorant of the Book they claim to follow.

Some of the readers of this study may be accustomed to a less direct style. They may even find the language in some parts overly blunt. This book is meant to be read by everyone irrespective of their religious background. Certainly there are sincere and intelligent Muslims all over the world – or perhaps even among the Arabs themselves - who are searching for the truth and the right *deen*. I wish to appeal to them not to read to contradict and refute, nor to believe and take it for granted, but to weigh and consider.

Most importantly I do not wish to cause offence to any reader and I would be grateful if this aspect of my delivery were regarded as deriving purely from the strength of my conviction.

To conclude this introduction, I must state that Aidid Safar is a pseudonym or *nom de plume*. The Arab religion today is insanity itself riddled with an absence of logic, tolerance or even basic knowledge of the Book everyone claims to believe. From Morocco to the Philippines, over one billion people have allowed themselves to be fooled to participate in this insanity.

People have had death sentences pronounced against them for saying much less than what I am saying in this book. In many so-called Muslim countries, the authorship of such a book would mean persecution, prosecution, imprisonment and maybe even death at the hands of enthusiastically insane followers of the Arab religion. Clearly, a sensible person must take precautions.

What is important here is the message, not who is saying it. Killing the message-bearer is a trait to which the history books attest. On the other hand, the bearers of messages have also been turned into something they were not on occasion by misguided followers – even idolised. I wish to preclude the possibility of either of these fates. Thus, I shall remain – with the reader's kind indulgence – simply Aidid Safar.

It is my sincere wish that interested persons read this book in the spirit in which it is written. In addition, I would also like to express my sincere thanks to those who have given me the moral support to undertake this work. I owe a debt of gratitude to my friends, associates and family who gave me the encouragement to undertake the writing of such a book. Please accept my greetings of peace. Thank you.

ANNEX

The context of the verses with regard to the 'Words':-

- God taught Adam His words. (2:37)

But the evil character duped him out of it, causing his banishment therefrom. We said, "Get out as enemies to each other - and on earth will be your temporary habitation and sustenance". Then Adam received from his Lord '**Words**', and then He liberated him. He is the one who liberates, and the merciful. And then We said, "Go away therefrom, all of you, and when guidance comes to you from Me, those who follow My guidance have nothing to fear, nor will they grieve. As for those who disbelieve and reject our revelations, they have deserved the fire; they will abide therein forever". (2:36-39)

- Abraham was tested with God's words. (2:124)

When Abraham was put to the test by His Lord **through 'Words**', he carried them out. God then said, "I am appointing you as the front for the people". He answered, "Will this include my descendants"? God said, "My promise does not include the wrongdoers". (2:124). And then We pointed to him the system as providence for mankind and as the security. Thus, you shall use the position of Abraham who was committed. We nominated Abraham and Ishmael to cleanse My system for throngs of people, and those who are devoted, and those who humbly submit". (2:125)

- God revealed the message to Moses with His words. (7:144)

God said, "O Moses, I have chosen you above the rest of mankind with **My message and 'My Words**'". Thus, take what I have bestowed upon you and be appreciative. And we wrote for him on the tablets all kinds of enlightenments, and detailed everything. "You shall firmly uphold these, and tell your people to observe the good lessons therein. I will point out for you the destiny of the wrongdoers". "And then, I will divert from My revelations those who commit pride on earth - without justification. Thus, even if they see all kinds of signs, they will not believe them. And when they see the path of guidance they will refuse to accept it as their path, and when they see the path of evil they will endure it as their path. That is because they have rejected our revelations and disregarded them. (7:144-146)

- The Jews perverted the meaning of God's words. (5:13)

God has taken a covenant with the Children of Israel, and We appointed for them twelve patriarchs; God said, "I will be with you for as long as you observe your commitments and continue to keep it pure (*Aqimus-Solaa-tawa-a-tuz-Zakaa*"). And, believe in My messengers and support them, and loan to God your virtuousness. I will forgive your mistakes, and admit you into the bliss with flowing streams. Anyone who disbelieves after this, has indeed sidetracked from the straight path. Because they violated their covenant, we put a curse on them, and we hardened their hearts. Then, **they distorted the 'Words'** given to them, and disregarded part thereof. You will always see prejudices from them, except from few. You shall forgive and forget about them - for God loves the compassionate. (5:12-13)

- John the son of Zechariah confirms God's scripture by words. (3:39 & 19:12)

Zachariah then prayed to his Lord, saying, "My Lord, please grant me righteous descendants. You are the hearer of all prayers". Thus, the energy responded while he was upholding his commitment in coercion, "Surely God gives you good news with John who is truthful with **'God's words'** and he is honourable and chaste. And he is a prophet from among the righteous". (3:38-39). He went out over to his folks from the duress thus he signalled them that they glorify day and night. O John, **uphold the scripture** firmly. And we endowed him the love and we purified him, and he was observant. And he honoured his parents, and he was not arrogant or rebellious. And peace be upon him on the day he was born, and the day he was dead, and the day he is resurrected. (19:11-15)

- Mary upheld God's words and His scripture. (66:12)

God brings forth for those who disbelieve the example of the wife of Noah and the wife of Lot. They were two righteous servants from those who served us, but their wives betrayed them. Consequently, they could not protect their wives from God. The wives were told; "Enter the sufferings along with others". And God cites for those who believe - the example of the wife of Pharaoh who said, "My Lord, establish for me by you, a system in the bliss and save me from Pharaoh and from his works and save me from the unjust people". And Mary, the daughter of Imran; she guarded her chastity. Thus we blew into her from our soul and she was truthful with the '**Words' of her Lord and His scripture**. And she was obedient. (66:12)

- Jesus the son of Mary was confirmed a messenger and he was God's words. (4:171)

O people of the scriptures, do not transgress the limits of your way of life, and do not say about God other than the truth. The Messiah, Jesus the son of Mary is no more than **a messenger of God and 'His Words' - that He blew unto Mary and the soul from Him**. Thus you shall believe in God and His messengers, and never say "Trinity". You shall refrain for your own good. God is only One God, much too glorious to have a son. To Him belongs everything in the heavens and the earth, and sufficient is God as your only guardian". (4:171)

- Muhammad believed in God and His words (see 7:158)

Say, "O people, I am a messenger of God to all of you, the one who rules the skies and the earth. There is no god except Him. He grants life and death". Thus, you shall believe in God and His messenger, the gentile prophet, who **believe in God and 'His Words'**. And follow him, that you may be guided. (7:158)

- No man can change God's words. (6:115 & 18:27)

The word of your Lord is complete in truth and justice. **Nothing can abrogate 'His Words'**. He is hearer, the knower (6:115). You shall recite what is revealed to you from your Lord; **nothing can abrogate 'His Words'**, and you shall not find any other source besides it. (18:27)

- God wanted to establish the truth with His words.

And God promises one of the two groups that He will invigorate you when you do not have the strength to face each other. And God wishes that truthfulness to be the truth - with '**His Words**', and it will neutralize all those who do not believe. (8:7). God supports the truth with '**His Words**', no matter how averse the guilty might be. (10:82)

31

- God is able to erase any falsehood and re-establish the truth with His words (see 42:24)

If they claim that you fabricated some lies and attributed them to God, then God is able to seal your heart, erase any falsehood, and **re-establish the truth with 'His Words'**. He is fully aware of the innermost intentions. (42:24)

- The Qur'an was written by the hands of those who were assigned. They were honourable and righteous.

It (the Qur'an) is recorded in an honourable scripture, exalted and unadulterated - written by the assigned hands who are honourable and virtuous. (80:13-16)

- God says He preserves His book.

Surely it is we who sent down the reminder, and surely, we will preserve it. (15:9)

- The Qur'an is a sign from God (see 29:51)

They said, "How come no signs were sent down to him from His Lord"? Say, "The signs come only from God, and I am no more than a warner". Is it not enough for the signs that we sent down upon you the scripture which is being recited over them? Indeed it is a mercy and a message for those who believe. (29:50-51)

- If we want to study the Book we have to focus on the words the way they are spelt and pronounced. In 7:204 it says when the Qur'an is recited we are to listen to it carefully.

And when the Quran is recited thus, listen to it carefully and reflect so that you may attain mercy. (7:204)

PART ONE

Misconceptions

Islam is one of the most abused and misunderstood words today. *Islam* effectively means ___peacefulness___ - accomplished through the observation of order or an orderly way of life, (which is the *deen*) from the providence in our Creator's system. This, however, is not the image called to mind when one hears the word *Islam*. True *Islam* is intended to be a life of blissfulness without religions, myths, superstitions, or 'holiness'. The religionists, however, have systematically destroyed this ideal, not by demolishing it, but by altering its form so that it is no longer manifested as its Designer intended. The introduction of the Arab religion misleads people, stunts their potential growth, and results in disadvantaged and dysfunctional societies. It propagates a way of life or a *deen* featuring violence, terrorism, extremism, idolatry, worship, rituals, animal sacrifice, pilgrimage rites, oppressive tribal laws, a caste system, exploitation, chauvinism, decadence, poverty and hermitism. This, they claim, is what God had decreed. This is provably contrary to the institution of *peacefulness* described in the Qur'an.

This book discusses the idol worshipping Arab religion. I will demonstrate that the current state of affairs is not at all what is envisioned in the *Islam* revealed to the Last Prophet. According to the Qur'an, a person can enjoy a blissful life without having to profess a religion. The evidence from the Book states that the enemies of every prophet will invent religions to divert mankind from the path of God. As shocking as it may be, the religionists have proven to the world that they are truly the enemies of the Last Prophet by virtue of the fact that they have replaced the *'peace'* with a *'sadistic'* idol-worshipping religion.

Before going on to support this claim, it is as well to define the terms within which this study operates. They are:

- The Qur'an (which translates as 'the Reading') is the word of God

- The Qur'an is the default document of authority for the Muslim people

- The contents of the Qur'an are true, without contradiction, precise and perfectly written

- The Qur'an easily exposes the distortions and anomalies that men perpetuate

Before we proceed let me explain briefly why I have chosen to address the subject of idol-worship. According to the Qur'an, God forgives all sins to whomever He will except that of idol-worship. A person's good deeds can be nullified if he or she falls into idol-worship knowingly or unknowingly.

> It has been revealed to you and those before you, that if you fall into idol-worship, all your deeds will be nullified and you will be a loser. Therefore, you shall serve God alone and be thankful. (39:65-66)

> God never forgives the idolisation of anything besides Him, and He forgives all lesser offences for whomever He wills. Anyone, who sets up any idol besides God, has forged a gross blasphemy. (4:48)

Moses for example killed a man during his younger days. God, however, chose him to become a prophet and forgave him the crime he committed as soon as he turned to serve the supreme God alone. The Qur'an gives full details about the history of Moses:

> "O Moses, I am your Lord, so take off your shoes. You are in the sacred valley of *Tuwa*, and I have chosen you, so listen to what is revealed. I am the One God, there is no god except Me. You shall serve Me and observe your commitments to remember Me" (20:11-14)

> "O Moses, this is I, God, the Almighty, the Judge. Throw down your staff." When he saw it move like a demon, he turned around and ran. "O Moses, do not be afraid, My messengers have nothing to fear." (27:9-10)

> "Now, put your hand in your pocket, it will come out white, without blemish. Gather your confidence, for these are only two of the proofs you will take from your Lord to Pharaoh and his elders. They are unjust people." (28:32)

> Moses said, "Lord, I killed one of them, and I fear lest they kill me." (28:33)

> God said, "Even to those who commit evil, but later substitute righteousness in place of evil, I am forgiving." (27:11)

Human nature is weak. We make many mistakes and transgress the limits of a normal life and thereby wrong our souls. The Qur'an on the other hand, gives an assurance that whatever wrongdoings a person commits can be converted into credit once he or she decides to lead a righteous life. Such a decision does not require a person to profess a religion.

As for those who repent, believe, and work
righteousness, **God will change their sins into
credits**, God is forgiving and merciful. Whoever
repents and works righteousness, **God redeems him
by a complete redemption**. (25:70-71)

That is the assurance from God Himself in the Qur'an.
We don't have to be religious to repent or to believe in the
One God. Similarly, we don't have to profess a religion to
do good deeds.

The Qur'an (or the Reading)

The first distortion is the religionist's contention that it
is *not possible* to translate the Qur'an into any other
language because the attempt will change the essence of its
meaning.

This is patently untrue, and is the first conspiracy
hatched by the religionists to prevent the people of the
world from understanding the word of God in their own
languages. It also has the effect of making the Arab
religionists the *de facto* keepers of the faith since all matters
related to the Arabic language have to be referred to them.
The inevitable result of this is that whatever they claim to
be the correct interpretation has to be accepted as God's
truth. The net effect of this is the gradual and insidious
replacement of God's *deen* with practices of the invented
Arab religion.

It is common knowledge that non-Arab Muslims
around the globe daily recite five ritual prayers in Arabic. It
is one of the idiosyncratic requirements of their Arab
religion – a requirement that is not to be found in the
Qur'an. The English, French, German, Russian, Japanese,
Chinese, African and other non-Arab speaking communities

are told that they must ritually pray to an Arab god specifically in the Arabic language. This presupposes that God cannot understand any other language, which by itself defies logic.

The religionists deliberately erected a language barrier to exert their influence over their religion and, by extension, over the people who practice the Arab religion. As a result, they created the Arab and Muslim culture, as we know it today. They prevent the faithful from serving the Lord of the Universe by systematically isolating them from understanding the Qur'an. Eventually, all translations of the Qur'an have to undergo their censorship before they can be circulated as legitimate translations.

This book hopes to systematically explore and destroy all these illogical Arabic illusions. We will refer to the Qur'an, armed with a healthy dose of common sense and logic. This means that anyone and everyone – Arab and non-Arab alike – can check and verify the arguments presented. The Qur'an can withstand any scrutiny or criticism. It is truly God's revealed word.

The followers of the invented Arab religion who do not use their common sense to discover the truth, or to question their priests, and who unashamedly call themselves 'Muslims' are the worst communities on the face of the earth today. God has condemned and humiliated them for their blind subservience to their obtuse religious masters. Their conspiracy is against the objective of the Lord of the Universe, the Creator of the seven heavens and the earth. It was through His mercy that He revealed His will to Abraham, Ishmael, Isaac, Jacob, Moses, Jesus and the other prophets. Each of them, obviously, received the revelations in his own language and, to date, mankind has never been instructed to serve God in only one particular language. The true objective of revelation has always been to make life simple for everyone so that they could all *serve* Him.

Serve God Alone

The message from God to all His prophets is consistent. It is simple and straightforward. It is simply a sanction of universal values listing the deeds to be observed by all. In simple terms, it is a master plan for a productive life.

Let us not forget that it is the Devil's purpose and nature to interfere. God has, time and again, reminded His servants *not to serve* him who imposes false limits beyond God's own sanctions[10]. God's revelation is all about this concept – nothing more and nothing less. There are no religious institutions, no religious obligations nor ritual prayers. God did not make provision for religious pilgrimages nor for the systematic collection of money in His name.   He did not command His prophets or messengers to *worship* Him in the ordinary sense of that word. There is no reference to *religious institutions* or *religious obligations* in His Scripture. None whatsoever. What better way for the Devil to subvert God's system[11] than by contaminating it!

---

[10] The Chambers 20th Century Dictionary amongst others defines "sanction" as "motive for obedience to any moral or religious law (ethics): a penalty or reward expressly attached to non-observance or observance of a law or treaty. In the context of the Qur'an, the limit to the orderly way of life is sanctioned. Thus it is called the 'Sanctioned Submission' or '*masjidil-haram*'.

[11] God's system does not operate through organized institutions. People were created as individuals, and each answers directly to God. Abraham, Moses, Jesus, and Muhammad were told to inform people that, *"No burden soul will bear the burden of another"*. Rabbis, priests, monks, and mullahs operate a false system created by the enemies of God and His messengers.

So, how did all these practices creep into *Islam*? Where in the Qur'an are these practices dictated? Let us examine the Scripture to see what God has enjoined upon us.

Inherently, all the prophets, messengers, and His servants – be they men or women – are required to *serve* God through their respective individual deeds both *in substance* and *in spirit*. *Islam* is concerned with deliberate and conscious obedience to God by the individuals to attain his or her peace in this world - not mindless automated behaviour. God's message conveyed to us by all His messengers simply says: *'You shall not serve other than Him'*. Within the framework of those words lies the truth of *Islam* or the *peacefulness*.

> *We did not send any messengers before you but with the message: **there is no god except Me**, therefore **you shall serve Me alone**[12]. (21:25)*

Thus, the key to Islam or peacefulness is by serving God alone.

There is no mention in the Qur'an of *worship* in the ordinary sense of that word or of ritual prayer be it three, four or five times a day or a week. It was but the religionists' conspiracy against God and the Last Prophet, which saw the introduction of religious institutions, houses of worship, ritual prayers and religious laws.

For example, the religionists have manipulated the meaning of the term 'way of life' or *deen* to mean

---

[12] Serving God alone is the main essence of all scriptures. Moses announced it in Deuteronomy 6:4 and Jesus repeated it in Mark 12: 29-30 and Muhammad in the Qur'an 17:22-23.

'religion', and 'I serve' (*ya'budu*) to mean 'I worship'. Whilst at first glance these changes seem minute, however, in realism they have had a tremendous impact on *Islam*. Sadly, the keepers of the faith have also perpetuated many other distortions. Among them are the *Ka'aba* in Mecca and the practice of mandatory pilgrimage.

God has declared the Arabs to be the staunchest disbelievers and the staunchest hypocrites. This will be demonstrated beyond all doubt by this book. The Qur'an confirms:

> The Arabs are staunchest in disbelief and hypocrisy, and most likely not to know the limits of what was revealed by God to His messenger, and God is Knower and Judge. (9:97)

Thus, the probability of Arabs being the caretakers of God's *deen* is close to zero. The current *status quo*, however, has the Arabs as the heroes and champions of 'religion' with non-Arabs putting their blind trust in the religionists who are obsessed with Arabic language.

God is not an Arab

It is wrong to promote the idea that one can only serve the Lord of the Universe in the Arabic language. Such an opinion (and that is all it really is) ignores the following material considerations:

- The Lord of the Universe is not an Arab.

- The Lord of the Universe understands English, French, Spanish, German, Russian, Thai, Tamil, Japanese, Chinese or any other language (including those of the ants and the animals).

Why then, the obsession with the 'political correctness' and emphasis on the Arabic language and culture in *Islam*? The Qur'an details the lives of great people of the past like Abraham, Ishmael, Isaac, Jacob, David, Solomon, Moses, Jesus and many others who served God. They did not speak the Arabic language but they were righteous people and the pioneer servants of God. They did not worship God in the ordinary sense of that word. Their relationship with Him revolved around upholding their obligations and keeping their commitments pure and chaste through deeds. All of this was accomplished without the facility of the Arabic tongue. Worship is a pagan ritual. Moses, Abraham, Jesus, David, and Muhammad were sent to teach us to stop worshipping through rituals. It is God's will that we submit to His deen by *serving* Him through upholding our obligations and performing righteous deeds.

Every living creature in the seven heavens and the earth are glorifying God in their own way. There is nothing that does not glorify Him. God understands their glorification and their languages. To demonstrate this fact, the Qur'an narrates an incident with regard to Solomon. Solomon was blessed with the understanding of the language of the animals, the birds, and the ants. One day, as he was passing a colony of ants, he smiled in amusement when he heard the ants communicating with each other:

> When they approached a valley of the ants, one ant said, "O you ants! Go inside your homes, otherwise Solomon and his troops may crush you unintentionally." (27:18)

Obviously the ants were not communicating with each other in Arabic. God translated the language of the ants into Arabic because He understands all languages. If He had

41

chosen a French prophet, He would obviously have translated the ant's warning to his comrades into French.

God revealed the scripture to Moses in his mother tongue i.e. the Hebrew, but when the Qur'an was revealed in Arabic to an Arab, the Children of Israel were told to believe in it.

> O Children of Israel, appreciate the blessing I have bestowed upon you and uphold My covenant, that I uphold your covenant, and reverence Me and believe in what is revealed herein confirming what you have, and do not be the first to reject it. Do not trade My revelations for a cheap price, and observe Me. Do not confound the truth with falsehood, nor shall you conceal the truth knowingly. And uphold your commitment and maintain its purity and humble yourselves with those who are humble. (2:40-41-43)

God's revelations had to come down in some language and there is no doubt that it is the message and *not* the messenger nor the language of the messenger, which is of supreme importance. Those who refuse to believe will regard the language as an encumbrance in accepting God's message. The Qur'an teaches that the language of God's Scripture is immaterial, and that God will put His message into the hearts of sincere believers irrespective of their mother tongue. The Qur'an says those who disbelieve are bickering about the language not the message. The Qur'an gives a good example about the people of the past who had disputed about the language of the Torah. There were instances of those who claimed to be following the teachings of Moses who squabbled about the language of the Torah and finally abandoned the Book. Instead, a small group of Jewish sages wrote the Babylonian and Palestinian

Talmud – the most influential documents they claim to explain the Torah – but the Jews are told not to 'read' the Talmud, but 'learn' like the music for a choir voices; it is sung. To understand the Talmud they must read the *Tosefta* which explains the *Misnah* (representing the thinking of Jewish sages) and also the *Gemarah* a commentary on the *Mishnah. Mishnah* was written by Judah the Patriarch, but it needs to be explicated by the disputing books of *Shammai* and *Hillel* – and that is the religion of Judaism as we know and see it today, a strange cult entity unknown to Moses. They created various sects because they differed in the interpretations and understanding of what they have invented. Similar disputes are, not surprisingly, raging within the Arab religion. The Qur'an predicts that people would have questioned God's revelation no matter in what language He chose to reveal it:

> Had we made it a non-Arabic *Qur'an*[13] they would have said, "Why are the verses not explained?" Shall we reveal a non-Arabic reading to an Arab? Say, "For those who believe it is a beacon and a guide. As for those who do not believe they will be deaf and blind to it, as if they are being called from afar." We also gave Moses the Scripture and it, too, was disputed. If it were not for a predetermined decision by your Lord, they would have been judged immediately. They are in great doubt thereof. (41:44-45)

> If presented in Arabic to the non-Arabs they could not accept it when recited to them. This is the way We render it to the hearts of the undeserved. Consequently, they fail to believe until the painful retributions strike them. (26:198-201)

---

[13] *Qur'an* means reading

Despite the fact that the Qur'an was revealed in Arabic, God has not preferred the Arabs over other races. He made it clear by resolutely condemning Arabs in the Arabic Scripture in the strong terms where He says they are the staunchest in disbelief and hypocrisy.

Certain people have accused the author of a hatred for the Arab people for his pointing out the existence of the verses in the Qur'an which do, in fact, describe the Arabs in exactly the terms mentioned above.

If we take 9:97-101 for example, critics of the views put forward here will insist that the words *a'robu* and *a'robi* refer to Bedouins or 'desert Arabs'. In addition, we have been furnished with the following interpolated translations that serve to prevent us from taking the words of the Qur'an at the normal value ascribed to them:

- The wandering Arabs are more hard in disbelief and hypocrisy, and more likely to be ignorant of the limits, which Allah hath revealed unto the Messenger. Allah is Knower, Wise. (9:97 – *Marmaduke Pickthall*)

- (The hypocrites among) the Bedouins are more hard in disbelief in (their) refusal to acknowledge the truth and in (their) hypocrisy (than the settled people), and more likely to ignore the ordinance which God has bestowed from high upon His Apostle, but God is all-knowing, judge. (9:97 – *Muhammad Asad*)

- The Bedouin Arabs are the worst in unbelief and hypocrisy, and most fitted to be ignorant of the Command which Allah hath sent down to His

Messenger; but Allah is All-Knowing, All Wise. (9:97 – *Yusuf Ali*)

God's Arabic in the Qur'an is perfect and is used precisely. In the language of the Qur'an, Bedouin Arabs or the 'desert Arabs' are referred to as *badu-naa fil-a'robi*.

When the Qur'an talks about the Bedouin Arabs, it says so:

Yah-sabu-nal ah-zaba lam-yaz-habu, wa-'in-yaktil-ah-zabu yu-wudu-lau an-nahum **badu-naa fil-a'robi** *yas-alunaa 'an-abaa-ikum walauka-nuu fi-kum ma-qor-taluu il-laaqor-li-lan (33:20). La-qad-kaa-naa la-kum fi-rosul-lil-lah-hee as-waa-tun hasana-tun lee-man-kaa-naa yar-jul-lah-hu wal-yaum-mil-aakhir-ral-lah ha-kashir-ran. (33:21)*

They thought their allies would not come, but when their allies came they wished they were Bedouins within the Arabs (*badu-naa fil-a'robi*) who were only watching you from a distance. If they happened to be with you they will not struggle (33:20). Surely there is best example for you in the messenger of God for those who seek God and the last day and who constantly remember God (33:21).

9:97-101 clearly uses the word 'Arab'. It does not qualify the noun. It does specify that these Arabs are of the city. They are not – and are *not* meant to be confused with – inhabitants of the desert. This is yet another example of how the Qur'an explaining itself and confounds those who would manipulate it.

It is true that the Qur'an also mentioned about the believing Arabs in Sura 9 Verse 99:-

"And from among the Arabs are those who believe with God and the final day and consider their contributions as means of drawing them nearer to God, and the commitments *(solaa-waa-ti)* of the messenger. Surely, it will bring them nearer to God, and God will admit them into His mercy. God is forgiver and merciful".

Understandably in order to qualify - the believing Arabs must commit themselves to the deen the way it was done by their messenger. They should be actively involved in contributing towards cultivating the deen for God. Nobody denies the fact that the messenger made a great effort risking his life against the disbelievers within his own community who refused to accept the Qur'an as the sole source of guidance. He struggled against the hypocrites and the idol worshipers. In other words, he took the challenge *(haj)* against his own people to promote *(u'mro-ata)* God's guidance to make it prevail over all other deens.

In 33:20 above we see that the Bedouins were not interested to strive in the path of God, then followed by 33:21 that says *'the messenger was a good example for those who truly seek God and the hereafter'* ...... Thus, the present day Arabs who think they belong to the group of people in 9:99 - should be doing exactly what their prophet had done. Obviously they know the true meaning of the verse in 9:19 that encourages them to *"Jaa-haduu fi-sabee-lil-lah bi-amwaa-lee-him waa-aan-fuu-see-heem"* or they must strive in the path of God with their money and lives. It is their duty to take the same challenge against their own people to promote what was sanctioned by God in the Quran to make it prevail over the present day idol worship practice in their homeland.

Unfortunately, in spite of their conversant in Arabic, many of them decided to move to the Western world for a better system of governance leaving behind the autocratic scheme in their own native land. Logically, if one wishes to qualify one must practice what one believes. No need to talk about it. They must follow the example of the prophet to establish the truth – (more than anyone else) because they understood the language of the Qur'an. They can physically sense the idol worship practice packed with Arab myth and tribal cult rituals in their country. Unless and until they demolish these false innovations - sura 9 verse 99 will remain indefinable.

Arabs from other countries are equally accountable to take the challenge to promote the sanctioned submission to cultivate God's guidance against the disbelieving and hypocritical Arabs. God told them in many places in the Qur'an, *"Do not fear the people, but fear Me instead, so that I may complete My blessings upon you, and that you may be guided."*

They must take into consideration that it was God's blessing that He sent a messenger from among the Arabs to recite for them the signs, and to sanctify them, and to teach them the scripture and wisdom, and to teach them what they never knew. Thus, it would be hypocritical for the believing Arabs to utter what they do not do because the Qur'an says, *"most abominable in the sight of God is uttering what you do not do"* (61:3).

Therefore, the language of the Qur'an does not bequeath the Arabs any advantage over God's Scripture despite their mother tongue, unless they follow the example of the prophet. Sadly, there are many non-Arabs around the world who seek to be more 'Arabic' than the Arabs. A non-

Arab henceforth cannot claim he believes and submits to God because he knows Arabic. In fact his insistence on Arabic exposes his wickedness.

If God understands all languages, language *cannot* be a barrier to magnify the Creator in any language whatsoever. God says even the heavens; the earth and the mountains are able to understand what humans say. Each time a person says that God has begotten a son - the heavens, the earth and the mountains react to such blasphemous utterances. I don't suppose this verse indicates that the heavens, earth, and mountains can only understand blasphemous utterances in Arabic.

> *They said, "God has begotten a son". Indeed you have uttered a gross blasphemy. The heaven is about to shatter, the earth is about to burst and the mountains are about to crumble upon hearing such claims about God most gracious.* (19:90-91)

In simple terms, the Arab religion insists erroneously and maliciously that everyone serve God in the Arabic language and in the 'Arab' way. This stand is not only devoid of authority from the Qur'an, but makes no logical sense whatsoever.

Ownership claim

The Qur'an remains simple and straightforward. The reigning confusion is entirely man-made. When people take the revealed words and alter their meaning to suit their situation, it is no longer true. The religionists promoted their invented Arabic religion and not the *Islam* that was revealed to the Last Prophet. This was done in order to support their claim of ownership over the Qur'an and declare themselves the rightful caretakers of religion.

Nowhere else in the world do we see such temerity. One wonders then, by extension, if the Devil converses only in Arabic.

Today, people who wish to serve their Lord by subscribing to God's way are driven into the complexities of the Arab religion. In other words, the religionists have set themselves up as the conduit pipe – a saviour and messenger no less – by which to reach God.

It is required of any subscriber to God's prescribed way of life (or the *deen-nil-lah*) to believe in the One God. The faithful know this and they know that God had revealed the Scriptures through many prophets to guide mankind. Somewhere along the line we have ceased to be vigilant against the enemies of God who are always waiting on the sidelines to derail us from God's path.

A student of the Arab language has to contend with the mullahs' interpretation to serve the invented Arab religion which, as has been indicated, is not part of the Qur'an and examples are provided in this book that show how the interpretation of certain, simple words in the Qur'an have been distorted to meet the requirements of this contrived man-made religion.

Sincere people who seek the grace and pleasure of God have been divided into violent conflict and hateful sects[14] under the mantle of the Arab religion. They fight and disagree over almost everything. As the supposed keepers of the Muslim faith, they bear poor testament to the privilege.

---

[14] In Pakistan the followers of the Ahmadiah sect are officially declared apostates by the Pakistani Constitution. Many of them are killed and their mosques burnt down. In Pakistan and India Sunnis are killing the Shiites while the Shiites are killing the Sunnis in Iraq - to quote a few examples.

The religionists continue to make fools of everyone by making them expend sizeable amounts of money to journey to the Arab soil so that they can walk in circles around a stone box. If it were not so catastrophic it would be laughable.

Create divisions among people

Those who believe the religionists do not realise that it is wrong to force divisions within God's way. It is not correct to assume that these changes were made to improve *Islam*. It is wrong to think that concepts need re-interpretation. We are just not supposed to meddle in something that is perfect in design and execution. A casual overview of the Qur'an will reveal a clear commandment warning the servants of God that following a way of life other than God's does not put them in the company of the Messenger. If anything, this alone should motivate Muslims to confirm that they are in the Messenger's company. In doing so, the truth shall be revealed.

> Indeed those people who change the *deen* into religion (*shi-ya'an*), you are not responsible for them in anything. (6:159)

Thus, the verse clearly says Muhammad had nothing to do with any Islamic religion or pioneered the Sunni and Shiite sects.

Our wish should be to lead a way of life as ordained by our Lord, who will ultimately take back that life and call us to account for it. To participate in this divine plan, He asks that we believe in the *unseen God* so that we can be certain of eternal life after death. We are told to be righteous in this life for as long as we shall live so that it will please the

Lord. As a people, our intentions are noble but we fail to perform the paramount obligation, that is, to read. None states this quite so elegantly as the verse following:

> **Read** in the name of your Lord who created. He created a person from that which clings. Read, your Lord is the most honourable. He teaches by means of the pen. He teaches people what they never knew. (96:1-5)

Instead of a life of righteous deeds and service, *Islam* today showcases a way of life that is centred on suppressing thought and talent and features the dogmatic rituals of prayer, idols, customs, traditions and pilgrimages. As regards pilgrimage, the only benefit the author sees arising from this arrangement is to the Arab tourism industry. Effectively, this ritual has doomed every single Muslim to a lifetime of servitude to a 'god' in a most ineffective and useless way. In an oblique sense, 'religion' is a major export of Saudi Arabia. There are countless faithful who do not have the means to perform the invented pilgrimage but have toiled, incurred debt and sacrificed ceaselessly to fulfil this purported obligation. Strangely, Saudi Arabia (which must have the largest percentage of pilgrims of any country in the world) is no shining example of God's just love.

These practices have divided both Muslims and mankind as a whole, causing dissent and instilling racial and religious prejudice amongst mankind. Perhaps its most damaging effect of all is that they have diverted mankind from the path of God. These ritualistic pre-conditions of the bigoted Arab religion have spread evil around the world by creating various religious sects to promote their Arab-centric, internal religious beliefs and customs. More importantly, the single most insidious aspect of the propagation of the Arab religion is to divide all those who are at peace (Muslims). Today, this enmity has not spared other religions that, to some extent or other, are at odds with Muslims. Why is the term 'fundamentalist Muslim' now not regarded as a positive term? Therefore the innocent Muslims or those who are at peace should consider returning to their Lord by submitting to His true deen to fulfil their obligations as the true servants of God. They should not be among the idol-worshipers who changed the orderly way of life (*deen*) into religion:

> You shall all return to Him and be observant to uphold your commitments. And do not be among the idol-worshippers who change the *deen* into religion (*shi-ya'an*). And each sectarian is happy with what they have. (30:31-32)

Students of the Arabic language are conditioned from an early age to unwittingly accept the teachings of their *u'lema* (priests) of the Arab religion, regardless of their pertinence or correctness. They are unaware of their wrongdoings and propagate the teachings of the Arab religion to each new generation of Muslims. When alerted to their folly, they respond by saying Muslims who denounce the Arab religion's discipline in observing God according to the Quran alone are apostates. It is absolutely horrendous that according to their Arab religion such 'apostates' are stoned to death. This anomaly alone is evidence of paganism. The true God does not impose double standards.

Stone-worshippers

The religion of pagan Arabs centres largely on traditions relating to the square stone house in Mecca mistakenly called the *Ka'aba* and its environs. The religionists make it mandatory for the faithful to worship it and this is why, to this day, Muslims around the world bow and prostrate in the direction of this particular rock structure wherever they may be.

The religionists say that *the stone house in Mecca is God's house*. They call the rock structure in Mecca the *baytul-lah* or *God's house*. The term *God's house* or *baytul-lah* is not found in the Qur'an. If this concept is so central to Muslims' belief, how is it that it escapes mention in the Qur'an? It must be another Arab fabrication.

From another perspective, were this supposition true, it would stand to reason that God, the Lord of the Universe lives in this tiny 627-square foot hollow rock cube in Mecca. Simply because *baytul-lah* is presented as an endemic Arabic term nobody has bothered to check the true meaning of the word. Muslims the world over do not question what they are saying when they utter the word *baytul-lah* because the word has been proclaimed '*divine*' and thus its significance cannot be questioned. To question this would invoke accusations of heresy.

Credit has to be given to the 'Arabs' for perpetuating myths of this magnitude. For non-Arab Muslims terms like this will always be 'divine' since they are uttered in combination with words like *Allah*. They will worship anything appended with that name. They will bow and prostrate to a stone house for the sake of the word *Allah*.

I visited the rock structure many years ago and felt humiliated after bowing and prostrating to it. Upon returning to my country, I asked for forgiveness from the Lord of the Universe and pledged to Him that I would never step foot on that soil again. It is inconceivable how millions of intelligent men and women including head of states and professionals consistently defy their common sense and serve a rock structure built by the Arabs. Although this point will be decried as heretical, it is nevertheless true: Mecca and Medina are the two largest idol-worshipping cities in the world.

There are Muslims who say: *since God owns the heavens and the earth, there is nothing wrong with saying there is a house of God.* However, it is a patent madness (invested with simple human pride) to assume that the Creator of the Universe owns a special house on the desert sand representing His glory. Yet the same foolish Muslims accuse others of being pagans by virtue of their idolatry. Do they not do the same when they worship a rock cube?

All this smacks of the Devil's touch. Consider the statement in the Qur'an portraying the Devil as the foremost expert in mind control. The Qur'an says that, God will assign the devil as companion to those who neglect His message and then the devil deludes them into thinking that they are guided:

> Those who neglect the message of God most gracious, we appoint the devil[15] to be their constant companion. Then the Devil will keep them away from the path and make them think that they are guided. (43:36-37)

All these linguistic and contextual ambiguities have successfully concealed the true message of the Qur'an. The Holy Book has been reduced to a choir book used solely for chanting and singing. To this day, many blindly follow the

---

[15] 'Devil' in not a form of creature but a person's negative character expressed through their words, thoughts and deeds. Human as devil 6:112 & 114:6.

'recipes' set out in these Muslim 'precepts' contained in a language foreign to them and perpetuate the same myths themselves. There are similar instances in many religions, but none quite so insidious and widespread. Many of these misconceptions are easily discovered with a little care and logic. It seems that common sense is hardly a common commodity.

Worship of mountain rocks

The rituals that have been instituted around the man-made *Ka'aba* have developed in a peculiar way. The faithful bow and prostrate to the stone house; they circumambulate it seven times, proclaiming to the Almighty, *'Oh God, I am here!'* increasing their volume as they near the 'sacred' stone cube. They kiss the idol, cry and wail to it. They do not deny they are worshipping their God *through* a stone house. But to make it palatable they say it is *'God's house'*.

The square rock structure in Mecca is constantly surrounded by thousands of people from all over the world twenty-four hours a day seven days a week. During the annual pilgrimage approximately two million people from all over the world worship it. This makes the *Ka'aba* the most successful idol on earth. In the following pages, we will demonstrate how the religionists conspired to change *Islam* – the *deen* – into a religion of idol-worship. In doing so, they have intentionally manipulated God's word in the Qur'an and sold it cheap.

The conspiracies

The list below shows twenty-seven crucial words in the Qur'an (although there are others) which have had their meanings twisted by the religionists to create the 'Arab' religion. The words are shown with their attendant translations:

Arabic word	Arab corruption	Fundamental meaning
Islam	Submission	peacefulness
Muslim	one who submits	one who is at peace
Asra	journey	captivated
Solaa	5 daily ritual prayers	commitment/obligation/ covenant
deen	religion	a way (or an orderly way) of life
bayta	God's house	a system
bayti-ya	My house (God's)	my system
baytal Harama	God's sacred house	the sanctions in the system
baytika-muHarami	God's Sacred house	your sanctions in the system
maqam	footprint	status, position or rank
musol-lan	a place of prayers	a committed man
musol-leen	people who pray ritually	people who are committed
Thor-iffin	encircle the house	throngs of people
a'kiffin	retreat to the stone house	Devote
wa-roka'is-sujud	bow and prostrate	submit in humility
masajid	mosque	submissions
masajidal-lah	God's mosque	God's prescribed submissions
masajidil-Harami	sacred mosque	the sanctioned submission
masjidil-aqsa	faraway mosque	proximity of submission
masajidi-lil-lah	mosque belonging to God	submissions for God
Hurumun	the pilgrim garb/pilgrim	restricted
ka'aba	God's house	ankles or lower foot

hadya	animal offerings	guidance
qola-ida	animal's garland	hunting rules
u'mro-ata	a visit to God's house	to prosper or to give life
Haj	the annual pilgrimage	to challenge or discourse
zakaa	paying of religious tithe	to purify, or keep pure

A quick perusal of this list leaves one incredulous. How on earth can the sense of these words have been corrupted to such an extent without people noticing? However, even basic research based on the Qur'an alone proves that the meanings of the words listed above have been deliberately distorted, misconstrued and falsified by the religionists with the intention of subjugating the *deen* to their lust for personal benefit and power, quite against the specific wishes of God and His messenger. A simple examination of associated meanings which appear repeatedly in the Qur'an should provide enough incentive for the true believer or scholar to undertake an examination of the Qur'an on the basis of personal and unbiased study, regardless of prevailing consensus. After all, the Qur'an is (to borrow the computer terminology of our day) the *default document* of the Muslim faith.

That a thinking person is equal to such a task is addressed in the Qur'an in no uncertain terms. This particular promise appears four times in a single *surah* alone:

Indeed, We have made the Qur'an easy to remember. Is there anyone who wishes to learn? (54:17, 22, 32, 40)

The fact is that the religionists have abused four key verses from the Qur'an to establish their claims. Having made these changes, the knock-on effect requires them to re-interpret other verses and words to retain the appearance of consistency. The end product is a reading of the Reading of God, which has become man-made corruption riddled with inconsistencies and fallacies. Clearly, the end result of such an onslaught has proven disastrous. Evidence of this is painfully apparent in verses: (2:124-129[16]; 5:1-5; 3:95-97; 9:17-20).

I invite the reader to accompany me on a journey of discovery to expose the conspiracy, using the Qur'an alone as a base of reference. As we go we should remember that the Qur'an is the only sure-fire revealed testament of God's will on earth accepted by all Muslims.

The fundamental Qur'an principles from which we will proceed are:

The Qur'an is consistent and there is no contradiction in the book.

> Why do they not study the Qur'an carefully? If it were from other than God, they would have found many contradictions therein (4:82)

The Qur'an is the best *Hadith* or message and it is consistent. The word *Hadith* is found in the following verses.

> God sent down the best *Hadith*/message a Scripture that is consistent (39:23)

> Which *Hadith*/message beside this would you then believe in. (77:50)

There is no priesthood or religious clergy in Islam.

---

[16] Eight words were distorted in 2:125 alone by the religionists to accommodate the rituals at the spot where the Arab god apparently lives.

They have taken their priests and the scholars as
Lords besides God (9:31)

No human can claim to be the sole authority of the Qur'an.

God Most Gracious, the One who teaches the
Qur'an. The One who created the human being.
(55:2-3)

Only God can explain the Qur'an since He wrote it.

Do not move your tongue to hasten this revelation.
We are in charge of putting them together into the
Qur'an. Once We recite it, you shall follow this
Qur'an. Then it is We who will explain it. (75:16-
18)

The Qur'an explains itself and provides the best
interpretation, beyond that of any human.

They never come to you with any example, except
We provide you the truth and the best interpretation.
(25:33)

There is no ambiguity to be found in the Qur'an.

A qur'an (reading) in Arabic, without ambiguity so that
they may attain success. (39:28)

The majority of Muslims will simply be afraid to
believe what is written in this book because they think they
are already on the right path - of the *religion of Islam*' - a
belief the majority of them inherited from their forefathers
who were effectively shackled by the Arab religious
masters. I would like to stress and to remind them again,
they can either remain to be what they are or search the path
to free themselves from the mental slavery. Read this book

with a critical mind. This book encourages them to think -
and think and think. Reflect on the purpose of life and see
the wonders of it.

Obviously what they are about to read is a dramatically
different idea about the Islam they believe. This study is
base on the document they cannot deny of its authenticity -
the Quran. My wish for them is - try not to be the groups of
people described by the Qur'an:-

Surely for those who disbelieve, it is the same over them -
whether you warn them or did not warn them - they will
never believe. God seals over their hearts - and over their
hearing and over their sight – are veiled. And for them – the
greatest suffering. (2:6-7)

And among the mankind there are those who say, '*we
believe with God and with the day of the hereafter*', whilst
they are not believers. They want to deceive God and those
who believe - surely they deceived no one – except their
own selves.   But they do not perceive. In their hearts a
disease – thus - God enhances their diseases. And for them
– a painful punishment - with whatever they are lying. (2:8-
10)

PART TWO

There is no 'religion' of God

There is a world of difference between the definition of the word *Islam* ordained by God and the Arab religion invented by the religionists which goes by the same name. The word *Islam* may possibly be the most abused word in the world today.

> Indeed, the *deen* by God is *Islam*. (3:19)

In one simple and straightforward sentence God states that *Islam* is a *deen*. The meaning of verse 3:19 literally says:-

> Indeed, the *way of life* by God is *Peacefulness*.

The word *Islam* means *peacefulness*. This word is derived from the root *S L M* or *Salam* that means '**Peace**'. In 6:54 we are told to greet one another by saying:-

> "*Peace be upon you*" or "*Salam-mun alai-kum*".

The word *ad-deen* means *the way* or *the order*. In no place in the Qur'an did God ordain *Islam* as a religion. This is a crucial point to consider.

What is the difference between religion and *deen*?

- A religion[17] consists of a belief in a god or gods, and the activities that are connected with that belief such as

---

[17] *Religion* is defined in the Chambers Encyclopaedic English Dictionary as 1. A belief in, or the worship of a god or gods. 2. A particular system of belief or worship, such as Christianity or Judaism. 3. Anything to which one is totally devoted and which rules one's life. 4. The monastic way of life. [from Latin *religio*]

prayer or worship or rites in the temple, church, synagogue, or mosque.

- A *deen* refers to a way: or method of doing something; or an orderly method of doing something designed (for an action or series of actions) to achieve an objective.

According to the Qur'an:

Religion is called *shi'ah*. It is a system detached from God's prescribed way of life – or the *deen-nil-lah*. Religion was created by humans for people to devote themselves to a common entity like – but not limited to – physical entities made from wood, stone, rock, metal or anything tangible. People serve these idols or icons by worshipping them through prayers and religious rites which eventually evolve to become institutionalised and regulated religious obligations.

The *deen* is a system conceived by the All-knowing, which allows people to devote themselves to the one, unseen God through His providence sanctioned in His Scriptures. True adherents to this system serve God by committing themselves to do the deeds required by Him in His system so that they can achieve the *peacefulness* in this world. These obligations require self-sacrifice but are free of the dogmatic practice of ritualised worship or rites. Men and women who believe in God, the final day and observe virtuousness in this life are called *Muslims* or ***those who are at peace***. *Muslim* is not a label but it is the state of being of a person who enjoys *peacefulness*.

In the Qur'an the history of Noah is narrated in a *surah*[18] by itself also entitled *Noah*. The history of the great

---

[18] Sura is chapter. In the Quran there are 114 chapters.

flood is known to all those who received something of God's Scripture. Noah was commissioned by God to reform a community, which indulged in serving false gods. His community belonged to a *religion*.

It is apparent that two quite different *systems* existed in Noah's time. The masses subscribed to the preservation and propagation of a traditional system of praying and worshipping as their way of life. Noah, however, observed his way of life or *deen* according to God's system without institutionalised prayer and worship. As soon his home was flooded, he turned to God, saying:

> My Lord forgive me and my parents and anyone who enters my system (*bayti-ya*) as a believer and all the believing men and believing women. And do not increase the wicked except to destroy. (71:28)

The religionists say the meaning of the word *bayti-ya* in this verse is *house*, the sense being, "… and anyone who enters my *house*". Yet, even the gentlest application of reason brings to mind the fact that Noah made his humble request during the great flood from within the ark, which he himself had built. At that very moment, his house was in all probability under the waters of God's retribution against those who had refused Noah's call all this time. It is equally clear that since all mankind had been drowned, there would be no one to enter his house. The word *bayti-ya* as we know it must mean that to which Noah subscribed. Incidentally, the word for ship in the Qur'an is *fulk*.

What then makes a house and a system different?

A *house* is commonly understood as a building in which people live, usually belonging to one family. It is inconceivable that Noah intended that God should forgive people just because they have entered his house, which submerged in the flood. When he implored the Lord of the Universe he was referring to his *system* which was different from the system of the idol-worshippers.

A *system*, on the other hand, is a way of working, organising, or doing something in which people follow a plan or set of rules. When a situation or activity has the semblance of a system, it means that it has a sense of orderliness or good organisation. It is also a way in which a whole institution or aspect of society has been organised or arranged.

In Noah's time people had already lived according to their own invented system of worshipping idols. Noah, however, was serving the Lord of universe alone and had committed himself to God's prescribed system. When he uttered the word *bayti-ya* it meant 'my system' – that is the *system* to which he was committed. We will shortly see that Abraham was directed to the same system, which God calls *bayti-ya*. Abraham and his son were instructed to cleanse the system of idol-worship for the benefit of the people who were devoted and those who humbled themselves in submission to the unseen God.

The Qur'an says those who observe the way of life marked by ritual prayer and worship belong to the *shi-ya'an*, (or religions). Those devoted to religion are termed *mushrikeen* or 'idol-worshippers'.

The history of Noah is again mentioned in *surah* thirty-seven alongside the history of Abraham:

> Noah implored Us, and We are the best of responders. We saved him and his family from the great disaster, and We made him and his family the

survivors and preserved their history for the later generations. (37:75-78)

The history of the retribution against Noah's people was preserved as an example to the people of Abraham. In spite of this, the people of Abraham similarly devoted themselves to false gods. They worshiped and prayed to the gods they created just like the people of Noah did.

The people of Noah drowned by the flood belonged to the *shi-a'tihi* (a religion). Similarly the community of Abraham were worshipping and praying to idols. They too, were *shi-a'tihi* and Abraham was excluded.

> Peace be upon Noah, throughout history. We reward the sincere people. Thus he was among the true believers and then We drowned the rest. And surely *from their religion **excluding Abraham** (min-shi-a'tihi-**laa-ibrohim**)* - who came to his Lord with a blissful heart while he asked his father and his people, "What are you serving? It is false gods besides God that you need? What do you make out of the Lord of the Universe?" (37:79-87)

The concept of religion requiring rituals or rites focused on physical icons enabling people to *see* what they worshipped. This singular attribute, according to the Qur'an, marks it as a religion. After all, who would choose to show the Glory of God in something tangible and man-made? Common sense tells us that there is no other god besides the One unseen God. He is over and above anything they associate with Him. *Deen* on the other hand, is a set system sanctioned by the supreme God. These sanctions were revealed to the various prophets. Hence, we find many passages in the Qur'an instructing people to obey God and obey the messengers so that they not be diverted from God's prescribed sanctions under the pretext of a particular religion. God's *deen* requires His servants to manifest their faith in practical acts of charity and deeds. His way is a series of decrees that must be followed to achieve a peaceful life. For example, God's covenant revealed through all the prophets requires His servants to observe the decrees listed below. Anyone can undertake to fulfil their covenant with God by upholding these prescribed decrees without consulting the priests of any religion:

- Your Lord has decreed that you shall *not serve* other than Him.
- You shall honour your parents for as long as they live, one of them or both of them.
- You shall not speak harshly to them nor mistreat them.
- You shall speak amicably to people and do not utter any lies.
- You shall regard the relatives, the orphans, and the poor.
- You shall not kill your children from fear of poverty.
- You shall not commit adultery, for it is a vice.
- You shall not kill anyone, for taking of life is made forbidden.
- You shall not touch the orphans' money except for their own good.
- You shall give full measure when you trade and weigh with an equitable balance.
- You shall not accept anything that you yourself cannot ascertain.
- You shall be perfectly honest when you serve as a witness, even if it is against yourself, your parents,

or your relatives whether the defendant is rich or poor.

- You shall give to charity from God's provisions, which He has entrusted to you.
- You shall strive in the path of God (*fi-sabi-lil-lah*) against those who strive against you, but not aggress.
- You shall fulfil your commitments and humble yourself with those who are humble.
- You are not to be arrogant, nor to walk in pride. God does not love the boastful, the arrogant. Be humble as you walk and lower your voice.
- Eat from everything that is lawful and good, and do not follow the step of the Devil, he is your ardent enemy. He directs you towards vice and evil and to invent lies and attribute them to God.

This is part of the prescribed way sanctioned by God in the Qur'an. People, from the times of Noah, Abraham, Moses, Jesus and Muhammad have been committed to these values. They observe these values in an *orderly* manner (as a *deen*). Common sense tells us that in order to achieve results these values must be translated into deeds. Worship or ritual prayers are irrelevant. Therefore, *religion* and *deen* are distinctly different.

People are expected to serve the Creator by observing the prescribed *way*.

He has decreed for you the same *deen* enjoined upon Noah and what is revealed herein, and what was decreed for Abraham, Moses, and Jesus. You shall uphold the *one* deen and not be segregated. It is simply too difficult for the idol-worshippers to accept what you advocate. (42:13)

You shall submit to God, beware of Him, uphold your commitments and do not fall into idol-worship. And do not be with those who change the *deen* into religion (*shi-ya-'an*) each sectarian is happy with what they have. (30:31-32)

Traditionally, the word *shi'ah* is translated as *sect*. Sects have long been associated with principal differences in a religious context. God however, has no interest in sectarianism. All the religions in this world are the same. The faithful congregate. They form groups to a common cause in public. They worship and pray ritually to different shapes of idols be it a wall, cross, star, crescent or a square house or other images made from the materials which themselves owe their existence to the true God. That is the extent of difference between *religion* and the *deen* as far as the Qur'an is concerned.

For example, while prescribing good and lawful foods God proclaimed that He has perfected the *deen*. He says: *'Today I have perfected the deen for you and completed My favour upon you, and decreed Islam (peacefulness) as the deen'*. This is in the middle of the subject about food.

Taken literally and substituting the concept of *deen* with *religion*, this decree becomes absurd. In 26:195-196 the Qur'an says: *'It came in the clear Arabic tongue and it contains the same message of the previous Scriptures'*. This means that the message in the Qur'an is consistent with all other previous Scriptures. God perfected a *deen* for His servants after detailing His covenant on food. God has not forbidden any food in this world except for the decaying meat, blood, carrion, any animal that dies through violent death and food consecrated to idols. This is the *deen* (or the *orderly way*) sanctioned by God in His system. There is nothing religious about it. It is merely a dietary restriction based on good hygiene.

> Restricted to you are the meat from the animals that die of themselves, blood, decaying meat[19], and food dedicated to other than God. Also, the animal that has been strangled to death, the animal struck by an object, the animal that dies from falling from a height, the animal that is gored to death, the animal that is partially eaten by a predator unless you have rescued it alive, the food dedicated to idols and meat divided by means of casting lots. These are abominations. Today, the disbelievers are in despair about your *deen*. Do not fear them and fear Me instead. Today, I have perfected the *deen* for you and completed My favour upon you, and I decree *Islam* as the *deen* for you. (5:3)

The word *deen* is mentioned three times in the verse above, instructing believers in simple and clear terms to observe the *deen*. There is nothing religious about not eating carrion or animals gored to death. Similarly, there is nothing religious about not eating decaying meat. It is simply an *order* prescribed from the One who has created you, and intended for your good. This directive supersedes all other dietary restrictions before it. That is the essence of the perfect *order* of life, the true peacefulness or *Islam*.

> We have revealed to you this Scripture truthfully, therefore serve God. Be sincere to Him in the way of life *(deen)*. (39:2)

---

[19] The word *Khin* literally means rotten - *Ziri* means that you see. *Khinziri* does not refer to swine - a livestock which is part of God's provisions to mankind (5:1 & 6:142). It is obvious the prohibition is limited to the nature and condition of food - not the species

Sincerely submitting to the prescribed limits sanctioned by Him in the *deen* is to *serve* Him. That is all it says. Simple. In this *simple* decree, God has reinforced the concept of His words to His servants around the world irrespective of colour or language. *Islam* is simple, the Qur'an is simple. However, bear in mind that simple here does not mean easy. In order to overcome the predicament we are told:

> Seek help through perseverance and be committed. This is difficult indeed, but not for those who are sincere who realise that they will meet their Lord that they will ultimately return to Him. (2:45-46)

I reiterate my stand that there is no such thing as the **Islamic religion**. There is, undoubtedly, the *peacefulness* of an *orderly way of life* sanctioned by God. It is our responsibility as His servants to submit to His will by observing His *prescribed way*. Let us now explore the logic behind this requirement of *Islam*.

- It is God who grants life and death.

- It is God who keeps the creation in perfect balance.

- It is God who makes us happy or miserable.

- It is God who creates the human, male and female, from a drop of liquid and then from *'something which clings'*, then He gives it life as an infant. Then some reach full strength and get to become old, and others die earlier. It is God who determines our time of life and death, nobody else.

- It is God who makes us rich or poor.

- It is God who provides everything in exact measure.

- To Him belongs the kingdom of the heavens and the earth.

- There is no god but Him.

Out of mercy He revealed His guidance to mankind so that they enjoy a peaceful life in this world and a peaceful life the hereafter. Those who are vigilant and submit to His will and believe in Him alone have grasped the strongest bond that never breaks. His message to all mankind:

> O mankind, you shall serve your Lord, who created you and those before you, that you might become observant. (2:21)

> I have not created the jinn and the humans except to *serve* me alone (51:56)

There are people who take God for granted by denying He is the Lord of the Universe. No matter how hard we try to deny His existence and power – we cannot escape from reality that He gives life and He takes it back. Our natural instincts as humans tell us that there is an unseen super power somewhere out there who has created everything in existence and maintains it in perfect balance. The Qur'an tells us that there is only one God and that God is common to all people. He is the Most Compassionate and Most Merciful and knows all our secrets. His names include: the King, the Sacred, the Peace, the Faithful, the Supreme, the Almighty, the Most Compassionate, the Dignified, the Creator, the Initiator, and the Designer. To Him belongs all the beautiful attributes. He is glorified every passing second by everything that exists in the heavens and earth, and whatever is in between them and whatever is beneath the soil. He gives us a very simple illustration in sura 2:258 of His power in the Qur'an by saying that He is the one that brings the sun from the east and that, if there is anyone who wishes to deny Him or challenge His authority, and then we should ask such a person to bring the sun from the west if they can[20].

It has been decreed that those who add even one extra ruling or regulation beyond that which was prescribed by God are His manifest enemies. They have rejected what God had sanctioned. And those who obey these additional restrictions are *not* submitting to God's decrees, rather, they have been misled by the Devil. The Qur'an is very clear on this matter when God says, *'Do not testify as they do, and do not follow their opinions'*.[21]

> Summon your witnesses who can testify that God has prohibited this or that[22]. Even if they testify, do not testify as they do, and do not follow the passions of those who reject Our revelations, those who disbelieve in the Hereafter, and set up idols alongside God. (6:150)

---

[20] Scientists have discovered within our small universe there are unknown galaxies millions of light years away. In this verse God gives a simple analogy by challenging anyone who think they can alter His creations. Although He could confuse us with other creations, but He mentioned the sun among His signs that we could physically see and imagine.

[21] i.e. those who create laws on food more than the Quranic injunctions.

[22] The Jews introduced the Kosher - Arab religionists rejected the Quran to follow the Jews and declared food as *Halal* and *Haram*. 6:138 says: 'They said, *"These livestock and crops are prohibited, and no one shall eat them, unless we say so"*, according to their claim'.

Those submitting to God must uphold their covenants and they may eat any food palatable to them except what He had sanctioned in His Scripture.

Deen does not mean religion

The principal idea of corrupting the word *deen* of *Islam* into the commonly accepted meaning of *religion* originated with the religionists. By means of this oblique device, the religionists effectively set themselves up to control the key to Paradise for all those who come to the Qur'an. Parallel situations are seen in the context of both the Jews and Christians in terms of their controlling priesthood. Religion, in the vernacular sense of the word, surely ought to have issued from *God to People* and not on any other basis.

Taken from the Arab cult perspective, 5:3 reads:

> 'Today I have perfected the religion for you and completed My favour upon you, and I decree Islam as the religion'.

By this simple trick and in the twinkle of an eye, Muslims[23] were enslaved by the concept of the Arab religion. Besides what has been prescribed in 5:3 there are no other decrees that regulate the restrictions in the *way* of life for people other than these simple injunctions:

• You are forbidden to marry your own mother, your daughters, your sisters, your father's sisters, and your mother's sisters, your brother's daughters, your sister's daughters, your foster mother who nursed you, girls

---

[23] Muslim literally means a person who is at peace. He attains peace by freeing himself from any kind of mental slavery. He decides his own way of life by his submissions, capitulates and relents to God's will.

nursed by the same woman as you, your mother-in-laws, your step-daughters, and women who were previously married to your sons. (4:23)

• You are forbidden to associate God with anything, you are forbidden to kill your infants from fear of poverty. You are forbidden to commit gross sins, obvious or hidden, you are forbidden to kill another person, you are forbidden to approach the orphan's money, you are forbidden from profiteering, you are forbidden to be a false witness for the benefit of yourself or your own relatives. (6:151-152)

• You are forbidden from doing evil deeds – obvious or hidden sins – or to go against the truth, or to associate God with idols and to attribute lies to Him. (7:33)

Any sensible person without religious guidance would know the above are morally wrong. Nobody needs a rabbi, or priest, or mullah to tell other people that they are bad. Of course, such injunctions require the application of common sense. However, the Arab religion is predicated on the absence of this very necessity. The *u'lema* will threaten their followers with hell-fire if they insist on using their common sense. Unfortunately, those who obey the religionists and the *u'lema* may understand too late and say:

> Had we but listened and used our common sense, we would not be among the companions of the blazing fire. (67:10)

The prohibitions above are the only clearly forbidden things in God's *way*. These four verses spell out all the restrictions or matters which are classified as *Haram* by the Lord of the Universe. The restrictions on food are repeated in two other verses. That makes a total of six verses

containing restrictions out of a total of 6348 verses. There
are no other restrictions in other verses in the Qur'an. If you
belong to the Arab religion you will find tome upon tome of
prohibitions written by men. Different sects in the Arab
religion have different prohibitions and in some sects the
primary victims are women. They are forbidden to expose
their faces, walk on the street alone, talk to men or travel on
public transport and in some extreme cases they are
forbidden from attending schools.

We are constantly reminded by God not to observe
ways from any sources other than His:

> To Him belongs everything in the heavens and the
> earth, and the way of life *(deen)* shall be for Him
> alone. Will you observe other than God? (16:52)

> You shall follow what is sent upon you from your
> Lord, and not follow any idols alongside Him. Only
> a few of you take heed. (7:3)

Sadly, those who have been misled by the Arab
religion observe a whole host of other things that are
purportedly forbidden or *Haram*. These other prohibitions
are based on nothing. Viewed logically, the *deen* is a
catalyst that allows people to discern the true Muslim by
observation. It is clear that no one who observes these few
simple restrictions can possibly participate in idol-worship.
God's values are perfect in form and function and universal
in application. There is no need for anyone to add to them.
Adding or taking away anything to these prescribed decrees
simply adds to idol worship.

The situation that people find themselves in today is
obvious. People must live **for** their Lord because He
advocates only justice. People are expected to be sincere

and focused their submission to God alone. The big shock
for the religionists at this point is that people of both sexes
have been granted total freedom of choice as long as they
keep these simple rules and do not defy truth and common
sense or invent lies and attribute them to God. What could
be simpler than that?

Total freedom

Each individual is given total freedom to choose the
path he or she wishes from the day God gives us life until
the day He takes it back. It is our right and responsibility to
choose wisely. There are two basic options:

- A way of life *for* God as ordained by Him (*deen-nil-
  lah*), or

- A way of life which is *not* for God (*Thoghut*[24])

God does not impose His *deen* on anyone. He describes
the Qur'an as the criterion between right and wrong. He has
said that the Qur'an is fully detailed and He has not left
anything out from it. Strangely, many think of *Islam* as a
religion bereft of choice and full of compulsion. But they
are confusing the Arab cult which masquerades as *Islam*
and the guidance outlined in the Qur'an for a peaceful life.
The choice to follow God is completely left to His servants:
'*there is no compulsion*'. It is in this spirit that the reader
should apply his or her logic and wisdom when discerning
whether a particular way of life *(deen)* is true in origin or

---

[24] The word *Thoghut* means idols. It includes humans 7:194, prophets and
messengers 3: 79-80, religious leaders 9:31, imam or mullahs 39:3, the dead
16:20-21, statues 2:93, personal property 18:42, ego 25:43, jinns 6:100 and also
by following a religion 30:31-32.

not. How you choose will determine whether you travel first class or coach in this life and onward to the life hereafter.

> There is no compulsion in the way of life *(deen)*. However, now [the difference] is made clear between right and wrong. Therefore, anyone who rejects the virtual idols *(Thoghut)* and believes in God, surely they hold to the strongest bond that will not break. God is Hearer, Omniscient. (2:256)

> There is no creature on earth nor birds that fly with wings except they are nations[25] just like you. We did not leave anything out of the Scripture. To their Lord they will all return. (6:38)

Those who believe in God and His messenger are called to focus sincerely and submit to God's prescribed way. The Last Prophet was made to declare:

> Say, "My Lord advocates justice. Observe your focus of submissions and invoke Him sincerely as a *deen* the same way He created you that you may return." (7:29)

> Whatever good happens to you is from God[26]. Whatever bad happens to you are the consequences of your own deeds. (4:79)

In other words, whilst a person is given the total freedom of choice in charting their way of life, God stresses the distinction between right and wrong, and there the golden rule applies: God advocates only justice.

---

[25] All living creatures in the heavens and the earth were created by God as nations of their own

[26] The Arab religionists teach their followers if a man jumps from the tenth floor or wraps his body with a bomb - it is God's will. There are cases when religious teachers rape a young girl - they tell the girl's parent it is God's will.

Virtual idols

Idol-worship can take many forms. For example, if a person chooses to make their ego paramount, their life will be controlled by their ego. They will idolise their own ego. If a person makes the accumulation of wealth paramount, his or her life will be controlled by greed and he or she will idolise money. If a person chooses to idolise other humans, his or her *deen* will be controlled by that conviction and others will dictate their way of life. Similarly, should a person choose to profess religion he or she will then idolise the religious leaders, and the rituals dictated by these religious leaders or priests will regulate their way of life.

The common factor here is idol-worship. There are clear instances in the Qur'an about people who idolise their prophets, messengers, energies and *jinn*.

> It is not possible for a human whom God has blessed with the Scripture and wisdom and prophethood that he should tell the people to serve him besides God. Nor will He ask you to idolise the energies or the prophets. (3:79-80)

Clearly, God's prophet and messengers are not to be idolised. Yet many prophets and messengers *are* – in effect – worshipped. And then there are others who idolise saints, gurus, priest and religious scholars.

> They have taken their priests and scholars as lords besides God. (9:31)

> What about the one who idolises his own ego? Can you do anything for him? (25:43)

The egotists have been forewarned. God's response to the question as to what can be done for them is:

> Do you suppose many of them hear or understand? Indeed, they are just like animals. No, they are worse than animals. (25:44)

The Qur'an does not mince words. As regards those who reject it, it is clear and unequivocal:

> The Qur'an is full of wisdom .You are one of the messengers, advocating the right path. A revelation from the Almighty, most merciful. To warn people, whose forefathers were never warned, they are unaware. It is predetermined that the majority will not believe. Consequently, We chain their necks to their chins, and thus they are forced [into the directions they choose]. And We place a barrier in front of them and a barrier behind them, so they can never see. (36:2-9)

The Qur'an urges people to consider the Creation:

> And the sun is moving in a specific orbit. Such is the design of the Almighty, the Omniscient, and We designed the moon to appear in stages until it reverts to a thin curve. The sun never catches up with the moon, nor does the night prematurely overtake the day. Each floats in its own orbit. (36:38-39)

In retrospect, if an undoubted source tells me that a set of instructions have arrived for me from the Being who created the sun and the moon and set them on their orbits, I would follow those instructions without question. To question such wisdom and ability would border on insanity. In contrast in 1969, the chief priest of the Grand Mosque in

Mecca was quoted as saying that the earth was flat and anyone professing the contrary was an infidel. This serves to illustrate the crux of the problem with the Arab religion, which goes by the name of *Islam*: ignorance. The Qur'an says:

> Will they choose other than God's *deen*, whilst everything is peaceful (*aslama*) in the skies and the earth either willingly or unwillingly? And to Him they will return. (3:83)

The word *aslama* in this verse is the same (i.e. has the same semantic root and is merely a separate conjugation of the root idea) as the word *Islam*. Everything in the seven heavens: the billions of stars, all the planets, everything on earth from every kind of creeper, plant and tree, every kind of animal and insect, every kind of bird, and kinds of aquatic life exist peacefully willingly or unwillingly. Thus, God poses the question that begs to be answered: *'Will they choose other than God's deen when His other creations are able to exist peacefully?*

The *deen-nil-lah* or – God's way – has been revealed to all His prophets (including Noah, Abraham, Ishmael, Isaac, Jacob, Moses, Jesus, and Muhammad). The message is clear, simple and the same in substance in every instance. No prophet was sent to deliver or start a religion. Their job was simply to deliver God's message, the gist of which is the *deen*.

Serve God through commitments

Again, this is a frighteningly simple concept. We are encouraged to remind ourselves from the teaching of the Qur'an:

My commitments, my sacrifices, my life and my death are for God, Lord of the Universe. He has no partner. These are the commandments given to me and I am among the first of those at peace. (6:162-163)

The Qur'an teaches a way of life that espouses self-sacrifice for the benefit of all those around us. People are repulsive in committing themselves to the fundamental values prescribed by God in His deen. They are not willing to sacrifice ego, greed and arrogance by observing their obligations to do good deeds to their parents, amongst themselves, their associates, their close or distant neighbours, their relatives, the poor, the needy and the oppressed.

When we are confronted with those who dispute this simple concept, we are encouraged to tell them:

Shall I seek other than God as a Lord when He is the Lord of everything in existence? Whatever anyone earns is for his own account. No burdened soul will bear the burden of another. To your Lord is your ultimate return and then He will tell you of everything you disputed. (6:164)

The Lord of the Universe did not reveal His Scriptures in vain. The revelations are His signs, His good news, and His guide to mankind. The Scripture is non-negotiable and cannot be manipulated.

These are the signs of the Reading, a profound Scripture, a guide and good news for those who believe. They uphold the commitments and keep

them pure. And they are certain about the Hereafter.
(27:2-3)

Those who recite God's Scripture and uphold the
commitments and give to charity from our
provisions, publicly or secretly, they seek a
transaction that never loses. (35:29)

Charity, donations, amicable treatment of people,
equitable trade, moral discipline and the fulfilment of
promises are just some of the guidelines encompassed in
God's way. It is, ultimately, the perfect recipe for mankind.
However, we have not embraced these prescribed values.
The history from the Qur'an tells us that from the beginning
of time, upon receiving God's Scripture people have
insisted on following religion rather than a way of
uprightness which promotes good deeds and good works
among themselves. They do not promote civility, sincerity,
honesty, humbleness, compassion, love or the treatment of
each other in the most amicable manner as a way of life.
They insist on worship at specific times with the hope that
they may be pardoned by their Creator of whatever
wrongdoings they have committed. The majority of them
prefer to idolise their children, property, *imams*, priests,
religious scholars, prophets and tangible idols. They reject a
simple concept of a way of uprightness or *deen-al-hunafa*.
All that is enjoined upon them is to uphold God's
commandments, be sincere in committing themselves to the
prescribed deen by doing the good deeds and good works. It
is a plain and simple way of life. There is no hardship
imposed by God. Of the idol-worshippers the Qur'an says:

Those who disbelieve among the followers of the
previous Scriptures and the idol-worshippers will

never believe even after proof comes to them. (98:1)[27]

All that is enjoined upon them is to believe in God by devoting themselves to serve God's in sincerity in the way of life *(deen)*, and to uphold the commitments and keep them pure. That is the way of uprightness (*deen-al-hunafa*). (98:5)

The way of uprightness is measured by personal commitment to the deeds as detailed in His Scripture. We know this from 98:5. One recommended way of upholding the commitment is to observe the following:

Your Lord has decreed that you shall not serve other than Him, and honour your parents for as long as they live, one of them or both of them. You shall not speak harshly to them, nor mistreat them; you shall speak to them amicably, and lower for them the wings of humility and kindness and say, "My Lord, have mercy on them, for they have brought me up from infancy." (17:23-24)

If we serve God and keep this one simple rule, try to imagine the global impact of such a movement. This is the world that *Islam* envisions. We are required to submit to what He has prescribed: uphold these commitments and keep them pure. This decree is not a new revelation to the Last Prophet. The same decree was given to Moses for the Children of Israel:

We made a covenant with the Children of Israel, "You shall not serve other than God. You shall

---

[27] The people of the previous scriptures who follow a religion under a brand name and those who receive the Qur'an but follow a religion are termed as idol worshipers. There is only one way in life for mankind to observe i.e. God's way

regard parents, the relatives, the orphans, and the poor. You shall speak to them amicably. You shall uphold your commitments and keep them pure. But you turned away, except a few of you, and you became averse." (2:83)

2:83 says the majority of the Children of Israel became averse and aborted their covenant with God. They did not fulfil their obligations.

Similarly, we are expected to uphold our commitments by observing the requirements of the following commandment:

O mankind! You shall observe your Lord, who created you from one person, then created from her, her mate, then from the two of them He spread many men and women. You shall observe God whom you swear by, and regard your relatives. God is watching you. You shall give the orphans their due properties and not substitute the bad for the good, nor shall you consume their money by mixing their properties with yours. This would be a gross injustice. (4:1-2)

Whatever decree had been revealed by God to the children of Israel was again revealed to the Last Prophet, and those who submit are reminded to uphold their commitments and to keep them pure. He repeats many times throughout the Qur'an that those who believe in Him should *serve* Him and observe His will through fulfilling their commitments, and that they should keep these commitments pure. God's covenants are those matters He prescribes in the Scripture. He constantly reminds us about His servants' obligation to fulfil the covenants:

You shall not touch the orphan's money, except for
their own good until they grow up. You shall fulfil
your covenants. You are responsible for your
covenants. You shall give full measure when you
trade, and weigh with an equitable balance. This is
better and more righteous. Surely your hearing,
eyesight and your heart will be questioned about
them. (17:34-36)

In other words, everything that we do in our life like
caring the orphans or even our trading activities will be
taken into account. In the hereafter we simply cannot deny
what we have done to ourselves in this world because our
ears, eyes and heart will testify against us. For example, if
we accept anything blindly without using common sense
our hearings, eyes and hearts will testify against us.

A Muslim's claim of submission to God can therefore
be put to the litmus test by observing his commitment to his
covenants. *Islam* is, by the Creator's design, a way of life
characterised by deeds and merit. And by a person's deeds
shall you know them.

The religionists (who insist that their followers recite
God's Scripture in Arabic) would have people parrot the
verses of the Qur'an without ever fulfilling their
commitments or gaining any merit. Praying ritually is not
part of the *deen* revealed by God. His prescribed way
demands service by deeds. Anyone can perform ritual
prayers.

The champions of the Arab religion insist a good
Muslim must *pray ritually*[28] five times a day facing Mecca.

---

[28] This is the most important pillar of faith in the Arab religion. A person's
character is judged by his compliance in performing these sets of body
movements. A criminal can be a good Muslim as long as he or she observes the

This is the most important commitment and the first pillar of their religion. There is no basis for this assertion since the Qur'an does not state a need to fulfil commitments by ritual prayer. Indeed this is a fact and there is no getting away from it.

Thus, they have corrupted one of the most important words in the Qur'an (and subsequently one of the most important concepts in the deen) by twisting the word *Solaa* (which means commitments) to mean *ritual prayer*. And they prevent people from upholding their commitments according to the covenants prescribed by God in the Scripture.

Before exploring the misrepresentation of the word *Solaa*, we would do well to explore the Qur'an and its instruction regarding worship. This is important because the word *Solaa* was mischievously distorted to become ritual prayer and it is an act of worship[29].

God is not to be '*Worshiped*'

First and foremost: the word 'worship' is not found anywhere in the Qur'an. The religionists twisted the meaning of a simple word in the book.

The essence of the Book is that all humans need to lead a righteous way of life according to the prescribed covenants by upholding their commitments and keeping them pure. No one can fulfil these commitments through acts of worship or ritual prayer. A person should observe

---

ritual prayer everyday, wears the skullcap, or covers the head. In some countries, it is a serious crime for not praying.

[29] The word *'abdi* in the Qur'an means servant, *na'budu* we are serving, *laa-ta'budu* means 'do not serve'. Worship is a profane word.

his commitments through the individual act of submission to *serve* the Lord of the Universe.

> *Wama qolaq-tul jin-ni wal-ain-sa il-laa li-ya'budun.* (51:56)

> And I did not create the *jinn* and the humans except for <u>serving Me</u>. (51:56)

In one sentence, the Qur'an has explained our purpose here on earth. We are created to serve, not to worship. We have been created in the grand design to serve by deeds (and not merely by thoughts or words). The misrepresentation of the word *serve* (*ta'budu*) to mean *worship* has had a dire effect on the Islamic landscape.

The words *serve*[30] and *worship* have different meanings in the context of this discussion. The former signifies serving God by doing good deeds in keeping with what we know to be His laws. The latter is a concentrated feeling of respect or admiration and love for the dead idols or icons and is demonstrated through rituals, pilgrimages, and the singing of hymns, etc. The word 'serve' *ta'budu* or *ya'budun* is derived from the word *'abd* which means *servant* (and not *worship*). All humans are servants of God. Therefore they have to *serve* and be subservient or submit (*sujud*) to Him alone. There are several derivatives from the word *'abd* (servant). For example, the following verse is in reference to Jesus the son of Mary and the assigned energies (*mala-ika*)[31] closest to God.

---

[30] Collin Cobuild: Serve something such as a company, community or your country, you work for it in order to benefit it.

[31] The word *mala-ika* is derived from the root *MLK* which means functional energies or the unseen magnetic forces at work. There is no such thing as angels floating around the space. Religionists borrowed the description of the Bible to promote this wrong idea. *Malik* is one who is in power.

*Laiyas-tabkifu masih'u ai-yakuna <u>a'bdan</u> lil-lah wa-
lal-malaikatu muqor-robun. Waman yas-tankifu 'an-
<u>'ibada-tihi</u> was-yastakbir fa-sayah shuru-hum ilai-hi
jami'an.* (4:172)

Never will the Messiah disdain being a servant
(*a'bdan*) of God nor will the assigned energies.
Those who disdain serving (*ibada-tihi*) Him and are
arrogant, surely He will gather them to Him, all of
them. (4:172)

The Messiah was pure but he was not disdainful of
being a servant to God. It is the duty of a servant to *serve*
his master. The duty of a believer is to serve God by
upholding the commitments and not to 'worship' Him in the
sense of bowing and scraping. It would seem strange for
any household to have a platoon of servants worshipping
their employer. Where would be the logic in it?

As servants we are expected to look towards Him and
praise Him like the rest of His creations in the heavens and
the earth.

O mankind, you are the ones in need towards God,
and God, He is the affluent the praised. (35:15)

He does not need our petty sacrifices of food or self-
imposed pilgrimages. He does not need our presence in
Mecca. In fact He does not need our promises. If we have
pledged a promise, it is our duty to fulfil that promise for
our own good. He wants us to put His words into action. A
servant has to observe his commitments or he become
useless.

Of course, one can argue that God does not need our
service either. This is true. It is we who benefit from being

true in our service to Him. By these means, we justify the responsibility of free choice granted us and grow to our full potential. We become fully what we were meant to be. We become true to our truest nature. *This* is God's will, and it is for our good.

Similarly, there are energies that are specially assigned making them close to God and they also *serve* their master. The word *'abdan* in this verse means *servant*. The same verse also uses another derivative i.e. *ibada-tihi* to mean doing service for Him. The Messiah and the assigned energies did not worship God. They were too busy doing His work and *serving* Him.

We can also find a similar derivative from the root word *'abd* in the Qur'an which means *serving* and not worship:

> *Wa-nah-nu lahu a'bidun* (2:138)

> And Him are we serving (2:138)

> *Was-alman arsalna min qoblika min-rosulina aj'alna min-dunir-rohman ali-hatan ya'budun.* (43: 45)

> And ask those whom We have sent from before you among the messengers if We have set other than the Merciful as gods for them to be *served.* (43: 45)

Simply put, all service is through deeds. The world is full of good intentions but intentions alone are not enough.

The seven verses in the introductory *surah*[32] of the Qur'an are recited by the followers of the Arab religion

---

[32] *Al-Fatihah*, the first *surah* of the Qur'an.

during each of their five 'mandatory' daily prayers. The religionists deceived them by ascribing the word *na'budu* (serve) in 1:5 to mean *worship*. This word is derived from the root *'abd* which means *servant*. Instead of declaring to God that they will serve Him alone without associating Him with anything, they say they 'worship' Him. God has never commanded anyone to *worship* Him.

The essence of the first part *Al Fatihah* is that God's attributes encompass His dominion over the *deen* of everything in existence in the heavens and the earth. He is the absolute ruler of the orderly system in this world and in the Hereafter. The first four verses say, '*With the name of God, the Most Compassionate, the Merciful. Praise be to God the Lord of the Universe, the Most Compassionate and the Merciful. The Ruler of the day of the order'*. And then, as servants to our Lord we pledge that we will uphold our covenant to serve him from what we are about to read from His guidance – a guidance which says at the outset of the very next chapter, '*This Book is infallible, a guidance for the observant who believe in the unseen, and they uphold their obligations......*'

1:5 should properly be read as:

Eiya-ka-na'budu wa-eiya kanas-ta'ain. (1:5)

You alone we serve and You alone we ask for help. (1:5)

This is followed by:

Guide us in the straight path, a path of those whom you blessed, and not of   those   who   deserve wrath, or those who strayed. (1:6-7)

90

Here, the request is to seek His help in guiding us on the straight path that He had blessed. Logically, the only way God guides His servants is through His revealed Scriptures; certainly not through the performing of ritual prayer. Instead of translating their services into practical acts according to what He has ordained in His Book, the religionists offer only lip-service by repeating: *'You alone we worship, and You alone we ask for help'* seventeen times per day (the five daily rituals consist of 2, 4, 4, 3, 4 units in each ritual prayer at dawn, midday, afternoon, evening and night).

These verses clearly say we declare that we will serve Him alone, put our trust in Him to seek His mercy and blessings to guide us to the right path in His *deen*. God is the only one who can guide His servants to the straight path. No one else can do this, not even the prophets:

> You cannot guide those you love. God is the one who guides whomever He wills because He is the only one who is fully aware of those who deserve the guidance. (28:56)

There is no such thing as 'holy people' who can guide another to the straight path. These so-called holy people will ultimately themselves become idols to their followers.

> God is the Lord of those who believe. He leads them out of the darkness into light. While those who disbelieve, their lords are the idols. They lead them out of the light into darkness. They have deserved the Fire as their eternal retribution. (2:257)

The Qur'an is telling us that the 'holy men' will take people out of the light into darkness and lead their followers into hell-fire. None of us can escape from these 'holy men' as long as he belongs to a religion.

Upon a critical reading of the Qur'an it becomes clear that we cannot 'butter up' our Master – the one who gave us this life – by worshipping Him through rituals. There is no barter system involving the performance of rituals. We receive the guidance from God through His mercy – mercy to which we are not entitled. In order to qualify we are simply required to serve God by fulfilling our covenant with Him. That is the contract with Him, and is binding upon us until we breathe our last. There is not a single verse in the Qur'an commanding humans to worship the Creator.

Moses and Jesus did not worship God

According to the Qur'an, all the revealed Scriptures stress one singular important message: that mankind is to serve no other than Him. The history of Moses is vividly described throughout the Qur'an. Jesus the son of Mary was sent to the same community to confirm what had been revealed to Moses.

> And We gave Moses the Scripture, and made it as guidance for the Children of Israel, saying, "You shall not take other than Me as your protector." (17:2)

The Qur'an tells us in various places that the Children of Israel violated their covenant (having pledged to uphold it) after they had distorted the words of God, and that many of them disregard parts of the Scripture. Moses left his people in anger after they refused to enter the Holy Land designated to them. Finally, the land was forbidden to them and they wandered in the wilderness for forty years without Moses. (5:25-26).

92

They created the religion of Judaism and called themselves Jews. Anyone who reads the Bible will know that they established the temple and created the priesthood system. They introduced rituals, worship and offerings as their way of life and falsely claimed that God ordained it. The Qur'an says the Jews say Ezra[33] was the son of God. As a mercy, God sent Jesus the son of Mary, supported him with the Holy Spirit and demonstrated signs through him. Jesus declared:

> "I come to confirm what is with you from the Torah, and to permit for you what was prohibited you, and I come to you with signs from your Lord. Therefore observe God and obey me. Indeed, God is my Lord and your Lord, therefore *serve* Him. And this is the right path." (3:50-51)

They were not able to accept any messenger of God who came to them with commandments contrary to beliefs they had concocted for themselves. They were arrogant and rejected – and even killed – some of God's messengers. This is the picture that emerges from their history in the Qur'an.

In reality, neither Moses nor Jesus required their followers to worship the Lord God. Jesus told the Children of Israel to *observe and serve* the One God. But today, the

---

[33] In the Old Testament Ezra was a Persian from Babylon whose main objective was to protect the interest of Artaxerxes, the king of kings of the Persian kingdom. He commissioned Ezra as the chief priest for Trans-Euphrates continent including Judah and Jerusalem. He was given full authority to create religious laws, taxes, rituals, and worships. His laws were sanctioned as sacred including death penalty for apostates, banishment, confiscation of property and imprisonment. In the New Testament Jesus condemned the teachers of the law of the Pharisees or Farsi and said, 'unless the people denounce the Persian influence there will be no salvation for them.

people who disagree with the Jews' rejection of Jesus are virtually worshipping the very man whose message was to *observe and serve* the One God. Everybody seems to need a religion so that they can *worship* something, whether it is the Christians deifying Jesus or the Jews deifying themselves and their own 'chosen' status. Both of these perversions of truth have their cousins in the religion created by the Arab religionists, the enemies who took and twisted what the Last Prophet was given to deliver to mankind.

According to the Qur'an, the Children of Israel conspired against God, Moses and Jesus. They introduced a system of priesthood and a culture of *worshipping* the servant of God. Today, the people who subscribe to the religion of Christianity cannot say with certainty whether Jesus was the son of Mary or the son of a man or the son of God or even God Himself. However, we know from the Qur'an the facts about this man:

> Because they said, "We killed the Messiah, Jesus the son of Mary the messenger of God." Nay, they never killed him. They never crucified him. But they were led to *believe* that they had. Those who dispute in this matter are doubtful thereof. They have no real knowledge. They follow only conjecture. In truth, they never killed him. (4:157)

The followers of the Christian religion were *led* to believe that Jesus was crucified, but they are not sure about it. All that the Christian priests can say is: *you must have faith*. But faith based on rhetorical propaganda promotes a way of life full of superstition, myths and tradition. The true life is the life of commitment to our brethren, our parents, our families, our relatives, the poor, and the orphans.

94

Rhetoric, worship, ritual prayers – that is, *religion* – is a side-show at best and a pernicious blight on humanity at worst.

It is, therefore, strange – not to mention downright blasphemous – to construe *'abd*[34] *(ta'budu)* as *worship* accompanied by sets of physical movements: facing a certain direction (or a statue or a wall or a stone building or image) and walking around a stone structure, and so on. These are simply pagan worship rituals, created by people to simplify what they cannot comprehend.

The ideal concept of peacefulness or Islam, an *'abd* is a servant who serves *(na'budu)* his Lord by fulfilling the prescribed covenants through his commitments. He does not fulfil his commitments by worshipping. His deeds *('amal)* are the service, or *ibadah*. The verb *na'budu* means 'we serve' and *ibadah* is noun signifying the service we render when we uphold our commitments by fulfilling the prescribed decrees. Such submission equals service to the Lord.

> And strive[35] in the cause of God with true striving. He is the one who selected you without imposing hardship upon you as the *deen*, the principle of your father Abraham. He is the one who named you Muslims *(those at peace)*. Thus, the Messenger will be a witness to you and you will be witness to the people. Therefore, uphold the commitments and keep them pure *(Solaa-ta-wa-atu-zakaa)* and hold

---

[34] Arab religionists insist this word means worship. But some sincere translators do translates this word as 'serve'.

[35] The religionists abuse the word *Jihad* (strive) Qur'an to instigate their followers to kill other people. In 25:52 God's calls people to strive in His cause with the Qur'an - the *biggest Jihad (Jahidu kabi-roo)* - without violence. The cause of violence in the world today is caused by them - not what God wants.

fast to God. He is your protector, the best protector
and the best supporter. (22:78)

This is the service that the servants of God must render
to serve Him. The act of fulfilling these prescribed
covenants and striving to further His cause through their
commitments and keeping them pure is *Solaa-ta wa-atu-
zakaa*.[36]

Therefore *ya'budu* is not worshipping but *serving*.

Religion is man-made

By reading the Qur'an with care it becomes obvious
that God did not intend that there be any 'religion' at all.
The Qur'an promotes a way of life which is acceptable with
God and which promotes the wellbeing of people. There is
no need to define it as a religion. It is clearly stated in the
Qur'an that no prophets or messengers brought 'religion'
from God. God revealed a *deen* to them so that the people
around them would serve the unseen God by observing
righteous deeds amongst themselves for their own benefit in
this world and the Hereafter. And, thus informed, people
would also know and avoid the unholy and the hypocritical
behaviour of 'religion' by the deeds of those who profess
and practice it. The *surah* of the Qur'an attributed to Noah
states that he worked day and night calling the people to
abandon religion. Noah told them they should not serve
anyone or anything except God. They should observe a way
of life *for* God. His neighbours and friends did not heed his
call.

---

[36] That is what is wrongfully rendered by the religionists as: *pray five times a
day and pay your tithes to the mosque.*

> Noah said, "O my people, I come to you as a Warner.[37] You shall serve God and work righteousness and obey me." (71:2-3)

The response from his community was:

> They said. "Do not abandon your idols, do not abandon *Wadd*, or *Suwa*, or *Yaghoot*, or *Ya'ooq* and *Nasr*." (71:23)

The people of Noah were probably rich, prosperous and comfortable with their way of life. They did not suffer any poverty in their 'religion' of worshipping idols. Noah did not fit into the popular pattern of the day. The Qur'an teaches us that following the masses ends badly:

> If you follow the majority of the people on earth they will divert you from the path of God. They follow only conjecture and they only guess. (6:116)

Muhammad espoused the same message as Noah. He was simply the *messenger* of God, he was not a *worshipper*. He worked to spread the word of God and hope it prevails over other *deens*. One would logically assume that Muslims the world over would want to emulate the Last Prophet and embody the teaching he brought. It is illuminating in that regard to read what the message he received was:

> We have decreed for you the same *deen* as was enjoined upon Noah and what is revealed to you herein, and also what was enjoined upon Abraham, Moses and Jesus. You shall uphold the *one* deen and not be divided. It is simply too difficult for the idol-worshippers to accept what you advocate. God is the one who will bring towards Him whomever He

---

[37] The Qur'an refers to God's messenger as a *warner* on occasion

wills, and He will guide towards Himself those who would return. (42:13)

Read that again: *'It is simply too difficult for the idol-worshippers to accept what you advocate'*.

That statement is self-explanatory: people who profess religion are regarded as idol-worshippers, they will simply not be able to fathom God's true *deen* (as advocated in the Qur'an alone and discussed in this work).

In addition, their almost certain adverse reaction to this book will bear testament to veracity of this statement.

PART THREE

The Arab religion

There is no historical record written by the Arabs of their own race prior to the revelation of the Qur'an. The Qur'an, however, says that the Messenger was sent to a race whose forefathers were ignorant of God's system. The people around the Last Prophet were gentiles and at a total loss as far as God's guidance was concerned (62:2).

The modern-day Arabs acknowledge that they belonged to a *jahiliah*[38] race before the Qur'an was revealed to the Last Prophet. This is a subtle way of saying they were pagans. In 53:19-22 God questions the Arabs about the three idols *Al-Manat*, *Al-Uzza* and *Al-Lat*, which may have been connected to stone idols. Non-Arab historical sources indicate that the Arabs were commonly known to be polytheists many centuries before Muhammad went to them to deliver the message of the Qur'an.

Of their many deities, the principal sacred object in Arabian religion was the stone, either a rock outcropping or a large boulder, often a rectangular or irregular black basaltic stone without representative sculptural detail. Such stones were thought to be the residences of a god. The nomadic tribes refer to these deities as *Hagar* or 'stone'. Often there would be a well or cistern with water for ablutions and a 'sacred' tree on which offerings to the gods or trophies of war would be hung.

In the Arabian temples the image of the deity sometimes stood in the open air and sometimes it was sheltered in a *qubbah*, or vaulted niche. Such a niche might

---

[38] *Jahiliah*: ignorance or fools

be portable. Such a portable shelter is represented graphically on a Palmyrene relief. Not to be confused with the *qubbah* is the word *ka'aba*. The word *ka'aba* (which actually means *ankles*) was warped to come to mean a cube-shaped walled structure. Such an awkward-looking empty square house was constructed possibly in the shape of tents, and served as a shelter for the black Arabic sacred stones.

The principal public celebration of the nomadic tribes was an annual pilgrimage in which tribes who shared a common bond through worship of a particular deity would reunite at a particular sanctuary or *station*. The pattern of ceremonial procession around stone idols was common and is a pattern we see today continued in the Arab custom of the pilgrimage to Mecca. However, present scholarly knowledge of ancient Arabia remains fragmentary at best and there are many substantial gaps in the picture that has come down to us.

Unlike certain other Scriptures, the Qur'an does not give the details of the personal life of the person who delivered the message. It emphasises the significance of the message rather than that of the messenger. But the Arabs have promoted the opposite tendency.

Despite their claims to the contrary and the sheer tonnage of 'learned' books (supposedly about the life of the prophet) that the Arab religion now rests upon, in reality the religionists do not have a reliable biography of the ancestry and early life of the Messenger except what they themselves cobbled together from the conjectures of story-tellers and fragments of tribal myth. The information to hand[39] was not compiled systematically but was manufactured years after

---

[39] The information about the supposed practices of the prophet is called *Hadith*, and highly spurious biographies have been created based on the same.

the fact to insinuate that this man was a charlatan who behaved in an illogical and strange manner which inspired fanaticism in his followers and a fiercely intolerant way of life towards those who rejected the Arab religion.

By the Arab religionists' own admission, this 'information' was transmitted orally for more than a century before being committed to writing. No one denies that not a single one of the known and revered biographers had any personal acquaintance with the Last Prophet whatsoever. Each of the fragments claims a pedigree of authenticity by dint of its alleged train of transmission. A typical formula goes something like: *"According to so-and-so, who heard it from so-and-so who is the nephew or uncle of so-and-so, who overheard so-and-so being told by so-and-so that the messenger of Allah said such-and-such-and-such."* This smoke-and-mirrors trick is pulled off by means of this kind of 'chain of transmission'. The 'chains of transmission' work wonders on the Arab mind given their obsession with their place and relatives within the tribal structure.

Despite all the uncertainty, it is a known fact that whatever the compilers claim to have heard (of what the Prophet is supposed to have said or done in his personal capacity) is always received from individuals who themselves honestly claimed to have received it from earlier sources. Beginning around two hundred years after the death of the Prophet, demented compilers began going from town to town asking people about the Prophet's personal behaviour. They would have been served better by applying themselves to the message he delivered. Since the collections of the *Hadiths* are spurious at best and pernicious at worst, we must admit that the dates and details of the Prophet's early youth and personal beliefs remain unknown.

The religionists have no details about the Prophet's father. Even the date of Muhammad's first revelation is debatable. Stories concerning important stages in his life are varied and contradictory, including the spreading of the revelation and even the circumstances of his death. Many of the events recorded are pure hearsay in which even the relater himself admits the frailty of the case, a frailty which the scholars will acknowledge using the formula: *'Only God knows best whether this is false or true'*.

What was finally recorded in writing from the mountain of material obtained from hearsay was decided by four major priests who led what are today the sunni schools of thought. The Shiite had their own stories to tell. The relevant parts of each of their selections were in turn accepted or rejected by other schools, as they thought fit. Each priest sought to improve on his forerunners and supersede them as a standard authority.

Arab Tales about the present Ka'aba

Perhaps in order to foster their many pagan associations, the religionists gave the square stone house that they call the *ka'aba* a history of its own. The Qur'an's mentioning of the word *ka'aba* relates only to the washing of one's ankles in 5:6, and in 5:95 to the restriction of hunting young animals. Clearly, given the prevalent tradition-based interpretation of 5:95 to mean the stone building at Mecca, this elucidation of the text based on itself is going to come as a bit of a shock. Nevertheless, the subject it deals with is the conservation of wildlife stocks. Anyone who kills wildlife on purpose during the restricted period must pay a fine.

The key fact here is that a hunter can distinguish the maturity of animals by observing their movements before deciding whether to shoot. Animal conservation is part of God's decrees as we shall see, and people are to uphold the decree not to hunt the animals during the restricted months. The ankles show both the way the animal moves when it is alive (and provide conclusive data when it is dead) and the state of maturity of the animal. This very important piece of information is found at 5:2 and repeated in 5:97. The word *ka'abata* simply means *ankle*. More is given on this in chapter eleven.

However, to return to the fictions of the Arab religion: according to their own traditions some mullahs (gurus) believe that the *ka'aba* was built by angels (a myth plagiarised from the Bible), whereas other mullahs say the *Ka'aba* was built by Adam (common conjectures in the Arab religion), destroyed in the flood of Noah, and rebuilt by Abraham and his son Ishmael. The religionists claim that Abraham's association with the stone house in Mecca dates from the pre-Qur'anic period. According to their own tales, it remained a pagan pantheon until Muhammad destroyed all the images it housed except the black stone.

By their own testimony the temple has been subject not only to periodic flooding, but because of the use of lamps in the shrine, to fire as well. In the course of its long history it has been damaged and destroyed by flood and fire scores of times, and has often had to be rebuilt from its foundations up. Many alterations to its shape and size were made centuries before and after Muhammad. This is what the mullahs say. No story of any related sort is mentioned in the Qur'an.

Since the Qur'an denounces all kinds of physical rituals and worship, the idea of 'God's house' and the cherishing of a black stone in Mecca are clearly fabrications by the religionists. An illuminating comparison can be made between the present-day pilgrimages at the square rock structure with the apparently older religion of Hinduism. Hinduism has travelled from India to many countries. Its influence can be found as far as Bali in Indonesia. Arabia was considered India's immediate neighbour (requiring only a relatively short journey across the Arabian Sea). There was a claim by the Hindus that the present day Arab religion has many things in common with them. Among other things they say:

- As the pilgrim proceeds towards Mecca he is asked to shave his head and to don special sacred attire that consists of two seamless sheets of white cloth. One is to be worn round the waist and the other over the shoulders. Both these rites are remnants of the old Vedic practice of entering Hindu temples clean and wearing seamless white sheets.

- Muslim pilgrims visiting the *Ka'aba* go around it seven times anti clockwise. In no other mosque does such circumambulation prevail. Hindus invariably circumambulate their deities anti clockwise. This is another indication that the *Ka'aba* shrine is a pre-Qur'anic Indian Shivan temple where the Hindu practice of circumambulation is still meticulously observed.

- Recital of the *namaz* five times a day is similar to the Hindu Vedic injunction of *Panchmahayagna* (five daily worship - Panch-Maha-Yagna) which is part of the daily Vedic ritual prescribed for all individuals.

Even without the Hindus claim it is an undeniable fact that the present day pilgrimage observed by the Arabs is the same ancient pagan religious practice focusing on stone and rocks in Mecca, Arafat and Mina. It lasts ten days and is hedged by many taboos of the pagan faith most of which have been retained until today. The rituals and exclamatory formulas as well as the ceremonies observed at the various locations signifying the '*station*', can be traced back to pre-Qur'anic times. Before entering the shrine pilgrims must be in a state of sanctity by donning the two seamless sheets of white cloth *ihram*, the pilgrims announce their readiness to the lord of the cube house. This is called the *talbiya*. It is demonstrated by the cry of the *ihlal* an ancient formula called the *laa-baik* followed by the rituals below:

- Circumambulate (*tawaf*) the square rock structure anti clockwise seven times.

- Each circuit the pilgrims must kiss the oval 'Black Stone' (*Hajar Aswat*) (some with flying kisses).

- Upon completion of the seven rounds the pilgrims then perform the prayer body movements behind a gilded cage a few meters away from the stone house.

- And then proceed to another location within the mosque precinct to perform the *sa'ei* Here the pilgrims have to run to and from two rock outcroppings seven times.

- On the sixth day devotees travel to another location a few kilometres away called Arafat (another rock mountain). The *wukuf*, which is actually a remnant of pagan ritual of worshiping the sun is observed by pilgrims at this place by standing from midday to sunset. The pagan rite of standing is an essential part of the pilgrimage.

- On the setting of the sun at Arafat the pilgrims will rush (another form of ritual call *ifada*) to Muzalifah an open area three miles away from Mina. The majority of the non-Arabs do not notice another rock tower in the vicinity that is regarded as sacred by the religionists. They follow blindly the ancient pagan ritual by lighting a fire and keep vigil through the night, raising a great shout from time to time like the old Red Indian warriors in the movies. This happens until today.

- The concluding rite of the pilgrimage takes place on the tenth day in the valley of Mina. This is actually an ancient sacrificial site about half way back to Mecca. Here pilgrims will start throwing stones at some stone pillars conceiving mentally these stone pillars are the devils. This rite signifies the end of the state of sanctity and they can now return to normal life.

- The climax to the proceeding is the livestock sacrifice. This is a custom of the ancient Arabs performing animal sacrifice at a granite block on the slope of Mount Thabir, a place falsely claimed as the spot of Abraham's intended offering-up of his son. (The Qur'an condemns animal sacrifice 6:136)

- The point of convergence of animal sacrifices is the blood not the meat. The three-day period from the eleventh to the thirteenth day, following the end of the pilgrimage is called *'tashrik'* literally means 'associating' the 'dry blood'. The drying of the blood signifies that their god has consecrated their pilgrimage for the year.

Words like *ihram, talbiya, ihlal, laa-baik, hajar aswat, sa-ei, wukuf and ifada* are not found anywhere in the Qur'an. These are terms used by the pagan Arabs from the pre-Qur'anic period. In 22:26 God told Abraham he should *la-tushrik* or <u>NOT</u> to associate the Supreme God with anything, but the religionists say they must associate *(tashrik)* God with blood.

According to the Qur'an, Muhammad condemned all forms of idolatry. Therefore, performing rituals around a temple or devoting oneself to any form of rocks or stone was never part of the *peacefulness* propagated by him. The religionists mischievously portrayed the Last Prophet kissing the black stone. The religionists believe that people are able to communicate with the black stone. They say Caliph Omar whispered to the black stone, "I know you are nothing but a stone that neither can harm nor help...... If I have not seen the Messenger of Allah kiss you, I would never kiss you myself." This is meant to imply that the Last Prophet also kissed the black stone. By this and many other methods, the religionists attributed stupidity and idolatry to the Last Prophet.

The way of life promoted by Abraham as preached by the Last Prophet was to call the people to believe in One God, the Hereafter, and to work righteousness. This is the *sine qua non* of the prescribed way of life. Muhammad came to change the time-honoured elements of native paganism: stone worship and idolatry. He undermined the foundations of the original Arabic paganism and did not

make any concession or compromise. He was the first
messenger to warn the Arabs. They knew nothing about the
monotheistic commitment sanctioned by God in His system
pioneered by Abraham and Ishmael. Although the Qur'an
does not go into the details of the idol-worship of the Arab
tribes, it confirms the ignorance of the Arab race at that
time and that of their forefathers.

> A revelation from the Almighty, Most Merciful, to
> warn a race whose forefathers were not warned
> before, and they are unaware. Indeed it is truly said
> (*haq-qul-khau-lu*) that the majority of them will not
> believe. (36:4-6)

In no uncertain terms this verse indicates that the Arab
community around the Last Prophet was a pagan society
following their forefathers' religion.   It also says the
majority of them (Arabs) will never believe the Qur'an after
it had been revealed to the Messenger. Such an amazing
statement is consistent with the statement in 9:97: that the
Arabs were staunch in disbelief and hypocrisy.

The biography of the Last Prophet according to the
Qur'an reveals that the Arabs rejected him soon after he
recited the Qur'an to them. The Arabs refused to accept the
Qur'an. They went as far as to say that the Qur'an was a
fabricated falsehood. Instead, they accused the Prophet of
trying to divert them from the idols served by their
forefathers.

> When Our revelations were recited to them they say,
> "This is a man who wants to divert you from what
> was served by our forefathers." They also say, "This
> is fabricated falsehood." (34:43)

Today, we observe the religionists praising, cherishing and honouring the very man they treated with such contempt at the time when he called them to demolish their forefathers' stone idols. Contrary to the belief of those who idolise their messenger, the Last Prophet was not a popular man among the Arabs. The Arabs were hostile towards him and never acknowledged him *en masse* as the messenger of God. They despised the man, and they oppressed and banished him from his home. The same man who is glorified today was forced to take refuge in the cave to avoid the threat of death at their hands.

This is what is revealed of the life of the Last Prophet in the Qur'an. The Qur'an does not mention at all anything about the famous Arab tale of his purported migration to a place named Medina. Medina simply means a 'city' and is the same word used to refer to the city in Egypt where Moses lived. At one time, amongst all the people around him there was only one other man who believed him.

> When you did not support, God supported him when the non-believers banished him. He was one of the two people in the cave when he said to his companion, "Do not worry, God is with us." (9:40)

From the above, it is obvious the Arabs did not support him. Instead, during the peaceful period his people betrayed him by pretending to claim obedience but later plotting against him to change what he actually said to them. According to the Qur'an, God had appointed for every prophets enemies from among the human devils and jinn devils who invent and narrate fancy words in order to deceive the people (6:112). Thus, it becomes a system in God's deen.

109

And they claim obedience. Thus, as soon as they
move away from you - as of by a *system* (*min-a'in-
di-ka-Bay-yaa-ta*) a group from among them say
things that were not narrated to them. And God
records whatever they had systematically *(maa-yu-
Bayitu-naa)* invented. Therefore turn away from
them and put your trust in God. God suffices as
trustee. (4:81)

On the death of the Last Prophet, the pagan Arabs did
not adhere to the *peacefulness* propagated by him. Instead,
the black stone was reinstated as the central object of
worship. They withdrew from the true *Islam*, abandoned the
Qur'an, and then reanimated their ancestral faith focusing
on stone idols. They then deceitfully gave Muhammad a
prominent place in their forefather's religion. Muhammad
became a victim of their surreptitious designs. They simply
worked him into a makeover of the previous cult.

The cornerstone of the Arab religion today is a slavish
reliance on what is camouflaged as the custom *(sunna)* of
the Prophet[40]. The term *sunna* was commonly used by the
primitive Arabs to describe ancestral usage or model
patterns of behaviour established by the forefathers of the
tribe. They also introduced the consensus *(ijma[41])* of the
tribal assembly, which eventually embodied the beliefs and
practices of the whole community.

The information incorporating these former principles
and practices were falsely attributed to the Last Prophet
along with the claim that they were divinely inspired to

---

[40] Non-Muslims may not realise quite how the so-called sunna (or 'example') of
the prophet is used to dictate the pattern of life within '*Islam*' – no matter how
illogical, inappropriate or un-Qur'anic any given 'example' may happen to be.
[41] *Ijma* is equivalent to the Jewish *Halakhah* a consensus of rabbis' thought of
how life should be lived, society should be organized and God should be served.

him. This ragbag of hearsay was then handed down from
generation to generation as described above and now goes
by the name of the *Hadith* of the Prophet. This catalogue of,
frankly, fantastic and irrational myth forms the source of
(and justification for) the widespread intolerance,
fanaticism, terrorism, and extremism now attributed to this
man of God. It also is the determining factor in the equally
bigoted and pernicious meanings that the 'scholars' derive
from the Qur'an (and upon whose pronouncements all
popular translations of the Qur'an are based). The Qur'an
anticipates this state of affairs:

> God revealed the best message (*ahsanal-hadis-thsi*)
> in a form of a scripture that is consistent repeating
> itself. The skins of those who revered their Lord
> shudder from them and then the skins and their
> hearts soften towards remembering God. That (*best
> message*) is God's guidance. He guides whomever
> He wills <u>with it</u>. But the one who is misguided by
> God will not be able to find any guidance. (39:23)

> These are God's revelation that we recite to you
> with the truth; which other stories (*Hadis-thseen*)
> besides God and His revelations do they believe?
> Woe to every inventor, the guilty. He hears God's
> revelation recited to him, and then insists on his own
> way arrogantly, as if he never heard them. Promise
> him a painful retribution. (45:6-8)

Like all previous messengers, the Last Prophet's duty
was to deliver God's message. He had no authority to co-
author the message. His job was restricted to delivering
God's message, committing himself to live by it and to
conducting his daily life in accordance with it. His duty was
to remind the people, call them to God and then take the

challenge in promoting God's prescribed submission that had been revealed to him in written form in the Qur'an. He was warned in the strongest terms not to interfere with the message or utter any personal opinion in the name of God as far as the revelation was concerned.

> If he ever made up any utterances and attributed them to Us, We would hold him by his right hand and cut his artery. None of you can protect him. (69:44-47)

Contrary to popular belief, the Last Prophet was forbidden from providing any supplementary guidance to the Qur'an. But the religionists claim that they have in their possession thousands of utterances of the Prophet, utterances, which represent a catalogue of barbaric and pagan laws. For example, this body of extra-Qur'anic literature includes detailed instruction on all the accoutrement any self-respecting 'religion' will need:

- the observance of ritual prayers
- diverse forms of worship
- pilgrimages
- animal sacrifices
- illogical and unfair punishments (e.g. stoning to death for adultery)
- physical mutilation (e.g. male and female circumcision)
- detailed instruction on the minutia of what constitutes the personal hygiene of the righteous
- conduct of rituals to cure sickness
- details of death rites and burials
- restriction of women's value and freedom (beginning with the mandatory covering of women's

heads and ending with their practical isolation from society)

Of course there is much, much more.   But as all rational, intelligent seekers of ultimate truth will be glad to hear, not one of these teachings is to be found in the Qur'an.

Even the religionists agree there are no details of the ritual prayer – the first pillar of their faith – in the Qur'an. It seems that God somehow forgot to describe the kingpin of their religion in the Qur'an. This was quite some oversight on His part which they argue is why we need to submit to their priests' interpretation of a hotchpotch of thousands of old wives' tales: *for how else are they going to know how to pray?*

Religion is not from God

The intention of the enemies of all the prophets throughout history has been to deceive the people and to retain power. It is very simple. This is the basis of all the 'religions' around the world today. Of course, not everybody in each of these religions is consciously doing this. Many are sincere. However, dupes make the best deceivers because they genuinely believe their own propaganda. At the top levels, the leadership understands the game plan. The Qur'an describes the existence of human devils and the *jinn* devil as being the common enemies who will invent and narrate lies to spread falsehood in order to divert people from God's guidance.

> We have appointed for every prophet enemies from among the human devils and *jinn* devils who will invent and inspire each other fancy words in order to deceive the people. Had your Lord willed, they

would not have done it. You shall disregard them
and their invention. (6:112)

If we look around the world today, this verse is
particularly relevant to the Jews, the Christians, and the
adherents of the Arab religion. Falsehood (based on 'extra
information') abounds in these religions. It masquerades as
the 'extra' enlightenment, a helping hand to further explain
God's message – as if God's message were full of riddles
containing hidden meanings. In reality, there is no such
thing as the extra explanation or extra enlightenment to
God's Scriptures. If God had wanted to reveal it, it must be
in both the Torah and the Qur'an. Conversely, if it is not
mentioned in these Scriptures, it means someone has
created a new tradition and added to the words of God.

It is most unwise to heed the ungodly. As has been said
before, for those who claim to hold to *Islam* and believe in
God, the Qur'an is the *default authority* on earth.

The Children of Israel conspired against Moses after
God's Scripture was revealed to him. They abandoned
God's prescribed submission to follow the religion of
Judaism. Moses did not know anything about this Jewish
religion. The Jews have written volumes of books for
themselves instead of following the Torah alone.[42] The
Qur'an censures this in no uncertain terms:

> The example of those who were given the Torah and
> then failed to study it, is that of a donkey laden with
> books. Miserable indeed is the example of those

---

[42] The Qur'an states that the texts delivered to the Jews and the Christians – the
torah and the *injeel* – are now themselves corrupted, ref, 2:59 and 15:12. God
assured His reminder is protected only in its original language (ref 15:9) - not
the translations.

who reject God's revelation. God will not guide the wicked people. (62:5)

Out of His mercy, God sent Jesus to them to re-establish the original law. However, they could not accept him because doing so would have undermined the foundations of their own power since he was committed to demolishing the religion. In the end, they conspired against him and continued to promote Judaism for themselves while inventing Christianity as a new religion for those not blessed enough to have been born Jewish. Later, God revealed the Scripture to Muhammad. Again, his enemies abandoned God's prescribed submission to devise the Arab religion.

Obviously, Muhammad did not know anything about Sunnism, Shia, Ahmadiah or Wahabism the religious sects that follow anything and everything under the sun except the Quran. Instead of following the Qur'an alone, those who claim to be following Muhammad have – like the Jews – written volumes of books and laden themselves down with them. It would seem that the only lesson people learn from history is that people never learn from history.

Today, billions of people are devoting themselves to religions. All religions share common features. Whatever the details, the most important commandments are:

1. Thou shalt worship.

2. Thou shalt ritually pray according to thy priest's teachings.

3. Thou shalt pay the caretakers of thy religion.

4. Thou shalt believe that *we alone* have the Truth.

There will be a mass of further detail, but this takes care of the general landscape.

The Lord of the Universe in His wisdom has warned us about religion and its caretakers. The objective of religion is to cheat people and to divert the innocent from the path of God. All religious teachers share one common aspiration: they espouse a false system and then collect financial tribute from their followers.

> O you who believe, the priests and the religious scholars cheat the people out of their money, and they divert everybody from the path of God. (9:34)

As an example, it is very common these days for the funeral rites to cost as much as four or five thousand pounds (depending on the kind of religious experts you engage to perform the rituals). However, these priests and religious scholars cannot guarantee the dead man will get to Heaven (which is, inescapably, the stated objective of all religions). We also see that there is an array of religious rituals for new-born babies, yet our own eyes bear witness that many of these 'religiously' blessed babies grow up to become anything. No priest or scholar can guarantee a 'religiously' blessed marriage will not end in divorce. Those who follow religion will surely fall prey to the designs of their religious priests on their wealth sooner or later.

People expect value for money. Unfortunately for them, when they follow a religion they are buying a one way ticket to Hell through their religious teachers. There is no such thing as a right religion as far as the Lord of the Universe is concerned. He is not interested in any religion. Rather, He has repeatedly insisted on an orderly way of life based around good deeds.

The Qur'an gives a simple solution but a forceful message for mankind:

> Follow those who do not ask for any wage,[43] they are guided. (36:21)

Religion is big business, and the Qur'an says those who collect money in the name of religion are not guided. In many passages of the Qur'an we are told all bearers of good news who propagated the good values of life declared openly: *'I do not ask you for any remuneration, my pay comes from the Lord of the Universe'*. Noah, Abraham, Isaac, Jacob, Joseph, Moses, Jesus and the rest of the messengers said this to the people.

By their actions, the religionists and their scholars do not believe the Qur'an when it quotes Muhammad correctly where he says:

> "I have not asked you for any wage, my wage comes from God, He witnesses all things." (34:47).

Ironically, those who impose the 'good example of the Prophet' on everyone themselves do the opposite. That is the reason why the Qur'an says the priests and religious scholars are cheating the people out of their money. If all people submit to the Qur'anic injunction not to follow those who ask you for a wage, surely the shackle that is binding them will be removed instantly. The priests and religious scholars will disappear overnight.

People should focus their full attention on doing good works. Their money and time could be put to better use attending to parents, neighbours, relatives, orphans and the

---

[43] This is with regards to paying people who claim they can guide others to the path of God. In 28:56 states that the Prophet cannot even guide his own wife.

poor, in being humble and speaking and treating people amicably – as the Qur'an directs. That is what life is about. This is *Islam* or *peacefulness. Islam* is not about religion. People are recognised by their deeds, not 'religious faith'.

Arab religious laws

Beside ritual prayers and the ritual worship practices, the religionists who invented the religion also mandated religious laws that have nothing in common with God and His prophets.

God's way has a benchmark here on earth: the Qur'an. He called His book the *Criterion*.[44] It is a book among books, a criterion, a standard by which all else is measured. With this benchmark, one can decisively discern whether something is good or bad, true or false, sacred or profane, real or imaginary. Having given us a rule by which all can be measured, it is assumed that a person will use this God-given benchmark often. The Devil, of course, will try to make it inaccurate. He has already done this by obscuring the original intent and limits of the *Criterion*.

For example, in 2:224-242 we find eighteen verses, which outline amicable justice on the subject of marriage and divorce. They further illustrate the guidelines and methods for resolving marital disputes. These guidelines are self-explanatory and can be put into practice by anyone. In other words, God has directed His people to apply a behavioural etiquette that does not include priests or any religious authority whatever. Thus, there is no need for any

---

[44] According to the *Chambers Encyclopaedia English Dictionary*, the word 'criterion' means: a standard or principle on which to base a Judgement. The word *furqan* is used when Moses was given the Torah (2:53 & 21:48), and to Jesus in 3:4. The Quran is called the *furqan* or 'criterion' in 2:185 and 25:1. In the Arab religion the man-made 'syari'ah' is the 'criterion' not the Qur'an.

new, independent body of lawmakers to formulate 'Islamic' religious laws on marriage and divorce.

The very existence of supplementary human laws to 'augment' the word of God is horrifyingly arrogant. It places the justice of People on the same level as the decrees of God.

Even in vernacular law, the essence of the law is paramount. We cannot go beyond the limits set. For example, if the minimum wage for a worker is ten dollars per day, we are free to pay him anything as long as it is not less than the stipulated sum. This concept is not man-made. Any individual who believes in God and the Hereafter is free to observe God's guidelines as long as they do not exceed the limits prescribed by God. If they transgress the limits, God will judge them. If He be the Judge, it is redundant to have God's guidance anointed with the title 'Islamic' law, religious law or '*shari'ah*' law.

The purpose of Scripture is *not* to impose religious laws but to replace unjust human law. The Scripture is a law unto itself. It is complete in form and function.

We have sent our messengers with clear revelations and We sent down with them the Scripture as the measure (*mizan*) to spread justice among the people. (57:25)

Let us take this concept a little further along and consider the following:

- Legislators and lawmakers of any civilised government (not including, naturally, the lawmakers of the Arab religion) will agree that no man or woman who commits adultery should be executed.

- The same servants of Justice (*except* for the religionists and their cohorts and dupes) will agree a person is free to believe or disbelieve in God, and that he or she is free to change their belief anytime without being punished by priests (or anyone else) for their decision.

- Similarly, the legislators (*except* the same people mentioned above) will agree that a divorced woman should not be deprived of her freedom and she should have reasonable provisions until she is able to find other alternatives or reconciliation.

These are just some instances of guidance which are humanely spelt out in the Qur'an. They are correct principles, which work together for the advancement and cohesion of society. Civilised countries have come to practice them after many years of experimentation and observation. They have come to implement them because they are fair and because they work. The Qur'an gives us a shortcut to a generative rule of law. The basis is not religion. The basis is Life. The basis is rooted in providing a plan for a way of life, designed to accommodate the human condition fairly and firmly. All prophets taught this.

The question arises: if the Arab lawmakers were so keen to 'legalise' the law of God, why did they not then legislate requirements for other equally important aspects of the Qur'an like civility, politeness, consideration, respect, empathy, patience, humility, charity on human welfare, temperance and mercy? Shouldn't the Arab version of God's law appear God-like in nature instead of tyrannical? The only conclusion any student of Islamic law can arrive at is that 'Islamic' laws originating from the religionists are *not found in the Qur'an* and are far from divinely inspired.

It is no wonder that the Arab world is in confusion and chaos. The religious laws of the Arab religion vary from country to country: Saudi Arabia, Egypt, Syria, Iraq, Iran, Sudan, Algeria, Oman, Pakistan, Afghanistan, Malaysia, Indonesia, and many other places have differing laws all claiming to be inspired by God. How is it that a divinely inspired law varies so much by geographical location? It can only mean that each location has a different 'religious god' at the helm. This has reduced Islamic 'shari'ah' law[45] to a comical position. No two 'Islamic' countries have the same 'Islamic' laws. If it weren't so sad, it would be hilarious.

Let us now examine what God intended before people started meddling.

Example one:

> It is the incumbent duty of everyone to make a will for the benefit of their parents and children or their next of kin before death approaches any one of them (2:180-182)

This is a simple decree observed by most people with any common sense. It encourages planning and pre-meditation. It solves problems before they are created. It makes the bereavement less difficult on the grieving. It is just plain civil.

The religionists and their courts tell us that it is forbidden (or *Haram*) to make a will in the Arab religion. The religious priests or religious authority will decide what,

---

[45] 42:21 forbids instituting any religious laws. Every man has the full right and freedom to conduct his personal way of life. The law of Justice and matters of crimes and security of a state is to be formulated through consensus by the experts of each field, which can be amended to suit circumstances.

how, and to whom a dead person's assets should be distributed. And, of course, a certain portion of the assets may well be reserved for some invented religious purpose.

Example two:

> Any person who believes in God, then disbelieves, and then believes and then disbelieves and persists in disbelieve will not be forgiven by God (4:137)

People are given the absolute right to believe or disbelieve in God. If they reject belief and persist in doing so, God will not pardon them in the Hereafter. That is all.

> There is no compulsion in the *deen*. Truth is now distinguished from falsehood. Thus, those who reject idol-worship and believe in God have grasped the strongest bond that never breaks. God is hearer, omniscient. (2:256)

The people can exercise their right and freedom[46] to accept or to reject God's revelations, yet He will not punish them in this world if they choose to reject His Scripture:

> You can believe therein or disbelieve. (17:107)

The religionists, in their contorted wisdom, have declared that anyone who renounces the 'religion' must be sentenced to death. It is very much Jewish in nature.

Example three:

A person is expected to use his or her intellect and reason.

> God will not guide those who defy their common sense (10:100)

---

[46] There must not be any court of law to deny a person's right in matters of faith.

Yet, somewhere along the line an adherent of the Arab religion declared:

> Those who use their common sense will be burned in Hell. (*Sahih* Bukhari[47])

Many of these 'new' decrees in the Arab religion are diametrically opposed to the wisdom of the Qur'an. How could the system have erred to such a degree? One supposes that religious centrism and insecurities have been the primary drivers for this movement. After all, only the Supremely Confident would have allowed people total freedom of choice. People, on the other hand, seek to impose control and likes to do so through laws. It is even better when that control is manifested in 'religious' garb which makes these laws incontestable.

God tells us that *Solaa* is the fulfilling of commitments through righteous deeds. The Arab religion tells us, however, it means doing the regimented prayers five times a day in the prescribed direction of their homeland where their god apparently lives. Of course, those wishing to commune with God must first consult with the Arab masters who have mastered the art of the prayer 'procedures', actions, precursors, etc. For the benefit of the more than five billion people on earth who would have no idea what the author is referring to, the Arab prayer ritual is outlined below.

The Arab ritual prayer

These simplified instructions will enable anyone to complete the dance of the Arab prayer ritual. Born to a

---

[47] Bukhari's collection of some several thousand of nonsensical 'traditions' are considered *Sahih*, that is 'good and reliable'.

Muslim family, the author personally performed this ritual
countless times throughout his life before he called it a day
many years ago. I must remind the reader, it is vital that
every utterance in the Arab prayer ritual be in Arabic. The
English-speaking Muslims may not even say a simple
phrase like, "Praise be to You my Lord" in English.

Here, is a summary of the basic procedure for those
who have never performed an Arab prayer ritual:

- First, wash out your mouth with water, blow your
  nose, wash your face, your hands, your forehead,
  your ears, your neck, and your legs and then speak
  to God in Arabic and tell Him you are going to
  ritually pray to Him.
- Find a spot and make sure you face the stone idol in
  Mecca. If you are in Japan the direction is
  westwards, but if you are in Europe the direction is
  the eastwards, obviously.
- Then, stand properly with the hands folded on your
  belly. Various sects have their own specific ways of
  placing the hands, and the tutored eye can tell a lot
  about your doctrine just by looking at the way you
  hold this position, though variations abound
  throughout the mosques of the world.
- Then pronounce '*Allah hu akbar*'.[48] The word *akbar*
  means *bigger*. So it is: '*God is bigger*'.
  (Interestingly, the phrase *Allah hu akbar* is not
  found anywhere in the Qur'an). Then recite some
  Arabic verses (which you may or may not
  comprehend).

---

[48] Saying *allah-hu-akbar* is done during each body movement and in a group
session is said by the man leading the exercise as a cue to tell the people when
to move from one position to another.

The prayer starts with a recitation of a set of speech formulated[49] by the religionists before beginning the compulsory recital of Al *Fatiha* (the first *surah*, consisting of seven verses). Typically, this will be followed by a short *surah* from toward the end of the Qur'an. *Surahs* 111, 112, 113 and 114 are particular favourites as they are very short and generally considered the minimum (along with *Al Fatiha*) that a Muslim should be expected to memorise[50]. The religionists say they are praying to God. Yet each of these last *surahs* begins with an instruction to the Prophet: *'Qul!'* or *'Say!'* followed by exactly what it was he was required to say. However these verses which begin with a direct instruction are habitually addressed to God in the Arab prayer ritual. For example:

> *Say!:* He is God, the only one. The absolute God. He never begets, nor was He ever begotten. There is none equal to Him. (*surah* 111)

There are many verses in the Qur'an that start with an imperative addressing a second person commanding him to recite to a third person or persons. That is the nature of the Revelation. However, the religionists teach their followers to recite these orders back to God in their prayer ritual. In one of their favourite *surahs* for this purpose, they tell God:

> *Say!:* O you disbelievers, I do not serve what you serve, nor are you serving what I am serving. I will never serve what you are serving, nor will you ever

---

[49] The recitations differ from one sect to another. The opening passages of the prayer do not come from the Qur'an except when they utter part of 6:79, 6:161-162. Abraham and Muhammad uttered these verses to the people but the Arabs address them to God.

[50] When people are willing to memorise without understanding it is a sign of their willingness to be shackled without thinking. If we train a parrot to say 'good morning', it will say good morning to people even during the night.

> serve what I am serving. To you is your own way, and to me is my own way. (*surah* 109)

However, if they choose to recite *surah* 108 in their prayer, they will tell God:

> We have given you many bounties. In appreciation, you shall serve your Lord and be charitable. Your enemy will henceforth be the loser. (*surah* 108)

Obviously, not all non-Arabs know what they are saying to God in their ritual prayers. Maybe there is some excuse. But even native Arabic-speaking Arabs including religionists and Arabic scholars say these things to God every day!

Having finished the liturgy of (frequently inappropriate) verses, you should raise both hands and say '*allah-hu-akbar*' or '*God is bigger*' again.

Then you bow forward for a few seconds before standing erect and calling out 'God *is bigger*' again. Then you prostrate – placing your forehead on the floor – and recite more Arabic words. Then you should sit up and then prostrate again before rising to the standing position. This procedure represents one unit of prayer. The number of units and whether what you say will be aloud or quiet will depend on a number of factors devised by the religionists such as time of day and 'type' of prayer. Generally, (although there are variations depending on whether you perform the 'extra' night prayers) a Muslim is required to bow seventeen times and prostrate thirty-four times in a twenty-four hour period.

At the end of any one particular set of units, you are to sit and send greetings to Prophet Abraham and Muhammad and their families (no need to wait for them to reply, however), then greet the *'two angels sitting on both of your shoulders'* (again, no reply is expected).

Qur'an clearly says:

You cannot be heard by those in the graves. (35:22)

Yet, the followers of the Arab religion the world over are greeting only the dead prophet Muhammad and their families five times a day! We are not supposed to make any distinction between the prophets[51]: but Isaac, Jacob, Ishmael, Joseph, David, Solomon, Moses, Aaron, Zachariah, John (*Yahya*), and Jesus were somehow left out of this private club. How very rude.

---

[51]As for those who believe in God and His messengers, they make no distinction among any of them. God will recompense them. God is Forgiver and Merciful. (4:152)

It is our freedom that decides
who we are and who
we choose to be.

We do not have to be who
we used to be.

People who make a different
choice are people who
make a different
world.

PART FOUR

Solaa (commitments) is not ritual prayer

When looking at other words which have had their meanings twisted in the Qur'anic context, we can usually get back to the true meaning by looking at extant words in modern Arabic surrounding the root. *Zakaa* is a good example. All the root meanings of *zakaa* refer to purity and sincerity. This can be verified by looking at any good dictionary. As we shall see – the Arab religion has created the un-Qur'anic tax and ascribed this to the word *zakaa*. The deception is relatively easy to spot since the key meanings of the word *zakaa* have remained intact.

Solaa is no different. Firstly, when we look up the word in a dictionary we find a word that is mispronounced by the Muslim world – Salaat – under the root S-l-w. It is worth noting that this root has no other meaning directly ascribed to it other than the '***ritual prayer***'. There is nothing else.

Whereas almost any key Qur'anic term has related terms which balance and integrate it into the waft and web of the language (and by means of which we can sense deceptions as and when they occur) this important – some would say *central* – Qur'anic concept has no 'context' in the language by which to verify the claims made for it by the Arab religionists other than the one created for it by those self-same religionists.

There are no related meanings that one can point to and say: *Solaa must mean what such-and-such because it integrates into the language on the basis of the sense we derive from the word*. This is not possible because the word simply has no semantic context in the religion of the Arabs as we know.

Now, it could be argued that the reason for this is that this word has only one meaning – unconnected to anything else in the vast and interconnected web of Arabic semantics – and that the meaning the Arab religionists ascribe to it is, in fact, the correct one. In this case, we would respond by pointing out that since the ritual prayer or **Salaat** (by the religionists' own measure and admission) is not in the Qur'an, their own definition of it is of no special value.

The situation we find ourselves in is: there is a word – '**Solaa**' – that exists in a semantic vacuum, and the leaders of the religious system say it means X based on their non-Qur'anic writings (the *Hadith*). Since their non-Qur'anic writings say some patently ludicrous things, and given that the religious elite promotes these non-Qur'anic sources to achieve ends which are usually advantageous only to the religious elite, a thinking person is left wondering what possible use their definition of this word can be to anyone except them.

Just to clear up the point of roots. The root of *Solaa* is S-L. It is a two-root word. They are many such words in the Qur'an. Examples of other two-root words found in the Qur'an are *haq* (truth, root: h-q), *abu* (father, root: a-b) or *yad* (hand, root: y-d) or *Qama* (the keep vigil or attentive, root: q-m).

However, knowing that the word *Solaa* does not come from S-l-w or S-l-y but from S-L it does not help us a great deal. S-L is not in the dictionary and S-l-w has only the '**ritual prayer**' meaning ascribed to it. In the Qur'an S-l-w means 'to roast' and (S-l-y) refers to 'fry or burn'.

The root word for S-l-w is found in 69:31 meaning 'to roast' not ritual prayer. It generates *yaslau* (4:10, 14:29, 17:18 and eight other verses). *islau* in 36:64 & 52:16, *siliya* in 19:70 spelt with S-l-alif-y. Here we must pronounce the word with the third letter 'waw' or 'ya'. Therefore it is wrong to assign a third letter to the root of S-L to read as S-l-w.

To recap: *Solaa* comes from the root S-L which does not exist in modern Arabic and which defies definition by modern methods. Yet the Qur'an treats its meaning as self-evident. The religious elite have ascribed its own meaning to this word, a meaning which fails appallingly in certain Qur'anic contexts.

Since the Qur'an is the only place we know of which knows what this word means we have to look to it for the ways it uses this word and derive its meaning from the multitude of contexts. God says the Arabic in His Book is perfect. Thus, nobody should try to change its word constructions, spelling and grammatical forms.

> A reading in Arabic without any crookedness therein so that they might observe. 39:28

The word *Solaa* [52] or any of the derivatives from the same root word is *never* used in the Qur'an to refer to the act of worship or the performance of a set of body movements.

Its use always refers to the act of honouring, upholding, or observing of commitments by consenting person or

---

[52] This word is erroneously pronounced as '*Salaat*' by the followers of the Arab religion although the consonant of the root word is *Sod Lam* is found in 2:249, 75:31, which is pronounced as '*Solaa*'. Muslims who are shackled by their religious masters are shocked when I used the word '*Solaa*' instead of '*Salaat*'.

persons when the phrase '*aqi-mu*' is used. Literally the word *Solaa* means to 'commit'.

This root word (like all roots in Arabic) forms its various functions by use of vowels, prefixes and suffixes. The short vowels "*i*" or *"u"* (9:103,108:2 and 33:56) can be added resulting in '*Sol-lee*' or '*Sol-luu*' without changing the underlying, fundamental meaning of the word.

The word pronounced with a short vowel 'a' appears in the Qur'an three times, in 2:249, 75:31 and 96:10 respectively.

In 2:249 it appears as '*falam-maa Solaa thalut bil-junudi*'. Nobody dares translate this sentence as, '*Thus, as Thalut prays ritually with the soldiers*' - because the correct meaning is, '*Thus, as Thalut commits with the soldiers*'. Translators give different meanings to this word for reasons only known to them.

In 75:31 it is written as *Falla-sod-daqor-wa-Solaa* and in 96:10 as *A'bdan izaa-wa-Solaa* and translators insist the word Solaa in both verses refer to ritual prayers. They do not.

These words appear in other passages of the Qur'an, and no religionists or Arabic scholars dare translate them as '*ritual prayers*'. So the best one can say is, consistencies exist because the leaders of the Arab religion interpret this root concept in various ways. The paragraphs following will attempt to explain this particular quirk.

As mentioned, the Arabic language derives its vocabulary from the root words. Conjugations of the root word can produce new derivatives and generally, these derivatives are constructed in accordance with established

vocalic moulds or patterns to which certain prefixes or
suffixes are added. The Arabic verbs have two 'voices' –
active and passive.

A prefix is used in the grammar notes besides an entry,
which cannot normally be used by itself. It is common to
see in the Qur'an a prefix like '*Ma*' or '*Mu*', '*Ya*' or '*Yu*'
placed before a grammar note to form a new word in the
same class. The two parts are joined together and written as
one word.

A suffix is used in the grammar notes placed after
another word so that a new word is formed. The form of the
suffix dictates to which class the new word belongs to.

These appear only in the perfect and imperfect and they
are constructed according to established moulds or patterns.
The imperfect is formed by the addition of prefixes and
suffixes that indicate the form of the verb as well as by the
gender and number of the doers of the action. Arabic in the
Qur'an then, it is fair to say, is a highly developed language
with a complex grammar via which it is possible to express
concepts with a high level of accuracy.

The Arabic in the Qur'an is very precise and concise.
There are those who claim that Arabic in the Qur'an lacks
the ability to define sense exactly. It would be good to
remember that at the time of the Qur'anic revelation, Arabic
was among the most developed languages in the world. God
used the most expressive and up-to-date language of that
era to explain a simple and perfectly defined message. After
all, I doubt anyone on earth speaks God's language. He
wisely chose to use the parlance of the time.

However, the subsequent twisting of the Qur'anic
Arabic by those who would force it into a pre-prescribed

shape has marred many people's reading of the Qur'an. For instance, we read in 75:31: *falaa soddaqor walaa Solaa*. The patrons of the Arab religion say it means *'He was not truthful and not praying'*. The true meaning is *'He was not truthful and not committed'*.

In 2:43 God tells us that He instructed the Children of Israel: *Wa-aqimus Solaa-ta wa-atuz zakaa*. The religionists say it means: *'Observe the ritual prayers and pay the religious tithes'*. This instruction is spoken in the present tense asking the Children of Israel to do what they have done before. If we ask the Jews if they had at any time in history performed the five daily ritual prayers, they will answer in the negative. Even the Jews who received the earlier Scripture knew that five the ritual prayers were not part of the *deen* revealed by God. It is not in the Torah and it is also not the Qur'an. The true meaning of this particular passage is: *'Uphold the commitments and keep them pure'*. The Children of Israel understand this instruction very well because they have committed themselves to God's deen through the Torah long before the Quran was revealed.

In 6:162, the Prophet and those who submit to God are encouraged to remind themselves of their obligation as servants of God: *In-naa Solaa-ti wa-nusuki wamaa yahya wamamamati lilahi robil a'lameen*. This means: *My commitments and my sacrifices and my life and my death are for God the Lord of the Universe*. The religionists twist their tongue and say this verse means, *'My ritual prayers and my sacrifices and my life and my death are for God the Lord of the Universe'*.

Among the previous people who use the word *Solaa* in the Qur'an are the people of Shuaib. At 11:87 they say, *'Ya-shu-'aib aa-Solaa-tu-ka.....'* which means, *'O Shuaib, does*

134

your commitment...?'. But in the Arab religion they say the people of Shuaib said, *'O Shuaib, does your ritual prayer........?'*, even though the context of this passage says that Shuaib was calling his people not to cheat but to trade equitably among themselves.

The history of Jesus in the Qur'an is another clear example. Jesus mentions the word *Solaa* as an infant. In 19:23 we are told that Jesus was born of the Virgin Mary and he spoke to his mother soon after the pangs surprised her. The religionists ridiculously claim that Jesus performed the ritual prayer and paid the alms tax from the day he was born. At 19:31 whilst in his mother's arms Jesus says, "I was enjoined with the commitments maintain it pure for as long as I live" (*'Wa-asoy-na bi-Solaa-ti wa zakaa-ti ma dumtum hai-yan'*) which clearly implies that he will uphold his obligation diligently in reforming the Children of Israel.

Different words were used in various languages during over the centuries of prophets calling people to uphold their *commitments* or *obligations*. In the language of the Last Prophet it is called *Solaa* (or its derivatives). Abraham, the people of Midyan, the Children of Israel and Jesus were non-Arabs, but the Qur'an quotes interaction with them on the basis of an equivalent word in their own language to *Solaa*. In 21:23, for example, God instructs Isaac and Jacob with the same word, *'wa-iqama-Solaa-ti-wa-ie-ta-zakaa-ti*[53]*'* which means: *uphold your commitments and keep them pure* after their father Abraham.

---

[53] Although this word is to be pronounced as *zakaa* the Arabs twist the meaning and also the pronunciation and call it *zakat*. For *Solaa* they say *Salaat* and for *zakaa* they say *zakaat* (misconstrued in both cases) Please see chapter six.

None of the prophets before Muhammad were talking about ritual prayers when they uttered the equivalent of *Solaa* in their own language. Therefore, the word *Solaa* or its derivatives cannot be translated to mean ritual prayers. To think otherwise is to err on a very large scale contextually. The word *Solaa* and its derivatives appear in many verses in the Qur'an. Modern Arab 'translations' will have us believe that there are many different meanings for the same word in different verses.

This ambiguity has generated much confusion. As a result, the word *Solaa* revolves around the ritualistic prayer performed according to a timetable accompanied by ritualistic physical movements. It is presumptuous to think that God would enjoin on us something quite so mundane.

The priests of the Arab religion will ask: *So how can we pray if we depend on the Qur'an alone?* This is absolutely beside the point. Was there ever any question that we should need more than the Qur'an?

Many religions around the world have in common the fact that their priests have the right to question their followers but the followers do not have the right to question the priests on religious matters.

If we ask the Christian priest why they say Jesus is God whereas the Bible says he was serving God who created him, the Christian priest will jump. Similarly, if we ask the priests of the Arab religion why they pray ritually five times a day and face the stone idol in Mecca when it is not specified in the Qur'an, they will likewise find themselves on the back foot.

This amounts to the beginning of an acknowledgement by the priests of the Arab religion (soon to be remedied by the use of other 'authentic' sources) that there is no ritual prayer in the Qur'an. The truth is their ritual prayer was *not* revealed to the Last Prophet in God's prescribed way of life. We know because we read the Qur'an. *Solaa* as it appears in the Qur'an simply implies a person's commitment to observe his or her obligations as prescribed in the Qur'an. Nowhere does the Qur'an state that humans must perform any ritual prayer *to* God. This is a fact that Muslims need to bear in mind.

Solaa between people

We can support the fact that the Qur'an does not mean ritual prayer by the word *Solaa* and its derivatives by examining the different usage of this word in the Qur'an in its various contexts. What transpires is that *Solaa* has to be observed by everyone – even by the non-believers and the idol-worshippers.

One very clear example regards the witnessing of a will by strangers:

> O you who believe, you shall have witnesses when death is near to any one of you: to dictate your will in the presence of two equitable persons among you, or strangers in case there is a sudden danger to your life when travelling on the earth. If you are not certain of them, retain them after they have committed themselves (*Solaa-ti*) to make them both swear by God, "We will not take advantage to favour anyone even the closest relatives. We will not conceal any evidence before God. If we do, the sin will be upon us."[54] (5:106)

---

[54] The two men are strangers to the dying man, yet the verse says they qualify to make an oath before God. Their willingness to write the will and to become

The verse says: *'After the two strangers* [note: who can be Jews or Christians] *commit themselves (Solaa-ti), make them both swear by God'*. This does not call for the performance of a ritual prayer in the presence of a dying person. Instead they are taking on the responsibility of being witnesses to a will by making a solemn pledge to the person before God. This is an example of *Solaa-ti* (the commitment) between people.

The commitment between people is to fulfil such obligations before the one God. It is that simple.

Besides upholding the *Solaa* with strangers, believers may also do so with non-believers, and idol-worshippers. Surely, the following passages in the Qur'an are not meant to suggest that polytheists perform the ritual prayers:

> Except those among the idol-worshippers with whom you have a treaty and then do not breach anything with you and do not aid anyone against you, therefore complete your agreement with them until its term. Surely, God loves those who fear (Him). (9:4)

> Then when the prohibited months are over, you may overcome the idol-worshippers wherever you may find them. You shall capture them, encircle them and watch them carefully at every place and if they repent and uphold their obligations (*Solaa-ta wa-atu-zakaa*) and keep them pure then give them the freedom to move around. Surely God is Forgiver, Merciful. (9:5)

---

witness is their commitment *'solaa-ti'*. Like the Jews, the Arab religionists conceal this verse from their followers.

And if one of the idol-worshippers seeks help from you, protect him then let him hear God's words then convey him to a place of safety. This is because they are a people who do not know. (9:6)

At 9:4–6 we are directed to treat the idol-worshippers well and even convey them to a place of safety. Those that we shelter *may remain idol-worshippers*. We are charged not with discriminating upon the basis of this prejudice. Rather, we are commanded to be a beacon of light and understanding. Understanding and carrying out the commandment in this verse alone would change the entire Islamic landscape as we know it.

We see that if and when the polytheists repent and agree to peace, it is the people who are at peace or Muslims' duty to uphold that peace and grant them their freedom. Again, the Qur'an enjoins civility and kindness in the face of hostilities. *Islam* does not condone the mistreatment of those who are under our power or control (9:5). Ultimately, *Solaa-ta* in this instance refers to the idol-worshippers agreeing to keep to their end of the bargain.

The prophet Shuaib provides another example of *Solaa* clearly signifying commitments. He committed himself to reform his people. Those who rejected his commitments challenged him.

He begins:

"O my people! Gives full measure and full weight equitably. Do not cheat people out of their things, and do not corrupt the earth. A smaller provision from God would be better for you, if you are really believers. I am not a guardian over you." They said, "O Shuaib, does your *Solaa* (commitment) prevent us

from idolising what our parents have idolised, and
from doing whatever we want with our money? Surely
you are too clement and too wise." (11:85–87)

The commitment that Shuaib was trying to bind upon
his people was that they should not cheat or corrupt the
earth. It was a simple precept that was not accepted by his
peers. Hence, they said to Shuaib:

"O Shuaib, does your commitment (*Solaa-tu-ka*)
prevent us from idolising what our parents have
idolised, and from doing whatever we want with our
money?"[55]

Solaa here clearly refers to committing to good deeds
and upholding a good moral order. The commitment called
for his people not to cheat, not to corrupt the earth, and to
be fair. There is no other reading without abusing the sense
in the text beyond belief.

What we can better understand, however, is why the
Arab priests themselves emphatically declare that the
Qur'an has no information at all about the five daily prayers
(thus contradicting themselves on what they proclaim to be
the first absolute pillar of the religion of Islam) – because
they are right! Their own lips condemn them. There is no
such thing as the five daily prayers. How woefully correct
and wrong they are at the same time.

Solaa to yourself

The other clear example from the Qur'an is about the
Solaa observed by you for yourself – it is for your own
good. In this case you are told to commit to the good values
by refraining from the practice of excessive profiteering.

---

[55] Clearly the word *Solaa* here does not refer to ritual prayer.

God diminishes profiteering (*riba*) but encourages charity and God dislikes the disbelievers who are guilty. Surely, those who practice righteousness and uphold their commitments (*Solaa-ta*) and keep them pure (*wa-a-tuz-zakaa*), for them are rewards from their Lord. And there will be no fear upon them nor will they grieve. O you who believe, beware of God, refrain from taking what remains from profiteering if you truly believe in God. (2:276-279)

The subject of *riba*[56] (or profiteering) begins at 2:275 and ends at 2:281. Profiteering is a condemned practice and we are commanded not to get involved with it. God degrades profiteering, encourages charity and He dislikes the guilty disbelievers (2:276). Instead He commands virtuous commitments that should be observed (*Solaa-ta*) and kept pure (2:277). Any involvement in profiteering should be stopped immediately, even if there are any balances owed (2:278). Otherwise God and His messenger will wage war (2:279). If a debtor is in difficulty, we are to give him time, otherwise, treat the debt as charity (2:280) whatever we do, God knows everything and we are to beware of the Last Day. (2:281)

The *Solaa-ta*[57] mentioned at 2:277 is our commitment to stop earning income from profiteering (*riba*) and to maintain our commitments by abstaining from such practices. We do not perform ritual prayer to abstain from profiteering; instead we commit ourselves (*Solaa-ta*) by

---

[56] Some foolish scholars say Bank interest is *Riba*. They created the Islamic Banking and used the same Base Lending Rate like other Commercial Banks.
[57] *Sol-laa* is never pronounced *Salaat*. Today, when the mosque announces the five daily prayers they say "*Hai-ya-'alaa-Solaa*". *Salaat* is a profane word not found in the Qur'an, which the Arabs and the *u'lemas* have invented and attributed to God.

sacrificing our greed by doing the practical, good deeds prescribed by God and fulfil our commitment to ourselves.

The phrase '*Wa-Aqimus-Solaa-tawaa-Atuz-Zakaata*' or observe your commitments and keep it pure appears in the middle of the subject of profiteering.

Solaa is about doing *deeds*

Everything that a person does should be *for* God. We are not asked to perform any rituals or to pray to Him or to worship Him. All that is enjoined upon us is to believe in God, be sincere in serving Him by upholding our commitments and do good works. Ritual prayers and worship are the pagans' shortcut to give idol-worshippers a sense of satisfaction that they have discharged their obligations to God when what is really required of them is that they discharge their *Solaa* amongst fellow humans and themselves.

According to the Qur'an, the main essence of the message revealed to Abraham and Moses is:

> No burdened soul will bear the burden of another[58], and every person is responsible for what he or she does. For whatever things that they do, it will be witnessed, and they will be fully repaid. (53:36-41)

In other words, each minute thought and deed is taken into account and recorded. God is recording all the *deeds* (and not the regimented mutterings) of His servants.

---

[58] This is the fundamental concept of God's orderly way of life sanctioned to all prophets. Unfortunately Rabbis, pope, priests, monks and mullahs say they can cleanse people's soul. Only God can cleanse people including the freaks in religious garbs. In 33:15 it says, "No soul will bear the burden of another, when a burdened soul implores for help, nothing can be unloaded, not even by a close relative. So, what are these religious morons doing in our life?

> Since We created the human being, We are fully
> aware of his innermost thoughts. We are closer to
> him than his jugular vain. The two energies at right
> and left are recording *all his deeds*. Not a single
> utterance does he utter without a vigilant watcher.
> (50:16-18)

The majority of people do not believe God is
omnipresent and that He can be with every human all the
time, twenty-four hours a day. However, He knows every
single thing a person does, even his innermost thoughts. No
person can hide anything from the Supreme Being.
Everything is recorded. In the Hereafter, they are told to
read their own record of what they have done to themselves.

> You will see every congregation humbled. Every
> congregation will be invited to view its own record.
> Today you will be paid for your *deeds*. This is the
> record pronouncing the truth about you. Indeed, We
> have recorded all your deeds. (45:28-29)

Ritual prayer, unfortunately for those who put their
faith in it, is not in the category of good deeds. What it is, is
a form of religious worship, which goes against the essence
of God's revelations.

It is absurd to imagine a world where regimented
prayers have moral precedence over good deeds. Besides,
one can look around the world and see many places where
people regularly perform ritual prayers and where serious
crimes abound: rape, sexual abuse, cheating, stealing and
corruption. These people ignore the priorities:

> You shall uphold what was prescribed, and also
> those who repented with you, and not transgress.

Indeed, He knows *whatever your deeds are*, watching. Do not be inclined to those who are wicked – they will make you suffer the Fire, and there is none for you except God as a protector. Then you will not be helped. And uphold your commitments (*aqimi-solaa-ta*) through the ends of the day and the parts from the night. Indeed the *good deeds nullify the bad*. That is the remembrance for those who want to remember. You shall be steadfast. God never fails to reward the righteous. (11:112-114)

The verse clearly says we are to uphold what has been prescribed, and not transgress. God is recording all *deeds*. People must fulfil their commitment to do righteous *deeds* through the ends of the day and parts of the night. The concept is simple. Good deeds will nullify the bad and this is one way to remember God. Deeds can never be fulfilled through a fixed number of ritual prayers. If the concept of *deen* is correctly understood, it is clear to the devout Muslim that it is incumbent upon him to commit to these instructions, uphold and observe them. A simple definition of righteous deeds is clearly prescribed in the Qur'an and it does not include the act of worship or the performance of religious rituals.

Righteousness is not the turning of your faces towards the east or the west. But righteousness is to believe in God, the Hereafter, the energies, the Scripture and the prophets. And to donate of one's wealth despite one's love thereof to relatives, the orphans, the needy, those who are in hardship, to beggars, and to free mental enslavement by upholding the commitments and keeping them pure. And to keep the promises that are made, and to remain steadfast in the face of adversity, hardship, and war. These are truthful, these are righteous. (2:177)

The problem arises when a person's mind is pre-conditioned to believe that *Solaa* means ritual prayer. Thus, *righteous deeds* are totally ignored. One so conditioned often insists that *Solaa* does mean ritual prayer, although a contextual study of the subject demonstrates that such a position does not make any sense.

Surah 107 is a very short chapter with only seven verses the name of which is *Charity*. A person who commits himself to the prescribed *deen* should not neglect his commitment to do charity and good deeds as a way of life.

> Do you not notice those who are lying with the *deen*? They neglect the orphans. They do not advocate the feeding of the poor. Therefore curses be on those who are *obliged, while heedless of their commitments*. They only show off, and they are averse to charity. (107:1-7)

The religionists and the *u'lema* believe that God is cursing[59] the people who pray ritually. They then teach their values to others who will listen without question – just as they did. Compare this rendition with that sanctioned by the religionists' twisting culture:

> Do you know who the rejecters of faith are? They neglect the orphans. They do not advocate the feeding of the poor. Therefore a curse be on those who *pray ritually, while heedless of their ritual*

---

[59] This is the most ridiculous way of thinking - obviously not to the priests of the Arab religion.

prayers. They only show off. And they are averse to charity. (107:1-7)

All seven verses are interrelated: taking care of the orphans, feeding the poor and carrying out charity work can only be fulfilled by the deeds of a committed person. But the religionists say God is cursing those who pray whilst heedless of their prayer. They encourage their followers to pray ritually in order to solve the problem of the orphans, the poor and in lieu of charitable work. Instead of committing themselves individually and collectively to taking care of orphans, the poor and to doing charity from their own earnings, the Arabs trained their priests in the Arab religion to become income generators. They take illegal collections from the people by corrupting the word *zakaa* in the Qur'an to mean *religious tithes*.[60] The Qur'an spells out other examples of good deeds to be observed by those who are committed to the prescribed way of life from God:

> Successful indeed are the believers, who are upright in their commitments (*Solaa-ti-hem*) those who avoid vain talk, those who keep it pure, they guard their chastity except with their wives, and with those who rightfully belong to them do they have sex without being blamed. (23:1-6)

> They are trustworthy when it comes to deposits entrusted to them, or the promises they make, and they constantly uphold their obligations (*Solawa-ti-hem*) (23:8-9)

In this verse it clearly says that those who avoid vain talk, guard their chastity and *commit* themselves to these

---

[60] See chapter six.

values as a way of life are the successful believers. Additionally, they uphold their obligations diligently in fulfilling what they have promised and they are trustworthy when it comes to deposits entrusted to them. In other words, the Qur'an emphasises sincerity and honesty through deeds – not through ritual prayer. Unfortunately, we seldom see these good values in the Arab religion. Be that as it may, each time the word *Solaa* or the derivatives from this root word appears in the Qur'an, it appears in the context of good deeds that people are encouraged to uphold.

A further example:

> They fulfil their promises to God and they do not violate their covenant. They linked (*ya-Siluu*) with it what had been commanded so that it binds (*ai-yu-Solaa*) as they are concerned about their Lord and they fear the dreadful reckoning and they steadfastly persevere in seeking their Lord's grace. They uphold the commitments (*Solaa-ta*) and they give to charity from Our provisions to them secretly and publicly. They counter evil with good. They have deserved the ultimate abode. (13:21-22)

Here the two letter root *Sod Lam* signifies the fundamental meaning of '*link*' for the word *ya-Siluu* whereas *ai-yu-Solaa* denotes the '*binding*' and *Solaa-ta* is the proactive 'commitment'. A person upholds his covenant with God by committing himself in doing the deeds that binds him. The meaning of '*aqor-mus-Solaa-ta*' in this context is to 'uphold the commitment' for the covenant. It is ridiculous to assume that we uphold our covenant with God just through ritual prayers everyday.

In 23:1-9 quoted earlier the religionists has deliberately corrupted the meaning of the words '*Solaa-ti*' and '*Solawa-*

ti' in these verses to mean 'ritual prayer'. They trained their blind followers to ignore the context of the subject completely. Instead, they encourage their followers to concentrate on ritual prayers.

Abraham's commitment

There is nothing new about people upholding the commitment to do good deeds as in the way of life prescribed by God in the Qur'an. It is not an innovation of the Last Prophet. Mankind has been enjoined to observe its commitments from the time of Abraham. God called Abraham the 'committed man'. He served the one God by upholding his obligations through God's prescribed Way of life or *deen-nil-lah*.

Wat-taqizu min-maqam-mi Ibrohim-ma mu-Sol-lan.
(2:125)
Take from the status of Abraham the Committed (2:125)

Please note the word '*Mu-Sol-lan*' in this verse. It refers to the state of being of an active participle. For instance, Salam is peace, Muslim is the state peace of an active participle, Muslimin for many and Muslimat for many women. Similarly, Solaa is to commit, Mu-Sol-lan is the singular proper noun. Mu-Sol-leen is the plural, and Mu-Sol-leemat refers to many women.

Abraham settled his offspring on a barren valley and he wished for them to live according to God's prescribed sanctions in the system so that they too could uphold their commitments – or *Solaa-ta*.

Rob-bana inni askantu min-zuriati bawadi ghoi-ri zar-ghain I'nda-baiti-kal mu-Harami. Rob-bana li-yu-qimus-Solaa-ta. (14:37)

> My Lord, indeed I am settling my progeny in this valley without vegetation <u>by Your sanctioned system</u>. My Lord, let them uphold their <u>commitments</u>. (14:37)

Those who wish to be right with God are told to commit in similar fashion:

> Say, the truth has come from God, and you shall follow the principle of Abraham, a sincere monotheist, he never associated any idols with God. (3:95)

The religionists and the *u'lema* would do well to meditate on the following verse which Muhammad was told to say, revealed in plain Arabic:

> "Indeed, My Lord has guided me in a straight path, the principle of Abraham, the sincere. He never was an idol-worshipper." (6:160)

There is no doubt that after such a declaration, any form of idol-worship (including bowing to a square stone structure or kissing a black stone) is completely out of the question. Today the religionists and the *u'lema* make it mandatory for everyone to worship the Meccan rocks.

Moses' commitments

Moses was chosen from among the Children of Israel to free them from the oppression of Pharaoh. Before they left Egypt, they were told to keep a low profile and use their homes as their base to uphold their commitments. Again the word *Solaa-ta* is used for commitments.

We inspired Moses and his brother, "Let your people confine themselves to their homes in Egypt, and let them consider their homes their base, and let them uphold their commitments (*solaa-ta*)[61], and give the good news to the believers." (10:87)

Moses and those who believe with him were committed to spread the good news to the people - which was their *Solaa*. After they were saved from Egypt, Moses and his people were told to fulfil the covenants by upholding their commitments and to keep them pure. We see the same words used in this context: *Solaa-ta* and *zakaa*:

> *Wa-iz aqodz-na misha qor bani-Israela la-ta'budu-na ilal-lah wa-bil-walidai-ni ih-sanan wa-zil-qurba, wal yatama, wal-masakini, wa-qulu-lin-nas husnan, wa-aqimus-Solaa-ta wa-atu-zakaa'-ta.* (2:83)

And We made a covenant with the Children of Israel: you shall not serve any other than God. And be charitable to your parents and your relatives and the orphans and the poor. And speak to people amicably, and uphold the <u>commitments</u> and keep them <u>pure</u> *(solaa-ta-wa-atu-zakaa).* (2:83)

The Children of Israel were to serve God by honouring their parents and relatives and the orphans and the poor and speaking amicably to people. These were their commitments. God was not telling them to pray ritually and to pay tithes.

---

[61] A good example *Solaa* does not mean ritual prayer. Moses were reminded with the same word *Solaa* a few times - In this verse he and his people were told to keep a low profile in their homes and continue to commit themselves to pass the good news from God.

Jesus' commitments

The Children of Israel created the Jewish religion after they had distorted the Scripture revealed to Moses. The following verse says God will be with them for as long as they commit themselves *(Solaa-ta)* in believing God's messenger and to lend God a loan of righteousness by upholding the covenant they made with Him.

> God has taken a covenant from the Children of Israel and We appointed for them twelve disciples; and declared, "I will be with you for as long as you 'observe your commitments and keep them pure' *(aqom-tumuz-Solaa-ta-wa-atai-tumuz-Zakaa)* and believe My messengers and support them. And lend God a righteous loan of righteousness. I will forgive your wrongdoings, and admit you into gardens with flowing streams. Anyone who disbelieves after this has indeed strayed off the right path. Because they violated their covenant, we put a curse on them, and We hardened their hearts. Consequently they distorted the scripture given to them, and disregard parts thereof. You will always see betrayal from them, except a few. You shall forgive and forget (the few), for God loves the compassionate. (5:12-13)

Jesus the son of Mary was sent to them with the purpose of demolishing this artificial Jewish religion. He was strengthened with the Holy Spirit and demonstrated miracles as signs that he was from God. He told the people he was enjoined to commit himself to undertaking the re-establishment of the laws of the Torah. It is self-evident that he spoke in his own language (which is rendered in Arabic in the Qur'an). What he said is found in the Qur'an as

Solaa-ti-wa-zakaa-ti. The following statement was made while he was in the cradle:

> *Waja'al-lani mubarokah ainama kontu wa-ausorni bis-<u>Solaa-ti</u> wa-<u>zakaa-ti</u> ma-dumtu hiya* (19:31)

> And He makes me blessed wherever I go and He enjoined the <u>obligations</u> and <u>purity</u> upon me for as long as I live. (19:31)

When Jesus, son of Mary said *wa-ausomi bis-<u>solaa-ti</u>* he did not mean *I was enjoined with the ritual prayer* but *I was enjoined with the commitments.* And what were his commitments? To abolish the Jewish religion through the knowledge and the wisdom of the Scripture given to him by God.

Muhammad's commitment

We saw in verse 6:160 above that Muhammad was following the order of Abraham. The Qur'an is not a new revelation or a new guidance from God. It is the same set of decrees prescribed to Abraham and Moses. The essence of all the Scriptures is the same.

> *In-naa haza lafi suhufil ulaa, suhufi ibrohim wa-musaa.* (87:18-19)

> Indeed, this is what is in the Scriptures of old, the Scriptures of Abraham and Moses. (87:18-19)

We have seen that Abraham used the word *Solaa* in his own language, Moses in his and Jesus in his. The word *Solaa* appears for the first time in the Qur'an at 2:2-3:

> That book is infallible, a guide for those who are observant, they believe in the unseen and uphold

their commitments (*Solaa-ta*) and from Our provisions to them they give. (2:2-3)

The word *Solaa* at the beginning of *surah* 2 refers to those who are observant and believe in the unseen God. They uphold their *commitments* by being charitable from the provisions given them by God. This is part of their commitment. Reading further, one sees verses detailing additional commitments. 2:4 says, *'They believe in what was revealed to you from your Lord, and what was revealed before you, and they are positively certain about the Hereafter'*. We should also note: it also says *'those who believe in the previous Scripture'* which means, there is a link between the Qur'an and the previous revealed Books.

Those who believe that the Qur'an is from God are committed to accepting the whole of it. The word *Solaa* in verse 2:3 cannot mean ritual prayer because we cannot do charity through ritual prayers and we do not believe in God's books through ritual prayers.

If we believe the Scripture, we will see all the prescribed decrees in the Book. With God's blessing, He will open up our hearts to submission when our hearts say, *'We hear and we obey'*. That is the moment when we enter into agreement with God:

> You shall be appreciative of God's blessing upon you and uphold the covenant He has made with you when you said, "We hear and we obey." You shall observe God, and God is fully aware of your innermost thoughts. (5:7)

We do not see God, but He hears our innermost thoughts. The moment our heart says *we hear and we obey* to His prescribed way we have agreed to uphold our *Solaa*.

Recite what is revealed upon you from the Scripture and uphold the commitments. Surely your commitments will keep you from evil and it is also for the remembrance of God, which is even greater. (29:45)

God assures us in 29:45 that if we recite His Scripture and commit ourselves to the values prescribed by Him it will keep us from doing bad things or getting involved in evil works. It is a method of remembering Him, which is a great achievement. Our commitment is to remember God's presence. It is an ongoing process as a way of life *'from sunrise to sunset and during parts of the night'*. For as long as we remember Him we are committed to doing good deeds in our lives.

You shall uphold what was prescribed to you, and also those who repented with you, and not transgress. Indeed, He knows whatever your deeds are, watching. Do not incline to those who are wicked. That will make you suffer the Fire. And there is none for you except God as a protector and you will not be helped. And uphold your commitments (*aqimi-Solaa-ta*) through the ends of the day and the parts from the night. Indeed the good deeds nullify the bad. That is the remembrance for those who want to remember. You shall be steadfast. God never fails to reward the righteous. (11:112-115)

The meaning of *Solaa* in the above verses is crystal clear. It has nothing to do with ritual prayers. The *Solaa* is to be observed as a means of remembering our Lord the Creator and to commit ourselves to doing good deeds which will obviously nullify all the negative elements in our life. There is nothing magical about the process.

Ask for God's help without rituals

God is always near. We are told to seek His help directly and we are required to practice patience while continuing to be committed to focusing on the sanctions prescribed by God and to doing good deeds.

> When My servants ask you about Me, tell them, "I am very near. I respond to the call of *any* caller who calls Me." Therefore, they shall respond to Me, and believe in Me that they may attain guidance. (2:186)

> Seek help through steadfastness and commitments, this is difficult indeed, but not for those who are humble and realise that they will meet their Lord. To Him they are returning. (2:45-46)

We must put our trust in the Omnipresent God although we do not see Him. God Himself says it is a difficult thing to do, but not for those who are humble and consider that they will ultimately meet Him. People, however, are weak by nature[62], filled with frailties and insecurities. Rituals, customs, and traditions have a soothing and reassuring attraction for us. They function like pacifiers. They lead to worship. The faithful then externalise their fears, hopes, dreams, and desires onto something tangible. It is a lot simpler to go through a ritualised prayer session rather than to have a one-on-one, heart-to-heart, talk to God.

Idolaters put their trust in things: a piece of wood, a cross, a new moon with a star, a rock, a wall, a stone house,

---

[62] God wishes to make things easy for you, since the human being is weak in nature (4:28)

a mosque etc. These things help one to focus on a collective idea. There are those who put their trust in *people*. They magnify their demi-gods and idols through physical acts of worship. It is strange to think that such a simple truth eludes so many: that those who so choose can magnify and be testament to the unseen God simply by upholding their commitment to do good deeds. What could be simpler than being a testament to God by doing good deeds! Be a testament while leading by example. No need to talk about it. Just do it.

When human beings have a need to call upon God they can call upon Him at any time, day or night from absolutely anywhere. Ritual ablution and its attendant processes are unnecessary. In fact, the Qur'an reminds us that those too proud to call upon God will burn in Hell. If we remember God, He will remember us. It is, after all, a reciprocal relationship.

> Your Lord says, "Call upon Me,[63] and I will answer your call. As for those who are too arrogant to serve me, they will be committed to Hell."(40:60)

> Therefore, you shall remember Me[64] that I may remember you. And be thankful to Me and do not disbelieve. (2:152)

The calling upon God for help, wisdom, perseverance, assistance, money, guidance or anything at all is part of the conditions in effect for a person serving God. The offer of

---

[63] Although the Qur'an was revealed to the Last Prophet, the message in the book is addressed to all mankind irrespective of colour, creed or language.

[64] In 29:45 it says be committed to the orderly way of life to remember God. Our relationship with the creator is through the 'remembrance' of Him not through ritual prayer. He has provided us with all the signs in the heaven and earth. A good example is being provided in 3:190-194.

assistance and guidance has been given, yet many will call upon their messengers, saints – their dead idols in the graves – and some even call upon the *jinn*.

The other side of the coin is our way of remembering God. Intelligent, sentient beings are not in need of a set of body movements in order to reflect on the wonders of God:

> In the creation of the heavens and the earth, and the alteration of night and day, there are signs for those who possess intelligence, who remember God: while standing up, sitting down and lying on their sides. They reflect upon the creation of the heavens and the earth, and they say, "Our Lord, You did not create all these in vain. Glory be to You, so spare us the agony of the hell-fire." (3:190-191)

> To Him belongs everything in the heavens and the earth, and those with Him are never too arrogant to serve Him, nor do they tire. They glorify Him day and night. (21: 20)

Everything was created in perfect balance. Those who are close to Him glorify Him day and night. This is not accomplished by the performance of random pantomimed movements. They do this by adhering to a higher code of behaviour and being a testament to their God.

Zachariah made a special request from God to grant him a son. After granting the request, the energy that delivered the news told him to remember and to glorify God day and night. God did not ask him to pray ritually. In 3:41 Zachariah initiates a communication with God directly by saying, "My Lord, grant me a sign." An unknown energy assigned by God to deliver the good news then said, "Your sign is that you will not be able to speak to the people for three days except by signal. You shall remember your Lord frequently and glorify Him night and day."

We are required to magnify God as a means of serving Him in our daily routine. We are advised to be patient in the face of false accusations, slander or gossip by our enemies, for example. In 20:30 we are told, "Therefore, be patient in the face of their utterances, and praise the glory of your Lord before sunrise and before sunset, also during parts of the night and through both ends of the day, that you may attain happiness."

We do not have to ritualise the methods of calling, praising, remembering, or glorifying God. We do it by magnifying Him in our heart constantly or by speaking to Him softly. We can remember Him while driving, walking, standing, sitting or lying on our sides any time of the day.

Glorify God through commitments

Glorifying God is everything in the heavens and the earth. He is the Supreme Power, the Sacred, the Almighty, and the Judge. (62:1)

In addition, everything that exists in the universe and the earth is observing its *Solaa*. It knows how to uphold its *Solaa* without the aid of prophets or messengers.

> Do you not see that God is glorified by everything in the heavens and the earth as well as the birds in their flight? Surely every one of them knows its own commitments (*Solaa-ta-hu*[65]) and glorification. God knows what they do. (24:41)

---

[65] God says everything in the heavens and earth glorifies Him and they are doing their Solaa including the birds in their flights. These creatures exist as nations like us- but we don't see them glorifying and doing their Solaa through

158

> Glorifying Him are the seven heavens and the earth and everything in them. There is nothing that does not praise His Glory, but you do not understand their glorification. He is Clement, Forgiver. (17:44)

The verse clearly says that there is nothing that does not praise His glory. This means all the celestial planets in the sky; the wind, the electro-magnetic forces, and everything in existence beyond human's comprehension are praising the glory of God all the time. For various reasons people were led to believe that they are required to bow and prostrate physically to God.

Here, the religionists have overstretched themselves. They would have us believe that the word *sujud* in the Qur'an means prostrate. However, a logical investigation into uses of this word and the cross reference of similar words with the same root in associated verses show that the word *sujud* does not – and can not – refer to physical prostration. *Sujud* simply means being in a state of subservience.

The concept of performing ritual prayer is the result of a false teaching introduced by the pagan Arabs to reduce the status of the Supreme God to that of a local deity. Instead of serving Him by deeds they call everyone to worship Him.

Ritual prayer is not in the Qur'an

God did not prescribe a ritual prayer to the Last Prophet or to any of the prophets before him.

---

organised religion. This is how God teaches people about His Book making His message clear.

The Qur'an has 114 chapters with 6348 numbered verses. No verse tells the people: *you must perform a ritual prayer to God.*

- A ritual prayer is an act of worship. God never tells any of His servants to worship Him.

- The revelation to the Last Prophet is not a new revelation from God.

- It is not about religion or worship of God.

- No priest of the Arab religion has ever said that the details of their ritual prayer can be found in the Qur'an. Their position is that seeking to obey the Qur'an alone is a non-starter since one cannot pray five times a day based on the Qur'an alone since it neither makes such a demand nor gives details of how this should be done. This is the testimony of the Arab priests themselves. They are very proud of their bowing and prostrating to the stone idol every day. They are very proud of the invented religion they promote.

Ritual prayer is a conspiracy

The religionists conspired against the natural peacefulness or *Islam* by destroying the revelation as the source of the prescribed covenants between God and mankind. They replaced it with 'short-cut' pagan rituals that make people feel a false sense of having upheld their responsibilities (without, of course, having to do any practical, good deeds). Those who observe the ritual prayer five, four, three, twice or once a day are doing it for the religionists and *not* for God.

This book asserts that *Islam* or peacefulness is a simple way of life, that the Qur'an was written for all mankind, and that it is for all the peoples of the world, irrespective of their colour or race. The reader should be slow to draw the inference that to submit to the One God is easy. Simple does not mean easy. In 67:2 it says, 'God is the one who created life and death in order to *test you* to distinguish the righteous among you'. In order to qualify we must be willing to change out mindset to free ourselves from the shackles that binds us by taking the challenge to find the way to God's system. Once we are in His system we will discover the simplicity in conducting our way of life that pleases Him.

Without any scriptural basis, the Arab traditions say that the Last Prophet was called up to the seventh heaven to speak to God about 'the prayer'. Well, to *negotiate* with Him to be more exact. God wanted Muslims to pray fifty times a day but Muhammad managed to beat Him down to five. It would seem odd that God's messenger should question the content of God's message. It is equally strange that a messenger should choose to intercede on behalf of the addressee of the message. It seems impertinent that a messenger should challenge the will of God.

If negotiations had closed where they began, assuming a 16-hour day we would need to pray once about every 19 minutes. Assuming one set of five prayers requires one to bow and prostrate to the stone idol seventeen times, we would have had the faithful doing a total of 850 separate bowing and prostration movements per day. It would seem that the religionists were the inventors of aerobics. Given this sad state of credulity, it is no wonder that many Muslim nations – whilst bountiful in natural resources – are yet to take their place among the advanced nations. They are too busy trying to find new ways to pray.

This madness has been ascribed Qur'anic legitimacy by the manipulation of 17:1. Taken in isolation, nothing seems amiss. Taken in context, a very different picture emerges. The simple, verifiable truth is that 17:1-7 is a history of the Children of Israel and of the story of Moses who had a meeting with God one night to witness God's signs.[66] (Please see chapter nine).

However, the religionists cannot deny that the word *Solaa* is not even mentioned in the verse.

---

[66] There is no information about the 'METHOD' of performing the ritual prayer in the Qur'an. The religionists deceived the masses with a fairy tale saying the Last Prophet flew up to the seven heavens to negotiate with God about it and back on earth in one night. From 50 prayers a day, they say it was Moses who instigated Muhammad to demand for discount from God. Although God conceded - perhaps He forgot to tell the last prophet the methods.

PART FIVE
The *Solaa* shuffle

In this chapter I will demonstrate how one simple but crucial word from the Qur'an has been manipulated. As we have seen, Arabic words derive their vocabulary from roots. These can be a bilateral, trilateral or quadrilateral cluster of consonants from which words are formed. The derivatives are, in most cases, constructed in accordance with established vocalic moulds or patterns to which certain prefixes, infixes or suffixes are added. This is the basic foundation of the Arabic grammar.

Theoretically, the roots may be formed from any set of consonants in the language with an addition of a short vowel *'a', 'i'* or *'u'* after each consonant to generate the ground form (imperfective, active, third person, masculine and singular, e.g. *he did*). The meaning of this verb is determined by the consonants. Other verbal nouns may be developed from the same root word.

A verb has three states: the *perfect* and the *imperfect* (which are tenses) and the imperative, which is a *mood*. The *perfect* usually signifies an action that is done and completed at the time of speaking (e.g. *he has done*). The *imperfect* signifies an action in the process of being done or completed, or that will be done (e.g. *he is doing*), and the *imperative* an order or a command (e.g. *do!*).

Several grammatical forms derive from the root words to signify the perfect active, imperfect active, imperative, perfect passive, imperfect passive, verbal noun, active participle and passive participles.

Besides the three numbers of singular, dual and plural Arabic recognises three persons: first person (the speaker), second person (the one addressed), and third person (one spoken about).

There are only two genders in Arabic, masculine or feminine. There is no 'it'. Hence, God is referred in the third person as *'Him'*, *'His'* or *'He'*. When we say *'There is no god except Him'*, it does not mean necessarily that God is male.

While one root can have more than one meaning, there does need to be some consistency in the way meanings are approached. Arabic is a clear language. Its very make-up tends to expose abuse of its core rules and structure. It is just such abuse, which has been worked on the word *Solaa* by the religionists.

How the religionists do the '*Solaa* shuffle'

The word *Solaa* and its derivatives appear in the Qur'an many times. Let us see how the translators are forced to jump from one meaning to another for the same word or the derivatives. I call this *The Solaa Shuffle*.

Form	Occurs	Explanation
Solaa	2	In 75:31 and 96:10 stated as *ritual prayers*
faSolaa	1	In 87:15 & 108:2 stated as *ritual prayers,* but 2:249 as took command.
yuSolaa	3	In 2:27, 13:21 and 13:25 stated as *must tie or connect the relationship with God*

164

Sollee	1	In 9:103 stated (with regard to the Prophet) as *supplicated* or *said a prayer* for the people, not *ritual prayer*
tuSollee	1	In 9:84 stated as *ritual prayer* (Do not pray over the hypocrites)
faSollee	1	In 108:2 stated *ritually pray* to your Lord, but in Arabic *faSolaa lirobbika* means 'uphold your commitments for Your Lord.'
yuSollee	2	In 3:39 and 33:43 (a) In 33:43 it is means God and the Angels *'blessed'* the believers. Nothing about *ritual prayers*. (b) But in 3:39 it is stated as Zachariah doing the *ritual prayers*.
Solluu	1	In 33:56 stated as the people must *Solluu* or *honour* the Prophet. Nothing about *ritual prayers*.
YuSollee	3	Once in 33:56 and twice in 4:102. (a) In 33:56 stated as God and the angels *blessed* the Prophet for the word *'yuSollu'*. (b) In 4:102 the same word is stated as *ritual prayers*.
YaSillu	5	In 4:90, 6:136 (2), 11:70, 11:81, 13:21 and 8:35 stated as *people who connect a relationship with God*.

muSollan (sing.)	1	In 2:125 stated as *a place of worship*, not *person who performs ritual prayer*.
muSolleen (plural)	3	In 70:22, 74:43 and 107:4 not stated as *places of worship* but *people who perform ritual prayers*.
Solaa ta	46	No ritual methods in context.
Solaa tee	20	No ritual methods in context.
Solaa tu	1	In 62:10 stated as *ritual prayers*.
Solaa taka	1	In 9:103 stated as meaning the Prophet's *ritual prayer makes the people happy*. The Qur'an clearly says that no burdened soul will bear the burden of another. So how can this be?
Solaa teka	1	In 17:110 stated as meaning perform your *ritual prayer* in a moderate tone. But today, the noon and evening prayers of the Arab religion are performed in silence.
Solaa tuka	1	In 11:87 stated as the prophet Shuaib's *ritual prayers* (in the context of them being able to change the economic system).

Solaa tahu	1	24:41 is said by the Arab religion to mean that the birds of the air perform their *ritual prayer*. Think about that one for a moment...
Solaa tehim	5	6:92, 23:2, 70:23, 70:34 and 107:5 are stated with the sense: you can trust those people who perform the *ritual prayer*, and they also make others understand that the people who perform the *ritual prayer* will always fulfil their promises in 70:32-35. Experience tends to show otherwise.
Solaa tuhum	1	In 8:35 stated as meaning their *ritual prayer* is nothing but controversy and rebellion.
Solaa-waatee	3	9:99, 2:238 and 23:9.

(a) In 9:99 stated as: *their good deeds will take them closer to God and also the 'Solaa-waatee'* (ritual prayer?) *of the Prophet*. Another illogical statement. If we give food to a hungry man how does that take us closer the Prophet's 'ritual prayer'?

(b) In 2:238 stated as meaning we are supposed to safeguard our 'ritual prayers' *Solaa-waatee*.

(c) In 23:9 stated as meaning, "They observe their ritual prayers (*sola-waa-teehim*)." Here the religionists and the *u'lema* say they can fulfil their promises by performing the ritual prayer, they also say they are trustworthy because they pray ritually. What do you think?

| *Solaa-waa-tun* | 2 | 2:157 and 22:40. 2:157 –were there any consistency – would need to be rendered thus: as *'upon them shall be ritual prayers from their Lord'*, whereas 22:40 renders the word as *churches*. Some Arabic experts say *Solaa-waatun* in this context means *oratories*. What in the world is an 'oratory' in this context? |

This twisting of one root word in the Qur'an yields many differing definitions, some of which are totally unrelated to the root word. No Arab priest today can provide any logical explanation for this inconsistency. They just regurgitate the *Solaa Shuffle* as a knee-jerk reaction to any challenge on the subject.

Frequently asked questions

Proponents of ritual prayer are fond of saying that certain verses where this root verb appears prove the existence of ritual prayer. Their arguments tend to be like the following:

1. What about 5:6 where you are supposed to do the ritual ablution (which they call *wudu*) before *Solaa*? Surely, that proves that ritual prayer is needed.

    Surah 5 is to be read from 1 through to 7. Verse 6 is about being hygienic. The first two verses talk about food. People should observe the harmony sanctioned by God in the system. Verse 3 has more details on food, and then it says, *'Today the way of life (or the deen) is perfected'* after detailing unhygienic food. The fourth and the fifth verses also talk about food with additional decrees that Muslims can marry the people of the previous Scripture. That in itself should be an eye-opener.

    The subsequent verse says that we are upholding our commitments when we make ourselves clean. In verse 7 we are told to be appreciative of God's blessing upon us and we should uphold the covenants He made with us from the time we say, *'We hear and we obey'*.

    Hygiene is part of our commitments. And if there is no water to wash ourselves, God has prescribed an alternative i.e. to use clean dry soil to clean our hands. The point is, we are obliged to be as clean as we can – and here the limits are described with provision for extreme circumstances.

There is no such thing as the word ritual cleansing or *wudu* (this common term used by the majority of the Muslims is not to be found anywhere in the Qur'an). There is no ritual ablution. In 5:6 we are told it is good to wash ourselves up to the elbows, wash the face, and wipe our heads and feet. We must keep ourselves clean. This verse does not say that *Solaa* is a ritual prayer. The verse does not say after we 'ritually' clean up ourselves we must start praying ritually.

2.   What about 11:114 where we are told to uphold the *Solaa* at the ends of the day and parts of the night?

It is a mistake to quote verses out of context. Here, 11:114 should be read from *surah* 11 verse 112 through to 115. The verse does not say the *Solaa* should be done *at* two ends of the day and parts of the night. The verse actually says *through* both ends of the day and parts of the night. The verse is rendered here in its full context:

You shall uphold what was prescribed, and also those who repented with you, and not transgress. Indeed, He knows whatever your deeds are, watching. Do not be inclined to those who are wicked. That will make you suffer the Fire, and there is none for you except God as a protector, then you will not be helped. And uphold your commitments (*aqimi-Solaa-ta*) through the ends of the day and the parts of the night. Indeed the good deeds nullify the bad. That is the remembrance for those who want to remember. You shall be steadfast. God never fails to reward the righteous. (11:112-115)

The verse clearly says the commitments are ongoing throughout the day and parts of the night. Verses 11:112-115 emphasise the importance of doing good deeds throughout the day and parts of the night by focusing oneself in routines according to what is taught from God's prescribed decrees. It is a simple instruction.

3.   What about 24:58 where the *Solatil fajri* and *Solatil 'isha* are mentioned?[67]

This verse refers to the periods of undress when children must seek permission before entering their parents' room – from the time the parents retreat to their rooms (*Solatil 'isha*) until the next morning (*Solatil fajri*). We continue to observe our commitments during our private time. The same verse requires the seeking of permission to enter the room when parents are resting at noon.

The *Solatil 'isha* and the *Solatil-fajri* are not the names attributed to any ritual prayers but they are the parents' private time. Similarly, it is not right for parents to simply walk into their children's room once they retreat to their rooms. The verse teaches family etiquette, and as part of the obligations we are to teach children to respect their parent's privacy. There is no *ritual prayer* mentioned in the verse.

4.   What about 4:103 where God says the *Solaa-ta* are done at specified times?

---

[67] That is, they say the Morning Prayer and the night prayer. Strangely, the Qur'an mentions the word '*Salatil-fajri*' but the Muslims say '*Salatil-Subhi*'.

It is our duty to do certain deeds at specific times through the day from morning to dusk and also parts of the night, from the sinking of the sun at noon till the darkness of the night. That means 24/7. The verse says we are committed to do certain things at the specified times. We must do what we have to do when it is time and do it diligently.

If we are traders we must maintain our commitments not cheat or earn by excessive profiteering. If a beggar or a poor man comes to us at nine in the morning, we should not tell him to come back at 1 o'clock. If our workers have worked for us we should not delay or postpone their wages. If we promise to see somebody at 3.00 p.m. then we should uphold that commitment to the man by meeting him at 3.00 p.m. sharp because God says, *'They fulfil their promises when they make their promise'*. Fulfilling our promises is part of the commitment.

5.   › What about 17:110 when you are told to use a moderate tone in your *Solaa-teka*?

First of all we must read from 17:105-111. In the context we see that 17:110 is about the manner in which we should publicly avow our commitments and call people to God. We are not to go around either with a loud speaker or by being so quiet no one hears us.

In 17:110 specifically, the Prophet is asked to use a moderate tone when calling people to God.

Say, Call upon God, or call upon the Most Compassionate. Whatever you call, to Him belong the most beautiful names. Neither avows your commitment publicly loudly or quietly, but seek a middle course. (17:110)

Questions that the *religionists* cannot answer

The proponents of the ritual prayer can only pick five verses from the Qur'an on the basis of which – by quoting them out of context – they claim an imperative for the ritual prayer. However, they cannot quote any verse from the Qur'an to show the methods of the rituals, as they themselves concede.

Perhaps now it is time for them to answer some questions:

- How do you pardon the idol-worshippers when they continue to remain as idol-worshippers even though they have performed the ritual prayer? (9:4-6)

- How are idol-worshippers to perform the ritual prayer?

- How did the Prophet lead the ritual prayers for the non-believers according to (your reading of) 4:101-102?

    > In-naal kafirin nakanu lakum 'aduwun mubin, wa-izza konta fi-hem fa-aqom-ta lahum solaa-ta (4:101-102)

    > Surely the disbelievers are your manifest enemy, And when you are in their midst you shall lead them in Solaa (ritual prayer?) (4:101-102)

- How can the ritual prayer of the Prophet console people or make them happy? (9:103)

- When you are in sudden disaster or facing sudden death, how can the two strangers who are to be witnesses (and who may not know anything about the Arab religion) perform the ritual prayer before swearing to God that they will be truthful? (5:106)

- How did all the people of a town and those living in the surrounding areas preserve their ritual prayer *(wa hum alaa Solaa-tihim haafizuun)* as soon as they heard the message of the Qur'an (6:92)? It may have included non-believers, Christians or Jews.

- Why is it that *yuSollu* means *ritual prayer* in 4:102 but in 33:56 it means *honour and support*?

- Likewise, how does the word *yuSollee* in 3:39 turn into *ritual prayer* while in 33:43 it is said to mean *honour*?

- *Solluu* in *33:56* and *Sollee* in 9:103 have come to mean *honour and supplication*. In 75: 31 and in 96:10 the word *Solaa* is said to mean *ritual prayer*. Why is that?

- How do the birds in the sky and everything between the heavens and the earth (including frogs, termites and trees, for example) perform their *ritual prayer*? (24:41)

- How could the *ritual prayer (Solaa-tuka)* of Shuaib in 11:87 have changed the economic system of the people?

- Why are the same *Solaa-waatee* in 2:238 (*'guard your 'Solaa-waatee'*) and 9: 99 (the Messenger's *Solaa-waatee*) understood differently?

- Why are the same words *Solaa-waatun* in 2:157 (*ulaa ika alaihim Solaa-waatun*) and 22:40 (*wa Solaa-waatun, wa masaa-jidu*) stated with different meanings?

- Is there anyone performing the *'ritual prayer'* by controversial talk and rebellion (*Solaa-tuhum 'indal baiti mukaan wa tashdiyyan*) anywhere in the world? If so, where and how? (8:35)

- How did the word *muSollan* (singular) evolve to mean *location* or *place* for performing *ritual prayer* in 2:125 when the same word *muSollin* (plural) is understood as the *people* who perform the *ritual prayer* in 107:4?

It is inappropriate for the word *Solaa* or any of the derivatives (generated from the same root word) to be rendered as a *ritual act* by people toward God. Its meanings relate to the commitments which link a human being to God through their deliberate deeds.

Solaa is the commitment to observe the prescribed covenants. This encompasses the whole of God's commandments in the Qur'an to people. It covers obligations, relationships, agreements between people, a person's obligations to own self, and matters of cleanliness and diet. It extends to promises, dealings, relationships, families, and parenting. There is nothing 'religious' about it.

PART SIX

Religious tithe collection is a scam

We have seen how words – when distorted by irresponsible people – can be used to twist what was meant to be a practical mode of productive living into a religion. A critical study of the Arabic text from the Qur'an has demonstrated that:

- Religion is man-made and has no justification except by means of corruption of the revealed Scripture

- Worship is a form of religious activity appropriate only for man-made deities or idols

- Ritual prayer is an act of worshipping idols

None of this is sanctioned by the Qur'an. A religion needs money and the creators and maintainers of religion must get it from somewhere. The Vatican does very well off its flock, and so does the Arab religion. The so-called *Islam* has imposed a compulsory religious tax in the form of a tithe. Again, this is done through corrupting the semantics of God's words and shoring the result up with a large wad of non-Qur'anic hearsay and conjecture. This chapter and those following will document the facts behind this conspiracy against the common people and the good name of the Prophet.

As indicated, to achieve this end certain words in the Qur'an which appear frequently have had their meanings contorted. A key phrase in regard to the topic in hand is *aqee-mus-Solaa-ta-wa aatu-zakaa*. Textual, semantic and contextual investigation shows that this phrase means *'observe your commitments and keep them pure'*. Instead, the sense has been rendered as *'you shall observe your ritual prayers and pay the religious tithes'*. That keeps everyone coming to the mosque and paying for the privilege. How jolly convenient.

The above phrase is found in many places in the Qur'an. As always, it is the context that is the key to the sense.

> You shall not earn from excessive profiteering. And do not say, "This is the way of a trade." God allows trading and He forbids excessive profiteering. If you can obey this admonition then you must refrain from such practices. This is for those who believe and do good deeds, and for those who observe their commitments and keep them pure (*aqeemus Solaa ta wa aatu zakaa*). Their Lord will reward them. They have nothing to fear nor will they grieve. (2:275-277)

The phrase *'aqeemus Solaa ta wa atu zakaa'* when recited in isolation has no sense. It calls the reader to submit to the essence of what is being recommended in by the context. An analogous situation in English would be to say: *do it, and do it well!* What we must do can only be comprehended by intelligent reflection on the *context*. However, the religionists and the *u'lema* have ascribed this particular phrase a meaning all of their own and use it to keep the people obedient, unthinking and – as we will see – financially useful.

Zakat does not mean religious tithe

Most Muslims have been duped by their religious leaders to believe that it is their duty to perform the ritual prayers and pay the tithe or religious alms propagated by the religionists. They are told that the meaning of the first half of the phrase *'aqeemus Solaa ta wa atu zakaa'* means 'pray the ritual prayer' and the second part means 'pay the tithe' (now erroneously called *zakat*). There are two reasons why they fall for it:

- They are ignorant of God's Scripture.

- They believe that these human devils (whose only profession is to leech off and cheat the ignorant) have some sort of special knowledge in this regard.

We should be wary, however, since:

- It is wrong to believe something without verifying it (see 17:36). We should not accept anything or do something if we are ignorant of the facts.

- It is dangerous to attribute something to God premised merely on the strength of hearsay.

Bearing in mind that ignorance is no excuse, we will be held accountable for our deeds in this world. Serving masters other than God is a very serious offence and at a very deep level, we know it. There is no escaping this fact.

Basic universal values

No court in the world accepts a plea of ignorance as vindication: ignorance of the law is no excuse. By the same token, we cannot plead ignorance on the Day of Judgement or blame someone else for the wrong things that we have done. Nothing could be clearer than the statement in the Qur'an when it says:

> *Ain-taqulu yaumal qiamati ain-na-kun-na 'an-haza ghor-filin.* (7:172)

179

So that you will not say on the Day of Judgement, "Indeed we did not know about this." (7:172)

Muslims on the whole – and the modern Arabs in particular – are grossly ignorant of God's message in the Qur'an. They read without comprehension, believing that they gain merit for just chanting the Arabic verses aloud. They leave the understanding to the *u'lema*. On the whole, they are sincere and simple people who feel that they need to serve their Lord and lead a righteous life. They have been born into a suffocating inheritance of religion. While it is easy to empathise with this situation, we all have to take responsibility for what we do. We cannot blame our parents for our lot on Judgement Day.

> *Or you may say, "It was our parents who set up idols, and as descendants we followed their footsteps. Will You punish us because they strayed?" (7:173)*

Today, people depend on the *u'lema* for guidance, but more often than not, the *u'lema* misguides them. By their deeds, and words we know that these *u'lema* are agents of the same wicked religionists who invented the Arab religion to worship a stone idol. We have seen how these fanatics twisted the meaning of the words *deen*, *'abd*, and *Solaa*. They also twisted the word *zakaa* (so often mentioned with the word *Solaa*).

Understanding that the *u'lema* have more than a passing knowledge of the Arabic language, they are doubly guilty of abetting the non-believers and hypocrites to distort the effect of the Qur'anic message on the hearers. They have deviated from the true teachings of the Qur'an and continue to educate their followers not to understand the meanings of the message of the Book. If that were not enough, they impress upon their followers that salvation is contingent upon those who do not use their common sense or to question the religionists. It is strange that the *u'lema* rarely encourage their followers to perform charitable deeds according to God's way in the Qur'an. This should be the cornerstone of God's *deen*. They are, though, most diligent in the matter of collecting *'zakat'*[68] which they deem to be a lawful religious tithe. Contributors, on the other hand must not question what they do with this money. According to the Arab culture, it is a cardinal sin to question the *u'lema*.

Anyone with even elementary Arabic must admit that there is no firm reason why *zakaa* should signify paying out money. In truth, there is not a single reference in the Qur'an regarding any such financial contribution or contributions in kind. On the contrary, the Qur'an advocates non-prejudiced charity and donation as the act of self-sacrifice by men and women towards their fellows in society.

Charity is prescribed

The giving of part of the provisions granted by God is one of the commitments enjoined upon mankind. This instance of self-sacrifice is required of His servants for the benefit of all. Giving without compulsion or need for recognition within or without the boundaries of the *deen* should be encouraged at every level. Instead of sacrificing a portion of their income or their crop or livestock bestowed upon them by God, they instead sacrifice their eternal soul and succumb to greed by hoarding God's provisions. Again, the Qur'an warns us such behaviour is not acceptable.

---

[68] In many countries these collections are made through compulsory deduction of salaries from workers - every month. The Vatican survives with such a system and many so-called Muslim countries are doing the same.

What has happened is that an orderly way of life that promotes the well being of all has been subverted to provide for the few in what has become a rapacious oligarchy.

There are many verses in the Qur'an calling people to perform acts of charity and God expects us to commit ourselves to these values.

> God is the one who created you. He is the one who provides for you. He is the one who causes you to die and He is the one who resurrects you. Can any of your idols do all these? (30:40)

> O you who believe, you shall give to charity from God's provisions to you before a day comes wherein there will be no more business, no favouritism and no intercession. It is the non-believers who chose wickedness. (2:254)

> And race towards forgiveness from your Lord, and the paradise that encompasses the heavens and the earth awaits the righteous people who are charitable during the time of prosperity and the times of hardship. They control their anger, and they pardon people. God loves those who are charitable. (3:133-134)

> What is wrong with believing in God and the Day of Judgement and giving to charity from God's provisions? God is fully aware of everyone. (4:39)

> You can never guide anyone[69]. God is the only one who guides in accordance with His will. Any charity

---

[69] Every organised religion promised they could guide people to the straight path to God's way. The Quran makes it clear that nobody can guide anyone except God. In 28:56 the prophet cannot guide his love ones. Many Arabs claim

you give is for your own good. Any charity you give
shall be purely for the sake of God. And any charity
you give will be repaid to you without the least
injustice. (2:272)

These are the prescribed ways of God. We are expected
to commit ourselves to this ideal. This is a personal
commitment between a person and his or her Creator.
Nobody should police the fulfilling of another's obligations.
God has even detailed the deserving recipients of charity.
All the guesswork has been taken out. He in His wisdom
makes it easy for His servants to fulfil their charitable
obligations:

They ask you about charity. Say, "The charity shall
go to parents, relatives, the orphans, the poor, and
those who are on the path. Any righteous deeds you
do, God is fully aware thereof." (2:215)

He who is charitable in the cause of God is like a
seed that grows seven ears with one hundred seeds
in each ear. God multiplies the reward many fold for
whomever He wills. God is bounteous, omniscient.
(2:262)

These are only some of the sixty-odd verses in the
Qur'an on the topic of charity. However, the word used for
charity is **anfak**[70] and not *zakat*.

This word *anfak* is alien to all the innocent 'Muslims'
around the world. Very few of them have heard of this word

---

they are related to Muhammad and they think they are exempted from God's
judgement.
[70] The word *Anfak* can generate other words like *yun-fik, anfiq, infak* and *munfik*
to refer as to spend, the act of spending, spending or in the case of *munfik* is one
who spends.

in their life. The religionists concealed this important word in the Qur'an and the *u'lema* or the Arab priests assist in the deceit. They have substituted true charity with their corruption of the concept of *zakat*. The word *zakaa* actually means to purify. Try substituting that meaning in the many verses where *zakaa* appears to see how it reads contextually.

Religious tithes invented by religionists

The concept of paying *'zakat'* is permanently lodged in the mind of every Muslim because the religionists and the *u'lema* say this is one of the articles of the faith. Anyone who is able to read basic Arabic can detect the distortion, however. The word *zakaa* appears in the Qur'an many times. Not surprisingly, even the translators cannot avoid translating *zakaa* according to its true meaning in many instances since the context will allow for no other rendition without making the sense too ludicrous to bear.

In the following reference the Qur'an exposes the distortion in the meaning of the word *zakaa* where, interestingly, it reminds us not to follow the Devil's words. Here God uses the root word *zakaa* and its derivative in one verse. Its usage confounds the distortion by the religionists and the *'u'lema'*:

> *Ya-aiyuhal-lazi na-amanu, la-tat-tabi'u hu-dhu-wati syai-thon-ni waman yat-tabi' khu-dhu-watil syai-thon-ni. Fa-in-nahu ya'muru bil-fah-sha-ie wal-munkari walau-la fadh-lul-lah alai-kum wa-rah-matu-hu ma-zakaa min-kum min ahadin abadan. Wala-kin-nal-lah yu-zakki man-yasha wal-lah-hu-sami'ul alim* (24:21)

O you who believe, do not follow the steps of the
Devil. If anyone follows the steps of the Devil, he
will advocate evil and vice. If it were not for the
grace of God upon you and His mercy, nobody is
purified *(ma-zakaa)* forever from any single one of
you. And it is but God who purifies *(yu-zakki)*
whomever He wills and God is Hearer,
Knowledgeable.

The verse breaks down like this:

ma	nobody is
zakaa	pure
minkum	from among you
minahadin	from any single one
abadan	forever
walakin	and it is
nallah	but God
yuzakki	purifies
manyasha'u	whomever He wills

The word *zakaa* has no other meaning than *pure*. In this
particular verse we are told to be careful of the Devil, yet
the people (including the *u'lema*) do not take heed. We
have been clearly warned that the Arabs are staunch pagans
and hypocrites, but still the *u'lema* trust them. Let us
explore another verse. Nobody translates the word *tazakka*
as paying the alms or religious tithes in this verse.

In 79:17 God speaks to Moses, *'Go to Pharaoh, indeed
he has transgressed and tell him, "Will you not purify
yourself?"' (hal-laka-ilaa-ta-zak-ka).*

The key phrase breaks down as:

hal-laka   will you

ilaa   not
ta-zak-ka   *purify* yourself

Moses did not go to Pharaoh and say, *'Will you not pay your religious tithe'?* Here the religionists themselves cannot avoid but admit that the word has no other meaning except *'Will you not make yourself pure'?*

Thus, the words *zakaa*, *yuzakki* and *tazakka* represent *pure*, *purifies* and *purify*. There are no religious tithes, taxes or religious alms to be paid to the priests. In fact, the whole priesthood should be abolished. Let the people begin again to apply their money and their intelligence to the things God has ordained for them and cease sacrificing both for the sake of supporting this caste of important-looking parasites.

Another example of the misuse of this word by the religionists is apparent by comparing 19:19 and 19:30. The human looked energy appeared to Mary. It says:

> *Qaala, khul-in-namaa rosulu rob-bika li-ahba laka 'ghul-man zaki-ya.* (19:19)

> He said, "Indeed I am a messenger of your Lord to grant you a son who is *pure*." (19:19)

Both *zaki* and *zakaa* mean *pure*. The human-looking energy transmitted the message to Mary that she will conceive a son who is pure. When the son Jesus was born he spoke to his mother. They then met some people who accused Mary. Baby Jesus defended his mother saying:

> *Wa-ja'alani mubarokan ai-nama kuntu wa-ausorni bis-solaa-ti wa-zakaa-ti ma-doomtu hai-ya.* (19:31)

> And He made me blessed wherever I go, and He enjoined on me my commitments and *purity* as long as I live. (19:31)

Zakaa is not about money

Money *cannot* be connected to the word *zakaa* in the Qur'an. It is the obligatory duty of everyone to practice charity. God does not call this *zakaa*. For charity or donation, God uses different words such as *anfak* and the attendant derivatives of the word.

So what is the big deal? What does it matter which word you use? The point is that the religionists have created a brand new religious obligation for the people without any basis, the only benefit of which is that it fills up the religious pundits' coffers.

The idea that the duty of charity and donation (*anfak*) is a free-will issue has been circumvented by the *u'lema*. What better way to ensure their own parasitic existence than making financial support for them mandatory and a prerequisite for the attainment of Paradise?

The result is that the *u'lema* gets their cut from the 2.5% religious tithe they support as a key pillar of salvation and Muslims are completely alien to the concept of charity and donation.

The meaning of the word *zakaa*

Zakaa and its derivatives simply mean *pure* or *purify*. Much as the religionists may think they can get away with scheming against the Almighty, they still have to face the fact that there are many verses in the Qur'an in which they cannot change the meaning of *zakaa*:

Qod-af-laha man- zak-ka-ha. (91:9)

Surely, benefit is for those who *purify it* (*zakka-ha*). (91:9)

The Scripture was revealed to the prophets in order to *purify* the people around them and those who obey them. The word *yuzakki* (which signifies *purify*) appears on many occasions along with the word 'Scripture' and the word 'wisdom'.

> *Rob-bana wab-'ash fihim ro-sulan minhum yatlu a'laihim a-yaatika wa yu'alimu humul kitaba wal-hikmata wa-yu-<u>zak-ki-hem</u> in-naka anta a'zizul hakim.* (2:129)

Our Lord, raise among them a messenger who will recite to them Your revelations and teach them the Scripture and wisdom and *purify them* (*yuzakkihem*). Indeed, you are Almighty, the Judge. (2:129)

> *Kama ar-salna fi-kum rosulan minkum yatlu a'laikum ayaatina wayu-zak-ki -kum wa'alimukumul kitab wal-hikmata wa-yu'alimukum malam takunu ta'lamun.* (2:151)

Such as sending a messenger from among you to recite you My revelations and to *purify you* (*zakki-kum*), and to teach you the Scripture and wisdom, and to teach you what you never knew. (2:151)

The word *zakki-kum* in 2:151 means *purify you.*

In the next verse we see other derivatives with prefixes meaning *purify*. The religionists do not claim that the word *zak-ka* in this verse refers to religious tithes although the word *Solaa -ta* appears right next to it.

Wala taziru wazirotan wizror ukror wa-ain tad'u mish-qor-latun ilaa himliha laa-yujmal minha shai'ain walau kaana za-qurbaa. In-nama tunzirul-lazi yak-shauna rob bahum bil-ghoibi wa-aqormus Solaa-ta waman tazakka. Fa-inama ya-ta-zakka linafsihi wa-ilal-lah hil masir. (35:18)

And no burdened soul will bear the burden of another soul, and when a burdened soul invokes to carry it, it will not carry anything of it although they are close relatives. Surely, you are reminding those who fear their Lord and uphold their commitments and he who is purified (*ta-zakka*) is indeed purifying (*ya-ta-zakka*) his own self, and to God is the ultimate destiny.

In this verse (together with many others) they have had to acknowledge that the word *zakaa* means pure or purify. In all other verses, whenever the word *zakaa* appears beside the word *Solaa* the religionists contend that *zakaa* is religious tithe. Such distortion by the religionists and their translators can be easily exposed by a simple contextual reading of the Arabic Qur'an.

The word *zakaa* is a common instruction to the Children of Israel. In their time they received the same instructions as the Last Prophet:

Wa-aqimus Solaa-ta wa-atu zakaa-ta warr-ka'u ma'al ror-ki'in. (2: 43)

And observe the commitments and keep them pure and humble yourselves with those who are humble. (2: 43)

189

The injunction to *uphold the commitments and keep them pure* is found throughout the Qur'an and instructs us how to remain within the bounds of the dynamic way of life prescribed for us by the Creator.

PART SEVEN

The Prime target was Abraham

Abraham holds an honourable position in the monotheistic system. He enjoyed the privilege of becoming the model in **ALL** the revealed Scriptures. In Qur'anic passages he is seen to be the perfect example for those searching for the path to God's system – a journey that leads to a peaceful life.

Abraham decided to remain in the system and committed himself to keeping it pure from any form of idol-worship and ritual. Likewise, we have a duty to take up the challenge. Once we belong to the system, we are charged to fulfil our obligations and, by God's mercy, we will be granted peace in this world and in the Hereafter.

According to the Qur'an, Abraham used his intelligence and common sense when confronted with dogmatic practices steeped in tradition. He saw his father and his people devoting themselves to idols. Abraham rejected the concept because it simply did not make sense. When he discussed this with the people he again used his common sense. When they threatened him with their gods, he said:

> How could you serve what you carved? God is the one who created you and the materials that you make to become your idol. (37:95-96)

For challenging traditional practices, Abraham found himself the prime target of the Arab conspiracy. They carved a footprint out of a copper block and placed it right opposite the square rock idol in Mecca and claimed it was his. This, they say, is to honour the man who built their rock idol for them. They say Abraham was the first man to *worship* the stone idol in Mecca through the ritual prayers. That is the reason why the religionists say that the status of Abraham (*maqami-ibrohim*) is somehow equated with the footprint in the gilded caged opposite their stone idol in their mosque.

Next, they say Abraham – *the committed man* – (the word in the Arabic is *muSollan)* denotes a *place* of worship. Their special place of worship, naturally.

This particular brand of absurdity is the result of God's Scripture being twisted by a race that God has decreed the *'staunchest in disbelief and hypocrisy'* (see 9:97).

The significance of Abraham's status

So what is the significance of Abraham in this context? The Qur'an tells us that Abraham was totally committed to serving his Lord. He was a model to mankind of a monotheist submitting to the Lord of the Universe.

> Whose way is better than the one who peacefully focus for God while doing good deeds, and follows the principle of Abraham the sincere? God has chosen Abraham as a beloved friend. (4:125)

> Indeed, Abraham was a nation of being faithful for God in sincerity, and he was not among the idol-worshippers. Instead he appreciated God's blessings. God guided him to the straight path. We endowed him with goodness in this life and in the Hereafter he will be with the righteous. (16:120-122)

Thus, who would then forsake the principle of Abraham except those who fool themselves? We have chosen him in this world and in the Hereafter. He will be with the righteous. When his Lord said to him, "Be peaceful" he said, "I am peaceful for the Lord of the Universe." (2:130-131)

When Abraham was put to the test by his Lord through certain words, he carried them out. God then said, "I am appointing you the leader (*imam*) of all mankind." (2:124)

A good example has been set for you by Abraham and those with him. They said to their people, "We disown you and your idols you set up besides God. We reject you and you will see from us nothing but enmity and opposition until you believe in God alone." (60:4)

Abraham was sincere in his commitment to observing God's laws and he regarded idol-worship as the enemy. His focus was people's submission to God without intermediaries. God did not appoint Abraham as *imam* to lead the people into rituals and worship. He was appointed to provide an example of a person committed to the service of God alone. In the context of the Quran the word *imam* simply means an independent and progressive leader who can lead the people by stimulating their intelligence, striving towards a condition of collective well being while observing the limits of the prescribed restrictions in God's system. He can also have a strong influence on people with his intelligence or power.

Abraham led his progeny and the people to prosper in a barren land, which they made productive. He was against all forms of idol-worship and rituals and wanted the people to free themselves from the bondage of dogma. He was willing to sacrifice his life to take a stand against the idol-worshippers. Today, we are witnessing an Arab culture that has reversed the process.

Fairy tales to strengthen the conspiracies

The Qur'an does not say where Abraham was born or where he lived. But it does say that the Torah and the Injeel were not revealed until long after him. At the same time the Qur'an confirms that the Arab race had never received any messenger or prophet before Muhammad. Thus, simple logic dictates that Abraham did not go to Mecca with Ishmael (please read the sections on *U'mra* and *Haj*). With this simple realisation, the whole illusion the religionists would have us believe turns to dust.

The religionists contend that Abraham was travelling on Arab soil with his wife and son, Ishmael. They say he abandoned the wife and baby in the middle of the desert and went away – a poor testament to the *imam* of the people appointed by God.

The story goes on to say that while Abraham's son was crying, his mother left him in the desert and started running left and right between the tops of the two hills. As the baby was kicking his legs on the ground, suddenly a gush of water sprung from the ground.

The religionists have named this place the *Safa* and *Marwah* – actually rock outcropping deities found within the precincts of the temple. The Muslims around the world are not aware of the Arab love of worshipping rocks.

Today, the religionists make the Muslims worship the two rock outcroppings by making it mandatory to traverse between them seven times when paying homage to the square rock idol. They call such rites as the *sa'ei* – another religious rite of the ancient pagan Arabs. Again, it is important to note that this peculiar word is not found anywhere in the Qur'an.

They also claim that the water that gushed from the ground was sacred and have called it *zam-zam* water. The Qur'an neglects to tell us any of this. Today we see a systematic flow of reverse osmosis water drawn by a *water pump* installed beneath the stone house, which draws its water from the city to supply the mosque.

The religionists continue their deception with another tale. Abraham is said to have built God's house at the spot where the spring water was gushing. They corrupted verses 2:125 and 22:26 to strengthen the fairy tale. The life and death of the Arab religion depends on a contorted reading of 2:125. Even if the truth is not exposed now, sooner or later people will know. God's system is never changeable and the truth will always prevail.

If we read both verses we discover:

> *Wa-'ahidna ilaa-Ibrohima wa-Ismael-la an-tho-hiror bayti-ya lit thor-iffin wal-a'kiffi-na war-roka'is sujud.* (2:125)

> And We instructed Abraham and Ishmael to cleanse My system for throngs of people, and for those who are devoted and those who humble themselves in submission. (2:125)

> *Wa-izbaw-na li-ibrohim makanal bayti al-laa tushrik-bi shai-a'in wa-tho-hir bayti-ya lit-thor-iffin-na wal-qo-emeen-na war-roka'is-sujud.* (22:26)

195

> And when we appointed for Abraham a place in the <u>system:</u> that You shall not associate anything with Me, and cleanse <u>My System</u> for the groups of people, and those who uphold, and those who <u>humble themselves in submission</u>. (22:26)

Although many other words were corrupted in 2:125, I am highlighting only three words from this verse to show the repetition in 22:26. In the next two chapters I will demonstrate the fact that the religionists changed the meaning of these words from those they are meant to have. I will do this by comparing them with the usages of the same words in other verses. Let's get some basics down first. According to the Arab religion:

1. The word *bayti-ya* in the two verses signifies *God's house*. In other words, the 627 square foot stone house in Mecca belongs to God and is a place where He lives.

2. The word *lit-tho-iffin* in the two verses means *those who walk around it*. In other words the faithful walk around it (the stone house) anti-clockwise.

3. The word *war-roka'is-sujud* in the two verses means *those who bow down and prostrate*. As in point two, the faithful are required to add this to their liturgy if they are to be counted among God's people.

There are no verses that corroborate these assertions. The distortions have created a great impact on the lives of billions of people around the world. I hope the Muslims will come to their senses and see the seriousness of the conspiracy and the price they have had to pay for being ignorant of God's Scripture and for following the religionists blindly. Perhaps they will ponder on what the Qur'an says about the blindness of the hearts:

> It is not the eyes that go blind, but it is the heart inside the chest that goes blind. (22:46)

2:125 has been a very special verse to me. This is the same verse that made me ask myself the simple question about the very existence of God's house in *Islam*. I never believed that God lived in a house. It is my natural instinct – and I am sure many share my thoughts – that common sense dictates that the supreme God cannot be represented by any kind of symbol or icon on this earth.

As a Muslim, I was told the Qur'an was the book of guidance – a revelation confirming all the previous scriptures. When I was confronted with such a problem it was obvious that I should look for the answer within the Book itself.

The Qur'an clearly says:

> Shall I seek other than God as a source of law when He revealed to you the Scripture fully detailed? Even those who receive the previous Scripture recognise that it came down from your Lord truthfully. Therefore you shall not harbour any doubt. (6:114)

The word of your Lord is complete in truth and justice. Nothing can abrogate His words. He is the hearer and the knower. (6:115) If you follow the majority of people on earth - they will divert you from the path of God. They only follow conjecture - and they only guess (6:116).

PART EIGHT

The worship of a stone house

The following chapters focus on the analysis of many Arabic words. These words will be written according to their vocalic sounds. Readers not familiar with Arabic are asked to bear with me. It is important to refer to these words because most of the time the enemies of God and His messengers will distort words, which seem to be similar and yet are not.

> He is the one who revealed to you this Scripture with perfect verses as the essence of the book, and the rest are consistent. Those who are sick in the hearts are inclined to follow that which is not consistent with the intention to disparage and to interpret them. No one knows their interpretations except God. And those who are well founded in knowledge say, "We believe in all the revelations from our Lord." No one will take heed except those who are intelligent. (3:7)

The essence of the Scripture is that the verses are perfect. Perfect means without defect. If we perceive any contradiction it is not the fault of the Book, but we have to sincerely admit that it is perhaps our lack of understanding or that our comprehension of the message is less than good.

> Why do they not study the Qur'an carefully? If it were from other than God, they would have found many contradictions therein. (4:82)

In other words when God says, '*You must not serve other than Me*' it simply means that anyone who claims to have found a way to serve Him which contradicts His message must be in error. Arab or not. Likewise, if God says, *'You must not associate anything with Me'* it means we cannot do something to the contrary and provide excuses to justify our action. That cannot be too difficult to understand. It is a simple black-and-white statement. No one would dream of answering the question, "Are you pregnant?" with an evasive: "Just a little bit." Either you are or you are not.

In chapter three we saw how the religionists *shuffle* the word *Solaa* by giving it different meanings. They only end up contradicting themselves when they try to manipulate the same word elsewhere in the Qur'an. That is exactly why the verse says the contradictions are not from God but from other than Him.

Chapter 2:125 has been the singular misfortune of being the Arab religionists' main target to twist God's words to justify their Arab religion. I will prove by reference to the Qur'an that eight simple words in 2:125 have been corrupted by the enemies of God.

The word *bayta* is found twice. If we examine the word critically and compare it with other verses in the Qur'an we will discover why the religionists' claim that this means a physical house – and the so-called *Ka'aba* in Mecca in particular – has no basis.

There are many words, which require examination in this one verse alone. Each has to be explained clearly. This chapter will discuss only bayta and bayti-ya. Other words in the same verse will be discussed in the next chapter.

Abraham did not know anything about Mecca

It is easy to prove false the claim of the religionists that Abraham was given the responsibility of building a house for God in Mecca. Firstly, there are many verses in the Qur'an to show Abraham and Ishmael had never been to Mecca (see chapter twelve). Secondly, if the house were the focal point for mankind as a place to serve God, then all the prophets subsequent to Abraham failed to fulfil their obligation to go there. Lastly – and most crushing of all – is the fact that the Supreme God does not need a house. The idea is ridiculous.

By definition, a house is a place where people live. However, the idea of God's house came from the religionists after they had manipulated the following passage. According to them the meaning of the verse is:

> We then designated *the house* for mankind as the place of assembly and security. Use the station of Abraham as a place of *ritual prayer*. We gave instructions to Abraham to clean *My house* with Ishmael for the people who encircle it, retreat in it and for those who bow and prostrate physically to it. (2:125)

We now need to break the verse down into parts and to show how it was manipulated to give validity to a tribal system of idolatry.

Firstly the religionists would have it that:

> God showed Abraham *the house*.

In order to utilise this statement for their own purposes, the Arabs either built this house (or utilised an existing pagan temple, of which there were many) to complete the illusion. This they made the centre for their re-vamped religion.

Having twisted the meaning of the word *bayta*, they then insisted that the word *masha-batan* as '*a place of assembly*'. *Masha-batan* literally means '*providence*' an alien word to Arabs or their scholars. In the Qur'an 'assemble' or 'assembly' is derived from the root H SH R or *Hashar*. The root generates other verbs *yah-sha-ru, uh-shur, hus-shira, yuh-sharu, hasher*, or *mah-shu-rotan* and never as *masha-batan*. For meetings the Qur'an uses the word *maja-lisi* also not as *masha-batan*.

After giving a wrong notion to the word *masha-batan* they then manipulate the words *maqaam* and *muSollan* (which, in fact, indicate Abraham's *status* and his *commitments*) to mean:

> Use the *station* of Abraham as a place of *ritual prayer*.

To add credence to this assertion they carved a pair of footprints from a copper block and displayed it in front of the square stone idol. This, we are told, represents the station of Abraham. These footprints are taken as signifying a place of assembly for the performance of the ritual prayer. This level of idiocy and illusion is not even worthy of a bad Hollywood film.

Next:

> For mankind to *encircle*, to *devote to it*, and to *bow and prostrate* to it.

So the people follow: they bow, prostrate, and encircle the stone house. Their rituals do not help them see God because the huge door to 'His house' remains closed. The religionists call the square stone house *baytul-lah* or 'God's house'.

It is perplexing to note that it has a door that the occupant never opens or closes. If the case is that God does not use doors, then why is there one? This can either mean He has never left His house, or it could mean *He is not there*. But let's suppose the premise were true for a moment: God lives in a glorified porta-cabin. Shouldn't the bounds of decency dictate that a house of God should be built for every mosque in the world, preferably from imported Arabian rock?

This is how the religionists fooled the people into worshipping idols made of rocks, granite, wood, copper, brass, black cloth and Arabic calligraphy. They teach the people to cry loudly, *'O God here I come, O God here I come'* as though God were hard of hearing, focusing their full devotion to the idol resembling a house in the centre of their mosque. God has already told us that He hears what is in our hearts. These are nothing more than comical pagan rituals. The impact of manipulating one verse has distorted the whole concept of serving the One God as dictated in the Qur'an.

Somehow, millions feel a great exhilaration at performing this procedure. Yet, there are also thousands who do ask themselves privately *'Why are we doing all this'?* Yet they dare not abandon this practice. They will find that the answer to that question will elude them for as long as they put their trust in the religionists instead of God.

When we read the passage from 2:125 according to the intended message it says:

And when We designated the *system as providence*
(*bayta-masha-batan*) for mankind and security.
Take (learn) from the *status (maqam)* of Abraham
who was *committed(mu-Sol-lan)*. We contracted
Abraham and Ishmael to cleanse *My system (bayti-
ya)*, for *throngs of people (thor-iffin)*, those who are
devoted (a'kiffin) to it, and those who *humble*
themselves in *submission (wa-ruku'is-sujud)*.

The disillusioned religionists changed the meaning of
eight words from this one verse alone to denigrate Abraham
– the chosen man – who was supposed to lead all the people
on earth to God's system. Translators are forced to accede
to the erroneous application of these words although just
two verses – 2:125 and 22:26 – form the entire supposed
Qur'anic basis for this whole category of manipulated
lunacy. The net result from the distortion is that millions of
people believe that Mecca is the centre for the Islamic
world:

- The 'system' (*bayta*) is centred around a square
  shaped stone made from the mountain rocks
  standing in the centre of a mosque in Mecca, similar
  to stone idols erected in many of the temples around
  the world.

- The 'providence' (*masha-batan*) became a place of
  assembly. So the people from all over the world
  assemble in Mecca.

- The 'status of Abraham' (*maqami-ibrohim*) is a
  smaller idol in the form of a pair of footprints in a
  copper block mounted in a cage some ten metres
  from the door of the stone cube.

- The 'committed man' (*muSollan*) is a place of worship. The stone idol is the focus.

- The 'throngs of people' (*Tho-iffin*) is the religious rite of walking around the stone idol seven times in an anti-clockwise direction.

- To 'devote to' (*a'kiffin*) means visit and pay homage to the stone cube.

- To 'humble in submission' (*roka'is-sujud*) is a series of choreographed movements of bowing and prostrating to the stone cube.

The religionists say that according to 2:125, God showed Abraham the house. They then advance two verses ahead to say Abraham and Ishmael *built* the house of God. Nobody notices this simple fraud. The question that begs to be answered is: *how did God show a house to Abraham in 2:125 and ordered him to cleanse it and then, later (in 2:127), make him raise the foundation of the said house?* With this level of gullibility being requisite for membership of the Arab idolatry club, is it any wonder the 'Muslims' are in such a poor state in the world?

This is, of course, yet more Arab trickery. In fact, 2:127 means: *Abraham elevated the foundation from the system*, but the religionists twisted it to mean *Abraham raised the foundation of the house!*

They have eliminated the word *min al* ('from the') appended to the word *bayti* completely, which changes the whole context of the passage. To illustrate, we will break 2:127 down to its component parts:

wa-iz   and when

yarfa-'u	established
Ibrohimul	Abraham
qo-wa'ida	the foundation
minal-bayti	**from the system**
wa-ismail	with Ishmael

Literally, it says: *'And when Abraham established the foundations from the system with Ishmael'*. This is more consistent with the context when the subject is read from 2:124. Even if the religionists insist that the word *bayti* means 'the house', Abraham could not be raising the foundation of a house which was already there. The word *minal* simply means *from the*. When it is prefixed to the word *bayti* it means *from the bayti* which means *from the system*.

A 'system' is a way of working, organising or doing something in which you follow a fixed plan or a set of rules. For example, if a situation or activity has a system, it has a sense of orderliness or good organisation. People sometimes talk about a system to refer to the government or administration of a state. When they think that it is too strong and has too many rules and regulations they oppose the system. Those who observe or uphold the system are committed to live in an orderly way within the prescribed rules of the system.

In other words, they live *'by the system'* or in Arabic *'inda bayti'* which is exactly what Abraham utters in 14:37.[71]

---

[71] Abraham said, "My Lord I have settled my progeny in this barren valley according to the sanctions of your system. Our Lord, this is to let them observe their commitments. Therefore, make throngs of people incline to it, and provide them with fruits that they may be appreciative." This is a repetition of Abraham's request in 2:126: "My Lord, make this a peaceful land, and provide its people with fruits; provide for those who believe in God and the Last Day".

206

The religionists somehow wanted us to believe that the word *inda bayti-ka* means *near Your house*. To follow this reading to its logical conclusion, all the people of the world should live near God's house. Just try to group the entire Arab race from Morocco, Algeria, Syria, Libya, Yemen, Palestine, Jordan, Iraq, Kuwait, Oman, United Arab Emirates and Saudi together in one place for one week and see what happens! If one were to add the Shiite population, the fireworks would really start to fly. There would be no need for the Americans to invade any more Arab soil – they could just walk in and take it because there would be no one left alive to oppose them!

The religionists are ignorant of what God says about the settlement of human beings on the earth:

> *O My servants who believed! My earth is spacious. Therefore, serve Me alone. (29:56)*

When read as one subject, 2:124-127 give the meaning that Abraham and his son Ishmael were committed to *God's system*. Both of them established the foundation of their commitments *from the System*. It has nothing to do with a stone house in Mecca or anywhere else. As a matter of fact, neither the father nor son had any knowledge about a square stone structure attributed to God. It is just a figment of the primitive Arabs' wild imagination. The message conveyed by these verses is, in fact, that Abraham and Ishmael were the first to establish the foundation *from* God's system.

Let us see how the Quran uses the word Bayta to refer to it as the providence in His system for mankind. In some cases, the system works according to what we do with our work.

God replied, "I will also provide for the disbelievers. I will let them enjoy for a while, then commit them to retribution of <u>Hell</u>, and a miserable destiny."

Bayta is a system not a house

- The religionists say *bayta*[72] means a *house*. According to the Qur'an *bayta* in 2:125 means a system and the indefinite noun is *baytin* which is found in 3:96.

- The words *bay-yaa-ta* and *bay-yee-tu* are used in 4:81 to inform us about a *system* being the norms of the enemies of the prophet to change whatever was said to them and God had *systematically recorded (yak-tubu-maa-yu-bay-yee-tun)* whatever they have invented. This is consistent with the information in verse 6:112 when it says: "*And we made for every prophet enemies from among the human devils and jinn devils, who invent to each other with fancy words in order to deceive*".

- In 7:4 and 7:97, the same word pronounced as *bayaa-tan* to mean: mankind will suffer from natural disasters by their own wrongdoings as a *system*. But translators said *bay-yaa-ta*, *bay-yee-tu* and *bayaa-tan* means *during the night*. It is obvious from the Qur'an that many communities went through disasters at any time of the day. Besides, the Qur'an uses *Layl* to refer to night and this word is not found in any of these verses.

- A house is called *buyut*, which is found in 2:189 and the indefinite noun is *buyutan*, which is found in 24:29. The addition of the dual ending *-an* shows that the word relates to *two*.

- In 2:189 the phrase *buyu-ta min-thu-huri-ha* is used to indicate a house to express *do not enter the house from*

---

[72] The religionists abused this word and made Mecca a religious sanctuary. They say the word *buyut* is the plural of *bayt*. The fact is that these words are used in the Qur'an to signify different things. *Bayt* and *buyut* are both singular.

the back door which is an Arabic proverb equivalent to the English *do not beat around the bush*. The suffix *ha* after the word *thu-huri* signifies the singular form of the house representing the feminine gender in nature.

- In 24:29 the word *buyu-tan* is a plural indefinite noun mean *houses*. *'You commit no error by entering uninhabited houses wherein there is something that belongs to you. God knows what you declare and what you concealed'.*

- In 24:61 the word *buyuti* is mentioned ten times in a command spoken to many people to refer to their fathers, mothers, brothers, sisters, fathers' brothers, fathers' sisters, mothers' brothers, mothers' sisters and friends. Each of them dwells only in one house at a time. The word *buyuti* refers to the house each of them owns.

The religionists claimed the word *bayti-ya* means *My house* and then wasted no time in naming a stone structure which they built in Mecca *baytul-lah*, or God's house. According to the Qur'an *bayti-ya* in fact means *My system*.

Bayta according to Qur'an

Every one of us initially follows our own *system* or *bayta*. By God's will, He will remove us from our system with the truth to His *system* or *bayta* once we deserve a higher rank upon receiving His mercy and forgiveness, and also a good provision from Him. This is clearly stated in 8:5.

The verse breaks down like this:

kama   the way

aqrojaka   remove you
rob-buka   your Lord
min-bayti-ka   from your system
bil-Haq   with the truth

Your Lord removed you (or brought you forth) from your *bayti-ka* (or your system), with the truth. (8:5)

If we read the full text of the passage, we see why *bayti-ka* means *your system* instead of *your house*.

> Indeed the believers are those whose hearts cringe upon remembering God. And when the revelation is recited to them it increases their belief. They are observant towards God. They uphold their commitments and from Our provisions to them they give away to charity. They are the true believers and they deserve higher ranks, forgiveness, and also good provisions from their Lord, the way Your Lord removed you *from your system* (*minal bayti-ka*) with the *truth*. Indeed, there are those among the believers who are reluctant, and they will oppose you even after the truth has become evident to them as if they were driven to a certain death. (8:2-6)

We are told that the Prophet was removed from his system after the truth was revealed to him. Are we to imagine that God removed the Prophet from his physical house after the truth was manifested to him?

Similarly, the deserving believers may also be removed from their previous system with the truth. They will live by to the sanctions of the system or the *inda baytul-muHarami* in fulfilling the wishes of Abraham. (This will be explained later.)

210

The logic is that God is able to move a person from one system to another while that person uses his or her house as a base to study God's revelations and wisdom.

They continue to obey God and His messenger and uphold their commitments and be charitable. The following verse was addressed to the Prophet's wives:

> You shall use your house (*buyuti-kun*) as your base. Do not behave like the ignorant among the earlier people. And uphold your commitments and keep them pure and obey God and His messenger. God wishes to remove from you the impurity of the people of the system (*ahl-la-bayti*) and to cleanse you thoroughly. You shall remember what is recited in your house (*buyuti-kun*) from God's revelations and wisdom. Surely God is compassionate and cognisant. (33:33-34).

In 33:33 it says:

> *yuridul-lah li-yuzhiba 'ankumul rijsa ahl-lal-bayti wa-yu-tho-hiro-kum tadh-hiro.*

> God wishes to remove *from you* the impurity of the people of the system and to cleanse you thoroughly.

The Prophet's wives were initially native-born to the ignorant and unclean people of the system or *ahl-la-bayti*. God's wishes to remove the impurity of the *ahl-la-bayti* from them and asks them to use their houses as their base. They are told to obey God and the Messenger and to remember what is recited from God's revelations and its wisdom, and uphold their commitments so that God can cleanse them thoroughly. They had to stop the permissiveness of the ignorant *ahl-la-bayti*. For more than a thousand years, most Arabs have believed it an honour to be associated with the *ahl-la-bayti*. The Qur'an declares the opposite. They say '*ahl-la-bayta*' refers to the '*members of the house of God*'. But it is written in 28:12 that the family of Pharaoh belonged to the *ahl-la-bayti* and we all know Pharaoh was a tyrant.

The word *system (bayti)* and *house (buyu-ti)* are both mentioned in 33:33-34. It is misleading to say that God wishes to cleanse the Prophet's wives from the impurity of the people of the house (*ahl-la-bayti*), cleanse them thoroughly, and later use the houses (*buyuti*) as the base to obey God and His messenger.

The religionists say *Bayta* is singular and *Buyuta* is the plural. The misunderstanding is explained by the Qur'an in 29:41. This verse uses a clear term of *aw-hana-buyuti* to denote the singular.

> The example of those who take (*ta-qor-zu*) protectors from other than Allah is like the example of the spider that took a system (*ankabuti-it-ta-qor-zat-baytan*). And surely the 'most fragile house' (*aw-hana-buyuti*) is of the spider's system (*la-Baytul-ankabut*), if they knew. (29:41)

The Qur'an uses the word '*ta-qor-zu*' to signify the people 'take' other gods besides the one God as a system in their way of life. When the same word is used as *ankabuti-it-ta-qor-zat-baytan* it means the spider 'took' a system. It follows with *aw-hana-buyuti* which clearly denotes the '**most** fragile house' to describe a single type of 'house' not 'houses'. The word '**most**' can only mean, 'among the many there is only **one** unique type'. The word *la-Baytul-angkabut* after *aw-hana-buyuti* reflects the earlier statement of *angkabuti-it-ta-qor-zat-baytan*. It is wrong to assume the word *ta-qor-zat* as to build. In the Qur'an '*banu*' is used to refer as 'build', a derivative from the root '*bani*'. This word is not found in 29:41. Therefore *Buyuta* is not a plural of *Bayta*.

Bayti-ya in the Qur'an

This word appears in the Qur'an three times, in 2:125 and 22:26 (which refers to God's system) and in 71:28. In 71:28 it refers to Noah's way of life, a system different from his folks.

In the scriptural account of the prophet Noah, everything was totally destroyed when God sent down the Great Flood. The rising waters eventually drowned even a young man, who Noah thought was his son, who had refused to believe when he had decided to escape the flood by climbing up a hill. In 71:26 Noah says:

"Lord do not leave on earth a single disbeliever."

Once Noah was saved, God destroyed everything in his area: all the people in his community including the livestock and their properties.

Most of us are familiar with the story of Noah. Noah lost his *house* during the flood. Everyone lost their houses during the flood. When on the ark, he implored God:

My Lord forgive me and my parents and anyone who enters my system (*bayti-ya*) as a believer and all the believing men and believing women. And do not increase the wicked except to destroy. (71:28)

Clearly, Noah was not referring to his physical house, but to the system (*bayti-ya*) to which God had guided him. There were no houses left because everything had been destroyed. Noah was afloat on the ark when he made this request to God.

Noah asked God to forgive those who were with him in his system – or his *bayti-ya* – those who believed in God and *not* those who entered his home. There is no indication in the Qur'an that God can forgive a person just by entering a physical house belonging to a prophet of God.

In the Qur'an *al-bayta* means *the system* and *bayti-ya* means *my system*. Every one of us knows the unseen God does not live in a physical house and He does not need a house to live in.

The Arabs in Palestine changed the name of the old city of Jerusalem to *Baytul-mu-qadis* very recently. When they used the word *baytul* for Jerusalem they did not say the meaning here was *house* but *city*: *baytul-muqadis* meaning the Sacred City. The word *muqadis* is derived from the root *qudus*, which means *sacred*. The prefix *mu* before the root indicates a state of being.

There are also prefixes appended to the word *bayta* in the Qur'an signifying the state of the verb:

baytul-ateeq	in 22:29 (the original system)
baytal-Harami	in 5:2 and 5:97 (the sanctions in the system)
baytika-muHarami	in 14:37 (the sanctions in the system to be observed by Abraham's progeny)

The religionists say all these words refer to *house*. This is for no other reason than to justify their invented Arab religion and to make their followers focus their worship on their stone.

Those who read the Qur'an to understand it have been instructed:

- Rule number one: *Ignorance can buy you a ticket to Hell.*

  We have assigned for Hell multitudes from the *jinn* and humans, for them hearts that do not understand, and for them eyes that do not see, and for them ears that do not hear. (7:179)

- Rule number two: *Ignorance is not bliss.*

  Surely the worst creatures by God are the deaf, the dumb without common sense. (8:22)

- Rule number three: *Do not be dogmatic. Verify your facts.*

  Do not accept whatever of which you do not have any knowledge. You are given the hearing, the eyes and the brains. (17:36)

- Rule number four: *The foolish do not think.*

  And it will not be for anyone to believe except by the will of God. God has assigned filth upon those without common sense. (10:100)

Those who have read the Qur'an should know the prime commandment in the Qur'an:

'*You shall not associate anything with God*'.

A house is a building in which people live, usually people belonging to one family. To associate a man-made rock structure like the cubical stone house which the religionists call *Ka'aba* in Mecca with the Almighty God inflicts violence against our reason and our common sense.

The followers of the Arab conspiracy should ask why they associate a stone cube with God. To grasp the essence of God's Scripture we need only a normal dose of common sense. This will lead us to the conclusion that the religionists have fabricated a convenient lie for their own cultural and material 'well-being'. They say it is God's house, but in the same breath, they also say God does not reside in that house. The next time you meet an Arab priest, ask him exactly what it is they want us to understand about God's house here on earth. Ultimately, they intend us to think that it is God's house but that He does not live there.

However, having built the house, they would have it that the structure is sacred. Ask the religionists:

- At what point did the rocks from the mountains become sacred?

- If they were sacred before they were taken from the mountains, did the Arabs not defile the mountains by taking them?

- If neither of these points results in a clear conclusion, what exactly *are* they trying to say?

In truth, the religionists have no answers to these questions. Their grand plan was – and still is – to conspire against *Islam* and to destroy the peacefulness of a way of life revealed by God to the Last Prophet. First, they put up the idols. Then they got the gullible to believe in them.

216

Next, they– corrupted the common people's understanding of God's words in the Scripture to justify the conspiracy. Then they set themselves up as the keepers of the faith and language. The religionists have also misrepresented and misstated the words *baytil-Harami* and *baytul-muHarami*. They say that the words mean 'sacred house'. The next time you meet an Arab priest ask him since when the word *prohibited* or *restricted* (*Haram*) began to mean sacred? Along the same lines, what has happened to the word *baytul-muqadis*? Does not Jerusalem mean '*sacred house*' because they say *bayta* is a house and *qudus* is sacred? The retort will probably be in the negative. Since it is not in Arabia, it does not mean the same thing.

No Arab is willing to clarify any of these points, even the most qualified priest of the Arab religion. Since none is forthcoming, let us just use a higher authority, the Qur'an.

Haram[73] is not 'sacred'

According to the usage in Qur'an the word, *Haram* means *denied, deprive, restrict, forbid or prohibit.*

For example, there are three verses where the word *bayta* is suffixed with the word *Haram* to denote the specific restriction to the *bayta*.

When the same word is attached to the word *masajid* (submission) it signifies the specific restrictions of the *masajid*. For clarity, it is called the *sanction*: a course or way imposed by God intended to make the people obey specific restrictions. However, in normal usage it can be said to mean '*the sanctions of the system*' or the '*specified*

---

[73] The Muslims were deceived by the religionists that this word means sacred.

restrictions of the submissions' when referring to the restrictions in the *bayta*/system and *masjid*/submission.

For example, in 5:2 it says, *aminal baytal-Harami*. It means *the peaceful harmony of the sanctions in the system.*

Another way of saying it is *the peaceful harmony of the specified restrictions in the system[74]*. The sanctions in this verse refer to the limits imposed by God in respect of His decrees so as to maintain the perfect harmony in His system.

This word appears only once, in 5:2. This verse talks about the violations of God's decrees. In the same verse it also mentions *shahrul-Harama* indicating *the restricted months, hadya*/guidance, *qola-ida*/the indicator marking the restriction on hunting, which encompasses the harmony of the sanctions or the restrictions in God's system.

On a similar note, upon receiving the revelations, the Prophet was instructed to focus himself towards the sanctioned submission or the *masajidal-Harami[75]*. It includes the details of the sanctions prescribed in the Scripture.

> You shall focus yourself to the sanctioned submission (*masajidal-Harami*). Wherever you may be you shall focus yourself towards it. Even those who received the previous Scripture recognise that this is the truth from their Lord. (2:144)

---

[74] Do not upset nature. Wildlife conservation is one deed He sanctioned in the system or *Baytal-harama*. He created everything in the heavens and the earth in perfect balance. Thus hunting of wildlife should be allowed only during specific period.

[75] The Arabs deceived everyone that this word refers to their mosque in Mecca.

The word *Haram* – when used as the ground form independently – means *denied* or *deprived*. The word *Hurumun* is derived from the same root and signifies the indefinite noun meaning *restricted*. Other words generated from the same root for example, *Hurimat* or *yu-Harimu* when used as the ground form can either be a perfect or imperfect active and mean *forbidden*.

The Palestinian Arabs exposed the hypocrisy of the religionists when they gave a new name to Jerusalem calling the city *baytul-muqadis* by their reckoning. If – as the religionists contend – *baytal-Harami* also meant 'sacred house' then the Palestinians would have never used the word *baitul-muqadis* for Jerusalem, as it is incorrect in both form and function.

Changing the word *Haram* to become *sacred* is an attempt to alter the message of the Qur'an because the word *quddus* is used in the Qur'an to mean sacred. In the Qur'an this word is used to refer to the sacred land (*ard muqoddasa-talati*) assigned to the Children of Israel. In 5:21 it says they refused to enter the sacred land. In 20:12 and 79:16 the same word is used to refer to the sacred valley of Tuwa (*mu-qod-dasi-tuwa*), the location of the burning bush. Lastly, the *sacred self* or *rohil qudus* (which loosely translated means *holy spirit*) is used to describe the existence of the sacred spirit in Jesus the son of Mary. Other than these, nothing is sacred but God.

This word is attributed to God at two different places in the Qur'an.

Huwal-lah hul-lazi laaila ha-il-laaha il-laa huwa al-malikil <u>quddus</u> sus-salam-mul mukminu muhai-minul a'zizu jab-barul mutakab-bir, subhanal-lah hi a'm-ma yus-rikun. (59:23)

He is the God, there is no god but Him, the Supreme Power, <u>the Sacred</u>, the Peace, the Faithful, the Supreme, the Almighty, the Compassionate, the Dignified, God be glorified above what they have associated with Him. (59:23)

Yu-sabihu lil-lah ma-fis-samawa ti-wa-ma fil- ard, al-malikul-qudusi, 'zizil-hakim. (62:1)

Glorify God everything in the heaven and the earth, the King, the Sacred, the Almighty and the Judge. (62:1)

Here we see clearly that *quddus* is *sacred* and not *Haram*.

Baytal-Harami simply means *the sanctioned system* and *a'inda-bayti-ka-mu-Harami* means *by 'Your sanctioned system'*. The religionists, however, are willing to say *baytal-Harami* is *sacred house* and that *a'inda-Bayti-ka-muHarami* means *near Your Sacred house*.

The Qur'an tells us Abraham was led to this *bayta* or *system*. Those who wish to follow his way should commit themselves to the same system. Abraham used the word *a'inda-baytika-mu-Harami* in 14:37 to indicate he wanted his progeny to live *'by'* the sanctions in God's system, the same system to which he is committed. It is illogical to say that Abraham told God he wished that his progeny and all the people around the world who follow his footsteps would become God's neighbour.

- The word *bayti-ya*: in 2:125 God directs Abraham and Ishmael to cleanse *'My system'* referring to God's system, and in 22:26 it says Abraham was given a place in *My system* or *bayti-ya*. It is ridiculous to say Abraham and Ishmael cleansed a physical house belonging to God and then were given a place to share the house with God.

- In 5:2 the word *aminal-bayti-Harama* is mentioned to indicate God's sanctions in the system about wildlife conservation. The sanction was prescribed for the harmonious preservation of His system.

- In 14:37 Abraham said: *I am placing my progeny by Your sanctioned system* (or *a'inda-baytika-muHarami*) meaning to say his progeny should uphold their commitments according to the sanctions prescribed in God's system.

- In 3:97 it says: those people who are convinced may take the challenge to God's system or *Haj-jul baytin manis thadhor a' ilaihi sabila* if they can find their way to it. The verse also gives some indications that in the system there are profound signs regarding the status of Abraham.

Therefore, in the Qur'an *bayta* refers to *system* and not *house*. If we explore a little further the subject of the family of Abraham in the Qur'an we see the relevance of his position in God's system – and *not* in God's 'house'.

Take the challenge to find the system

It seems that in God's system nobody can inherit the *deen* from his forefathers. If the father submits to the way, it is his duty to exhort his children to submit to God. Abraham and Jacob reminded their children:

Moreover, Abraham enjoined his children and so did Jacob, saying, "O my children, God has pointed out

> the *deen* for you. You shall not die except as those
> who are at peace *(Muslims)*." (2:132)

Abraham and Jacob told their children they must not
die except to be those who are at peace in obeying the *deen*
prescribed by God. Abraham and Jacob did not tell their
children that God had pointed out a *religion* or a house for
them. They said:

> God has pointed out to you the *deen* (or the way of life).

None of them were told to make a pilgrimage to a stone
house or to start *worshipping* God, but they were told that
there was a *deen* of which they must be convinced and then
take the challenge to live by God's system, if they could
find the path. Their father Abraham was led to a system,
committed himself to it with Ishmael, and together they
lived by the sanctions in the system. Similarly, if we submit
to God's way, we are told to remind our family members to
also believe and submit to the orderly way of life by doing
exemplary good deeds. It stands to reason that if the role
model is at peace by upholding this system, the progeny
will follow suit.

> You shall exhort your family to be committed and
> persist in doing so. We do not ask you for any
> provisions. It is We who provide for you. The final
> victory belongs to the righteous. (20:132)

We are to tell our children the way of *Islam* is the
sanctions prescribed in the Scripture and that they must
focus themselves to these sanctions when they submit to
God's way to uphold their commitments. They must *not* fall
into idol-worship by following any religion. We cannot tell
our children the *deen* is somewhere inside a stone house
built by the Arabs in the desert. Luqman in his wisdom said

to his children:, O my son, do not set up any idol besides God; idol worship is a gross offence', then he continues:

> O my sons, observe your commitments (*Solaa-ta*) advocate righteousness and forbid evil, and stay steadfast in the face of adversity, this is the real strength. Do not be arrogant nor walk in pride, God does not love the boastful and the arrogant. (31:17–18).

There is no evidence that Luqman had received any revelation, but the Qur'an says God endowed him with wisdom. Thus, he had the ability to make sensible and reasonable decisions. In his wisdom, he knew the most serious offence in this life was to associate God with idols. Yet, the majority of the people on earth serve almost everything but God. They simply cannot seem to serve the unseen God whose domination encompasses the heavens and earth.

What is in the '*Bayta*'?

People do not realise that words like *fi-hi* (which means *inside it*) *bi* (which means *with*), *ilaa* (which means *to* or *towards*), *minal* which means (*from the*), and *li* (which means *for*) and a few others have had their meanings twisted or ignored in certain contexts by the gatekeepers of the Arab religion. These words are often appended to a verb as a prefix, but they make a lot of difference. For example, people fail to think carefully of the significance of *fi-hi* (*inside it*) in the following context:

> Inside it (*fi-hi*) there are clear signs (*ayatun bai-inatun*) about the status of Abraham, (*maqami ibrohim*) and whoever enters it is secured. And it is the incumbent duty of mankind to take the challenge

(*Hajuu*) to the system (*bayti*) for those who can find their way. And whoever disbelieves, surely God is self-sufficient, above any need of the worlds. (3:97)

The words *fi-hi* mean in the context, 'in the *bayta* there are Clear Signs (*ayatun-bai-natun*) about the status of Abraham (*maqamu ibrohim*) and whoever enters it will find security'.

If the word *bayta* truly meant a house then, logically, we have: '*In the house there are clear signs about the status of Abraham*'. Can the religionists or the *u'lema* prove to the world that there are clear signs about the status of Abraham *inside* the cube structure standing in the middle of their mosque? No, they cannot. But what they will show us instead is a piece of copper in a gilded cage standing outside the house where their imagination apparently left a footprint.

The *baytien* in 3:96-97 refers to a system, not a house and we can find in this system (*baytien*) the clear signs (*ayataun bai-inatun*) of Abraham's status (*maqamu ibrohim*) who was totally committed to the *deen*. Whoever embraces this system is secure. All humans are expected to take the challenge (*Hajuu*) to the system. They must try and to make their way to it.

For the sake of argument, if the word *bayta* actually meant a physical house and the *Haj* meant *pilgrimage* we would be confronted with a very serious problem. Each and every one of the 2,000,000 people who perform the 'pilgrimage' today must squeeze into the house to observe and sanctify the spot where Abraham stood for his ritual prayer. If this is the case, then the house the religionists have put up needs major reconstruction. It will also mean that if the number of Muslims increases, they will have to renovate God's house in order to accommodate the new faithful. As it stands, God's present 'house' can comfortably hold a couple of hundred at most.

That's right. All the Sunnis and Shiites from every corner of the globe would have to squeeze into the *'Ka'aba'* to achieve security. This is both illogical and impossible, but this is exactly what happens when we take the magnanimity of God's ideals and equate them with the pettiness of people's physical world. The result: an idol smack in the centre of a house of worship.

The religionists say those who worship God through images or icons are the pagans and idol-worshippers. Though quick to condemn and criticise others, the Arab religionists have never considered that they themselves do exactly the same. They also say the followers of other *religions* are *pagans* and *idol-worshippers* when they walk around their stone idols in their temples or around their temples. They do not pause to realise they are doing the same. The Qur'an tells us that it is not that their eyes that are blind, but their hearts.

Hindus, for example, walk seven times in an anti-clockwise circle around a *lingam* – or stone idol – at the centre of their temple. Hindus have been doing this for much longer than the religionists.

The fallacy of the religionists' claim that the word *bayta* means a house is totally contrary to the concept of serving the Lord of the Universe. Each time a word in the Qur'an is twisted, it renders the message absurd. In a further case, they insist *bayta* means a house and we have what the religionists themselves call the *Forbidden House* when they refer to *baytil-Harama*.[76] The question is why they make it a mandatory for everyone to go to a forbidden house.

To conceal the conspiracy they continue to distort the meaning of the word *Haram* to become *sacred*. The non-Arab Muslims around the world had never confronted the religionists with a simple question: how did a rock structure renovated as recently as 2003 become *sacred?* Which part of the building is actually sacred? They will soon discover it is not the square structure proper that is sacred, but the small black stone (or *Hajar aswad*) worshiped by their forefathers, that is sacred. The word *Hajar aswad* used in reference to the black stone is nowhere to be found in the Qur'an. But the religionists say it is part of *Islam*.

The Arabs have successfully reinstated their true stone deity of black basaltic rock as the focus of worship in Mecca to carry the torch of their forefathers' religion, a pagan community.

---

[76] i.e. what 'Muslims' call the mosque at Mecca.

PART NINE

The corruption continues

It is common knowledge that there are many followers of other religions who *worship* God through the images in their temples – the Orthodox Christians, for example. But how is it that the followers of the Arab religion call those people *pagans* and *idol-worshippers?*

The fact is the followers of the Arab religion have more than just *one* idol. Besides the cubical house in the centre of the mosque, the religionists also provide their followers with many other idols. The black stone embedded at one corner of the cubical house is the most revered icon. It is encased in a silver-frame portraying rather a vulgar image – make of that what you will. The design was perhaps to symbolise the female representation of the three chief Arab idols: *Al-lat, Al-Uzza and Manat.* Grammatically, these are female names, and the religionists said they referred to the daughters of Allah. The Arabs worshiped these female goddesses long before the Qur'an was revealed and the Last Prophet was commanded to ask the Arabs:

> What about *Al-lat* and *Al-Uzza*, also *Manat*, the third one? Is it for you the males and for Him the females? This is indeed an unjust distribution. Actually, they are nothing but names that you invented, you and your forefathers. God never revealed about it from His authority. They followed nothing but conjectures and what their own souls dictated when the sure guidance had come to them from their Lord. What is it that the human being wants? (53:19-24)

This verse confirms that the pagan Arabs had invented many new gods for themselves. In this case, these stones were assigned female names. These stones were touched, stroked, or kissed by the worshippers to acquire some of the stone's holiness.

The other idol is a twelve-foot tall cage protecting a copper casting of someone's footprints. It stands opposite the door of the *larger idol*. All these idols have their own purposes and functions.

Within the same precincts there are two rock outcroppings which the religionists have called *Safa* and *Marwa*.[77] During any visit or pilgrimage, the followers of the Arab religion will run between the two rocks after they have circumambulated the cube and kissed the black stone and prayed behind the gilded idol opposite the stone house. This latter rite, they claim, is to honour the suffering of Abraham's wife when she was searching for water within the same area. No one has asked a simple question: what has Abraham's wife got to do with *Islam*? The author does not see any logic in this ritual except to say the religionists used Abraham's wife as an excuse for their followers to worship the two rock outcroppings. The whole thing is another pagan Arab myth.

We will analyse the other six words in 2:125 and see how these words were distorted by comparing them with the usage of the same words in other passages of the Qur'an. We will establish beyond any doubt that the religionists have abused the meaning of these words to create the basis of all the ritualistic practices in their 'religion'.

---

[77] One Qur'anic verse refers to entities by these names. Clearly, the Arabs took the Qur'anic words and applied them to aspects of their local pagan rites.

Abraham's status (*maqami ibrohim*)

The word *maqam* appears in the Qur'an a few times. Since the Qur'an explains itself, we just need to look at all the pertinent verses to understand the meaning of *maqam*. The religionists say the meaning of *maqami-ibrohim* is the footprint immersed in the copper cast opposite the stone structure. If that were true, how would they explain *maqama-robbuka* or *Your Lord's maqam* in 55:46? Can it mean *the footprint or station of your Lord*? The same word is used again in 79:40. In this passage it is written as *maqama robbihi* which means *status of their Lord*.

The verse breaks down thus:

wa-am-maa	and surely
man-khor-fa	those who fear
maqama	the status
robbihi	of their Lord
wa-nahal	and they refrain
naf-saa	themselves
'anil-hawa	from their lust

When translated, it can be rendered:

> *And surely, those who fear the status of their Lord, and they refrain themselves from their lust. (79:40)*

Perhaps the Muslims should ask their Arab masters whether they translate the same verse as:

> *And surely those who fear the footprints/station of their Lord and they refrain themselves from their lust.*

Such primitive thinking is an insult to our intelligence.

The same word is mentioned in 17:79 as an assurance from God that He will raise anyone of us to a higher status upon fulfilling certain commands. And it is this same word which is used in 2:125.

Wat-ta-khi-zu min-maqami Ibrahim (2:125)

Take from the status of Abraham.

maqaman mah-mu-dan (17:79)

Raise you to an exalted status.

Maqam therefore simply means the status or rank of a person. It is *not* a place.

The word 'committed' corrupted

In 2:125, the word *muSolla* is derived from the root *Solaa* with a prefix of *mu* represents Abraham as the doer in the singular.

The enemies of the Last Prophet, however, say the word '*ibrohimi muSolla*' is a *place* of *ritual prayer* where Abraham stood to pray (and then somehow his footprints were miraculously appeared in a copper block at the same spot). We should note that there are three numbers in Arabic: singular, dual and plural. When the doer of *Solaa* is in the singular he is called *muSollan*, but when the doer is plural they are called *muSollin*. The word *muSollin* is also found in the Qur'an:

- In 2:125 *ibrohimi-muSolaa* informs us that a man by the name of Abraham was the doer of the *Solaa*. Abraham was called a *muSollan*.

230

- In 107:5 (see below) the same word is used to indicate many people (plural) who are the doers of their *Solaa*. They are called the *muSollin*. This is the plural of *muSollan*.

The same method was used by the religionists in their shuffle of the word *Solaa*. They say one thing in one place and then something else in another place. The word *muSollan* (in the singular) appears only once in the Qur'an and it refers to this particular person who was made the 'leader' for mankind.

It seems – in their haste to ascribe meanings to words in order to shore up their religion – the religionists overlooked the fact that the same word is used in the plural at three other places in the Qur'an. We will look at all instances now:

Min-maqam-mi   Ibrahima   *muSollan*   (singular) (2:125)
The status of Abraham, the committed.

Illaa muSollin (plural) (70:22)
Except those who are committed.

Lam-naku Minal muSollin (plural) (74:43)
We are not from among those who are committed.

Wai-lul Lil- muSollin (plural) *al-lazi-nahum ala-solaa-tihim saa-hun* (107:5-6)
Woe for those who are committed but they are careless of their commitments.

The last verse refers to those who take their commitments in jest: woe to them!

231

No Arabic linguist would dare say *muSollan* is a place of ritual prayers; but the religionists insist the word refers a physical location. So in 2:125 they prolong the corruption by claiming that *ibrohima muSollan* is *Abraham's place of ritual prayer*. There is a logical and grammatical contradiction here for which no priest or *u'lema* can provide any explanation.

MuSollan is nothing but the singular of an active participle who upholds the *Solaa*. *MuSollin* is the plural. This is simple Arabic.

An example: in 7:44 there is a *proclaimer* of an announcement. The word *announce* in Arabic is *azan* and the past tense is *azzana*. The person who proclaims or makes the announcement is called the *Mu-Azzin*.

> Then it is announced (*azzana*) by the announcer (*MuAzzin*), "God's curse has befallen the wicked." (7:44)

Similarly, Abraham was the upholder of the *commitment* or *Solaa* and he is called a *muSollan* – committed man. Even the scholars who know the Arabic language were taken for a ride by the religionists. Are they not part of the conspiracy, then?

Cleanse the system

Let's break down the key part of 2:125.

wa-ahidnaa	*and We contracted*
ibrohima	*Abraham*
wa-ismael	*and Ishmael*
an-Tho-hira	*to cleanse*
bayti-ya	*My system*

232

We can agree with all the translators when they say the word *Tho-hira* is to *cleanse*, but it is very difficult to understand why Abraham and Ishmael should clean a physical House.

Of course, today the King of Saudi Arabia (who calls himself *Keeper of the Haramain*) does clean the stone idol every year on the festival of Eid. He has become God's janitor or house-cleaner.

In the Qur'an, Abraham was committed to *serving* God and he was against all religious and idol-worshipping practices. *Tho-hira bayti-ya* does not refer to Abraham cleansing a non-existent *house*. Rather, he was enjoined to *cleanse* the system from idol-worship. This is why Abraham rightly broke the idols – or to borrow the language of the Qur'an – he broke the idols with his *right hand*.

'Group of people' corrupted

The religionists twisted another simple word in the same verse (which, in fact, refers to throngs of people) to mean *encircling a square stone house*. The word *Tho-iffin* mentioned in the verse is part of the message to signify the response of the people who will partake in God's system.

The religionists made a grave mistake when they tried to change the meaning of the word *Tho-iffin* since it is easily verifiable by means of comparison with other verses. Nevertheless, they have fooled people from all around the world into walking in circles round their stone idol.

The word *Tho-iffin* is generated from the root *Tho-if*. The word *Tho-if* means *a party* or *throngs of people*. This word (or other derivatives from the same root) is used in many parts of the Qur'an. They can be found in 3:69, 3:72, 3:122, 3:154, 4:81, 4:102, and 4:113. Some examples:

3: 69	*Tho-iffa-tun min-ah-lil-kitab* means *a group from the people of the book*
3:122	*Tho-iffa-ta-ni min-kum* means *the two groups from among you*
4:81	*Tho-iffa-tun-min-hum* means *a group from among them*

Tho-iffin, then, simply means a group (or groups) of people.

It is illogical that this same word means *walking around in circles* with reference only to the word *bayta*. Obviously, this deliberate misinterpretation is inflicted on readers year after year to support the invented pilgrimage rituals. There is no justification from the Qur'an for *Tho-iffin* to mean *encircling around* because in all other occurrences of *Tho-iffin* means *groups of people*.

The Arabic scholars will not be able to explain this contradiction either. There is no reason for the religionists to manipulate this word other than to preserve the traditional pagan religious rites of the nomadic period at the expense of God's Scripture. The word *li-Tho-iffin* simply means that it was Abraham's job to *cleanse* the system or the *bayta* for *throngs of people*. That is all.

Thawwaf

This word is not found in 2:125 or 22:26 but I have to mention it for clarity. The religionists called the seven

234

rounds of circumambulation at the cube house as *Thawwaf*[78] and they misconstrued the word *Tho-iffin* in the two verses to mean the same thing. *Thawwaf* is mentioned several times in the Qur'an with reference to the state of mind of being familiar or get used to certain things, but in contexts that are unrelated to stone structure. The first point which needs making in this regard is that the medial root of *Tho-if* and *Thawwaf* are different consonants, hence the meaning are not the same.

The religionists changed the meaning of this word *Tho-iffin* to make people think it refers to the activity of walking around the stone idol, and translators have had to concur with the religionists by translating it as *'those who encircle around'* it. This is but a terrible corruption.

The word *Thawwaf* is mentioned three times: in 2:158, 22:29 and 24:58.

> *Tha-waf-fu-na ali-kum* (they are used/familiar on you) (24:58)
>
> *Ai-yat-Tha-wa-fa bi-hi-maa* (so that you get used with them) (2:158)
>
> *Wal-yat-Tha-waf-fa bi-bayti-a-tiik* (And get used with the system of old) (22:29)

As mentioned earlier this word *thaw-waf* is not found in the all-important 2:125 or 22:26. What is stated in 2:125 and 22:26 is *Tho-iffin,* which means *throngs of people,* and not *Thawwaf.*

---

[78] This word is mentioned at this point although it does not occur in the verse under discussion – 2:125 – because the word *Thawwaf* is commonly used by practitioners of the Arabic religion to denote the act of circumambulating the *Ka'aba*

Once we understand the essence of the message in the three verses we discover the existence of a very serious premeditated distortion.

24:58 is to be noted. In this verse, children and servants must ask permission before entering the parents' room at three periods of 'nakedness' in the day. Other than these three periods, they are permitted to do so. Hence, *Tha-waf-fu-na ali-kum* in this verse means they are so used/familiar with the parents. This is simple domestic etiquette.

Please note that 22:29 follows up from the reference to Abraham in verse 22:26. There was already another system of the old (or the *bayti-a-teek*) before Abraham. That is why we found in 2:125 saying that God points out His system or *bayta* to Abraham. But the word *Thaw-waf* is not in the verse at all. Thus, 22:29 disproves the claim by the religionists that *bayta* is a physical structure built by Abraham.

If for the sake of argument, *bayta* were taken as meaning *house*, then we should understand by virtue of 22:29 that there was another '*house*' already in place before Abraham i.e. the *bayti-a-tiik*. According to the religionists, the only 'house' is the '*bayta*' (or today's *Ka'aba*) built – as they would have it – by Abraham.

Cleaving becomes retreating

The next word in our study is *a'kiffin*. The word *a'kiffin* means *hold strongly onto something*, but the religionists insist that it means *retreat to the mosque*. In the context of 2:125 it reads as:

> *An tho-hira bayti-ya li tho--iffina wal a'kifiina wa-rukai' sujudi*

The root of *a'kif-fin'* is '-k-f or *'akafa*. Each time this word is mentioned elsewhere in the Qur'an it is always explained by the religionists and also translated for the non-Arabs as *those who are devoted* or *holding fast onto something*, for instance: 2:125, 2:187, 7:138, 20:91, 20:97, 21:52, 22:25, 26:71 and 48:25. For example:

> *Ya'-ku-fu-na ala-as-nam*
> Hold strongly to idols. (7:138)

> *Lannab raha alai-hi a'kiffina*
> We will continue to hold strongly to it. (20:91)

The word *a'kiffina* in 20:91 is the same word as in 2:125. But here it refers to the Children of Israel who idolised the golden calf.

They said to Aaron the brother of Moses:

> "We will continue to devote (or hold strongly) to it."
> (20:91)

The religionists have otherwise consistently translated this word as meaning *to devote* or to *hold strongly onto something* – except in 2:125. In this only instance, they tell people the meaning of *a'kiffina* in 2:125 is to *retreat* implying that it is good if the people retreat to the mosques. The religionists condemn other people who retreat to their temples to tend to their idols as idol-worshippers, but in their own case – when we are talking about devoting oneself to the square rock structure – they appear to have received a special dispensation from God.

How does the religionists' physical 'house' differ from the physical 'idols' in the centre of other temples? Such is the hypocrisy of Arab religion!

'Humbly submit' becomes 'bow and prostrate'

The last phrase in 2:125 is *wa-roka'is-sujud*, which means *those who humbly submit*. The religionists have mangled the meaning here and say it means to physically *bow and prostrate*. It embroils a regimented body movement only worthy of pagan rituals.

Physical bowing and prostrating have become the critical components of the body movements in the Arab religion. Without these pantomimed movements their rituals will become redundant and useless. They believe the instruction of these body movements were ordained by God by virtue of 2:125 and 22:26.

For many centuries, non-Arabs who have mastered the Arabic language have allowed themselves to be subjugated by the religionists without verifying simple words by reference to other verses in the Qur'an. Having discovered this, I feel sorry for the Muslims who perform these silly body movements without verifying the correctness of their understanding from their own Book.

Since they are conditioned to believe that the word *bayta* in 2:125 means the *house*, naturally, *bayti-ya* in the same verse must mean *My house*. Although they do not physically cleanse God's house, they derive tremendous satisfaction by circumambulating the Cube. The Muslims were made to believe that the meaning of the passage in 2:125 is:

Thor-hira   *Cleanse the* [physical] *house.*

Thor-iffin   *Walk around the house*
                           (because they believe the

238

religionists who say that the word *Tho-iffin* has the same meaning as the word *Thawwaf.* However, these two words are not the same).

a'kiffin   *Retreat to a* [physical] *house.*

wa-roka' is sujud   *Bow and prostrate physically to a* [physical] *house* (since they also believe the word *roka' is sujud* is physical bowing and prostrating).

Since they proudly claim *Islam* abhors all images and icons, how can they not notice that the religious rites they faithfully observe are blatant idol-worship? Do they not devote their faith and bow and prostrate to a physical house?

If their answer is *no*:

- Then why do they say it is 'God's house'?

- Why do they use the expression *baytul-lah* which is not found in the Qur'an?

The truth is the innovators of the Arab religion have been very successful in deceiving people. They make their followers perform ridiculous body movements without telling them why. Yet they cannot even answer these simple questions!

No modern Arab or scholar of the Arab religion can provide intelligent answers to these basic questions:

239

- Is the stone house in Mecca God's house or *baytul-lah*?

- Why is God not inside His house – or is He?

- Why do they have to bow and prostrate to the stone house?

- Are they prostrating to God or to the stone house?

- Why do they walk around the house and in an anti-clockwise direction?

- If they are prostrating to God and not the stone house, can we move the stone structure to Japan, Australia, Canada, Mexico or other countries?

- Would their pilgrimage ritual and their five daily ritual prayers be nullified without the *Ka'aba* 'stone house' (whilst God exists twenty-four hours a day)?

Of course, the crux of the matter lies in simple logic. If they worship the house, they need to say that God is present in it. If that is the case – fine. However, if God does not live in the Cube, they are venerating the cube-idol. All they have to do is prove that God is in there.

If no sensible answer is forthcoming from the religionists themselves, why then should the Muslims continue to put their trust in the religionists? Perhaps they naively assume it is not harmful to follow the religionists blindly. The pertinent question is whether obeying such absurdity will save them from the Hell Fire? Is it worthwhile ignoring something so important by not verifying the correctness of its meaning by using one's own common sense? According to the Qur'an *'the worst*

240

creatures at the sight of God are those who do not use their common sense'.

Is it not time yet for the sensible Muslims to come to their senses and seek forgiveness and mercy from their Lord while they still can? Is it so difficult for them to be sincere to Him alone in pursuing for His grace and pleasure? These are some of the fundamental questions the non-Arabs should consider seriously.

The religionists have, indeed, twisted the meaning of many words in the Qur'an to divert mankind from the path of God including *wa-roka'is-sujud* in 2:125 which simply means to *humbly submit.*

The message in 2:125 is that Abraham was directed to the system and had diligently committed himself to devote and humble himself in submission to the will of God in the system. His son Ishmael was similarly committed, and both of them *cleansed* the system for *throngs of people* who are *devoted* and also those who *humble*[79] *themselves in submission* to the same system. Abraham and Ishmael were not devoting themselves to a physical house, neither have they *circumambulated*, or *bow* and *prostrate* physically to some rocks. Those who follow the footsteps of Abraham are not expected to *bow* or *prostrate* to anything. They should devote and humble themselves in submission to the same system by upholding their commitments to observe the *deen* prescribed by God. That is all that is meant.

There is no verse in the Qur'an that implies that *roka'is-sujud* carries the sense of physical *bowing* and *prostrating.*

---

[79] Humble, humbling or humbled is derived from the word ruku'. Humble people feel they are not important or good enough to criticise others or to have much attention paid to them by other people. God told the children of Israel to be humble to accept His revelations. In 2:43 He said, *'war-ka'u-ma'al-ror-ke-en'*

Sujud does not mean physical prostration

As mentioned in chapter three, in the Qur'an the word *sujud* means *submit* or *being subservient*. The religionists have consistently said that in many verses of the Qur'an this word does not mean a physical act of prostration, but they try to make it an exception when the word is used to refer to human beings. They realise it is ridiculous to say the sun, the moon, the stars, and the trees prostrate themselves to God when the Qur'an uses the same word *sujud*.

> *Qor-laqol-insan a'lama-hul bayan ash-shamsu wal-qomaror bil-husban wal-najmu wal-sajaru yasjudan was-sama'a ro-fa'aha wa-watho'a mi-zan.* (55:3-7)

> He created the human. He teaches him clearly. The sun and the moon with calculated movements, and the stars and the trees all are submitting (*yasjudan*) and the skies, which He raised with a just balance. (55:3-7)

God created human beings and He teaches them clearly that the sun, the moon, and the stars that they see in the sky are *yasjudan* (or *sujud*) all the time to God. This word is derived from the root word *sajada,* which means *to submit*. Perhaps the religionists and their Arabic scholars may want to describe how the sun and the moon prostrate to God before they insist that everyone should prostrate physically to the Lord of the Universe. The Qur'an clearly shows that everything in the heavens and the earth *sujud* and *aslama* or they are submitting (*yasjudan* from the word *sujud*) and peacefully (*aslama* from the root *Salam*) by God. The word *Islam* is also derived from the same root *Salam*. Thus if everything in the heavens and the earth are all Islam, can the religionists also tell us how the sun, the moon, the stars, the trees, and all of the animal kingdom become Muslims? Did they have to declare, "We bear witness that there is no God except Allah, and we bear witness Muhammad is the messenger of Allah?"[80] Then why is it that such a declaration has become the first pillar of faith in so-called *Islam*?

The billions of stars in the sky, the grass on earth, the vegetables that we eat, the Bougainvillaea we plant around our houses, the trees in the forest all *sujud* to the One God. We do not witness any of them prostrating physically. Everything we see obeys its God-given command; and God says it performs its *sujud* to Him.

If we read the Qur'an critically, we discover the same word *yas-judun* used in reference to the state of being of humans. In 84:21 it says:

> *Waiza quri-a' alaihim qur-anun la-yasjudun.* (84:21)

> And when the Qur'an is recited to them they do not submit. (84:21)

We have not seen any religionists or the Arabic experts prostrating themselves each time the Qur'an is recited to them, but at the same time they insist the word *sujud* means prostrate. *Sujud* here means only one thing: to acquiesce to the decrees of the Qur'an. As matters stand today, every Muslim upon hearing the Qur'an being recited would have to prostrate himself immediately. Now we all know that it is

---

[80] A phrase not found in this formula in the Qur'an and used by Arab religionists to trick people into their fold. What the phrase means, of course, is that the person pronouncing commits to accept (under the guise of the Prophet Muhammad's teaching) whatever the ruling caste dictates.

not done. One wishes the religionists would be a little more consistent.

Everyone can see the verse does not command us to prostrate physically each time the Qur'an is recited to us rather, that we should submit ourselves in substance every time we hear the message. There is an opposing verse that says the arrogant refuse to submit when the message is recited to them by the act of their rejection.

> Those who reject our revelations, and they are arrogant towards it, they are the dwellers of the Fire, and they will abide therein forever. (7:36)

Clearly the word *sujud* does not refer to any physical prostration. If what the religionists are saying about the physical prostration had any basis we would see Muslims prostrating themselves all over the place: in offices, inside their cars, shopping complexes or on the roadside each time they heard the Qur'an recited over the radio or television. This is patently ridiculous.

Here is another example from the Qur'an that clearly shows *sujud* does not mean physical prostration.

> *Wad-qulul ba-ban suj-jadan.* (2:58)
> And enter the gate in submission (2:58)

When the Children of Israel are told to enter the gates of a city the word *su-jadan* was a command for them to enter in a submissive state of humbleness. It does not mean they should enter the gate in a prostrating position (unless the religionists can demonstrate to us how this is done). The Children of Israel knew the word *su-jadan* did not mean that they should enter the gate crawling on their bellies.

The history of Joseph also demolishes the misrepresentation of the religionists that *sujud* is the act of physical prostration. Joseph told his father he saw eleven planets, the moon and the sun *sujud* to him in a dream which positively indicates these heavenly celestials did not physically *prostrate* to him.

> Recall that Joseph said to his father, "O my father, I saw eleven planets and the sun and the moon submitting (*sa-jidin*) to me." (12:4)

The forms *sujud, yas-judan, sujadan, sajid and masjid* derive from the root *sajada* which means s*ubmit*. None of these words refers to the act of physical prostration.

The Lord of the Universe is not interested in our body movements. There is no need for us to demonstrate a state of holiness at a specific time. He says He is omnipresent and we cannot hide any secret from Him. He knows everything in the heavens and the earth. No three people can meet in secret without Him being the forth nor five without Him being the sixth neither less than that, nor more without Him being there all the time.

Therefore we are expected to do the right thing and work righteousness all the time throughout our life and always keep in mind that every movement, deeds, utterances, thoughts or whatever we conceal in our heart is known to Him, Then, on the day of resurrection He will inform us of everything that we have done. God has recorded everything and He is fully aware of every single one of us. That's it!

> You should realise that God stands between you and your heart and that you will be gathered before Him. (8:24)

245

Contrary to popular belief, Abraham did not start this aerobic class. The Qur'an tells us that he submitted to the will of the Lord of Universe and led a righteous life as a monotheist serving the One God.

> When his Lord said to him, *"Be you at peace (aslim),"* he said, "I am at peace for the Lord of the Universe *(aslam-tu-li-rob-bil-'alamin)."* (2:131)

Abraham did not demonstrate his peacefulness through physical body movements but through his love of his Lord with all his heart, soul, mind and strength by doing the good deeds and personal commitments in fulfilling his obligations.

Unfortunately, he became the prime target of wicked people who accused him of being the first man to *worship* a stone idol in Mecca through physical bowing and prostration.

Ruk'u does not mean physical bowing

In the Arab religion they say the word *ruk'u* means bowing. Again, this is another misconception propagated by the religionists.

The word *ruk'u* means to humble oneself, to lower oneself in humility. There is absolutely no verse in the Qur'an which says a committed man must bow down physically at specific times of the day.

> *Woe on that day to those who lied. And when they are told to be humble* (irka'au) *they do not humble themselves* (laa yar ka'uun) *(77:47-48)*

Both *irka'au* and *yar ka'uun* derive from the root *ruk'u*. A person's sincerity is judged by his humbleness not through his actions of bowing up and down.

The Qur'an narrates the history of Mary who was about to receive news from God. God transformed the energy to appear as a perfect man telling her to submit and to humble herself with those who humble themselves in submitting to the will of God. Before the news is announced, she was told:

> O Mary, Surely God has chosen you and He purified you *(tho-hara)* and He raised you above all the women in the world. O Mary, obey God and submit *(sujudi)* and humble *(ruk'u)* yourself with those who humble *(ruk'u)* themselves." (3:42-43)

And then in 3:45:

> The human-like energy said, "O Mary, God gives you good news; a word from Him to be called Messiah, Jesus the son of Mary. He will be honourable in this life and in the hereafter, and he will be one of those who are close to God. He will speak to the people as an infant. And as a man he will be righteous". (3:45)

She humbled herself to accept the news. But it was strange to her that she could possibly conceive a son as a chaste girl. So she questioned the human-looked energy:

> She said, "How could I have a son, when no man has touched me?" Then she was told, "God creates whatever He wills. To have anything done, He simply says to it, 'Be' and it is'. (3:46)

Mary is not being asked to *ritually* or physically bow and prostrate with anyone whilst listening to the news.

Similarly, in 2:43 the Children of Israel were told to humble themselves with those who are humble in the following context:

> O Children of Israel, appreciate the blessing I have bestowed upon you, and uphold your covenant, that I uphold your covenant, and reverence Me. Do not be the first to reject what is revealed herein confirming what you have; and do not be the first to reject it. Do not trade My revelations for a cheap price; and observe Me. Do not confound the truth with falsehood, nor shall you conceal the truth knowingly. You shall observe your obligations and keep them pure. You shall humble yourselves with those who are humble (*war-ka'uu ma-al-ror-kee-in*). (2:40-43)

Here the Children of Israel were advised by God to humble themselves – together with those who are humble in conceding to what was revealed to the Last Prophet. The phrase *war-ka'uu ma-al-ror-kee-in* in 2:43 clearly instructs them to do exactly what was written from 2:40. It is their obligations to honour the revelation to observe God and they should not confound the truth with falsehood nor conceal the truth knowingly. Let not their prejudice against the Arab race hinder them from upholding their commitments to the Lord of the Universe. God's scripture is meant for the whole of mankind.

Hence, we see that *ruk'u* and *sujud* are not physical bowing and prostration, but are the humbling or lowering of oneself (*ruk'u*) in mind, heart and soul putting oneself in a state submission or subservience to something (*sujud*).

Therefore *wa-ruka'is-sujud* in 2:125 does not mean *and those who bow and prostrate (physically)* but means *and those who humbly submit (to God's System).*

Tho-hira Bayti-ya	cleanse My system
lit-tho-iffin	for throngs of people
wal-a'ki-ffin	and those who are devoted
wa-ruka'is-sujud	and humbly submit

The core of the corruption is found in this verse. The phrase *throngs of people* were *altered* to mean *those who circumambulate*, the word *devoted* became *retreat* and *humbly submit* became *bowing and prostrating*. The intent was clearly to make all these words relate to the performance of rituals.

The religionists found their way to reinstate their forefathers' religion by breaching the essence of the Scripture revealed to the Last Prophet to do it. We have seen evidence from the Qur'an that the distortion was deliberate.

To recapitulate, let us consider some of the proofs we have so far uncovered:

- *deen* or a *way of life* became *religion*

- *ta'budu* or *serve* became *worship*

- *Solaa* or *commitment* became *ritual prayers*

- *muSollan* or the *committed* became a *place of ritual prayers*

- *bayti-ya* or *My system* became *God's house*

249

- *Tho-iffin* or *throngs of people* became *walking around in a circle*

- *zakaa* or *purify* became *the religious tithes*

- *a'kiffin* or *cleave in submission* became *retreat to the mosque*

- *wa-ruka'is-sujud* or *humbly submitting* became *bow and prostrate* physically

- *maqami-ibrohim* or the *status of Abraham* became *the footprints of Abraham* in a copper casting displayed opposite the cubical stone house cut from the mountain rock of Mecca

According to the Qur'an, the Jews who distorted God's words are bad people and a rebellious race due to the hardness of their hearts. This notion is repeated over and over:

> Do you expect them to believe as you do, even though some of them distort God's words after hearing them with full understanding thereof, and maliciously? (2:75)

> When they are told, "Believe in these revelations of God," they say, "We believe only in what was revealed to us." Thus they reject all subsequent Scriptures even though they know it is the truth, and even though it confirms their own Scripture. Say, "Why did you slay God's prophets in the past, if you are really believers?" Moses came to you with profound signs, yet you idolised the calf in his absence and turned wicked. We made a covenant with you as we elevated the article above you,

saying, "You shall uphold strongly the commandments we gave you, and hearken." But they said, "We hear but we will not obey." Their hearts were filled with the adoration for the calf as a consequence of their disbelief. (2:91-93)

Because they violated their covenants We put a curse on them, and We hardened their hearts. Consequently, they distort the words from their original place and disregard part thereof. You will always see betrayal from them except a few. You shall forgive and forget about them, God only loves the compassionate. (5:13)

Everybody ignores the other truth from God when He said the Arabs are sick in their hearts, which perhaps is worse than the hearts of the Jews. We cannot deny that the groups of the people mentioned in 2:8-10 are the Arabs who had received the Scripture. God has categorically labelled the Arabs the staunchest in disbelief and hypocrisy.

The Arabs are staunchest in disbelief and hypocrisy. (9:97)

In truth, they exemplify the people described in 2:8-10:

There are those who say, "We believe in God and the Last Day," while they are not believers. In attempting to deceive God and the believers they only deceive themselves without perceiving. In their hearts is a disease, and consequently God augments their disease. They have deserved painful retribution for their lying. (2:8-10)

This verse perfectly describes the modern-day Arabs who say they believe in God and the Last Day. Although

251

the Qur'an abhors idol-worship, the religionists defied the instructions in the Qur'an. They claim it is part of the Islamic way of life to serve carved stones and rocks from the mountains, stone pillars and rock outcroppings. In their attempt to deceive God and the true believers around the world, they deceived themselves without perceiving. They have no reason to do all these things if they truly understand the message of the Qur'an and submit to the Supreme God according to the Qur'an alone. The Qur'an says that in their hearts is a disease. The disease was inherited from their pagan forefathers.

Ironically, many non-Arabs around the world – including women – are happy to follow the pagan way of life. Many are seen to dress like Arabs – men and women alike – even though the Qur'an declares that the Arabs reject God and are the worst hypocrites. For instance, the covering of the woman's head is plagiarised from the Bible. Today it is strictly observed by Muslim women around the world. They were deceived by their scholars who claim that such head covering is ordained in the Qur'an, but the true fact is, such instruction is not found in the Qur'an. They are upholding their commitment to keep the decrees in the Bible pure. In Corinthians 1 11:5 it says, *Any woman who prays or prophesises with her head uncovered dishonours her head – it is just as though her head were shaved. If a woman does not cover her head, she should have her hair cut off, for it is a disgrace for a woman to have her hair cut or shaved off, she should cover her head'*. Head covering is definitely not the requirement by the Qur'an but the Bible.

Instead of serving the Lord of the Universe through good deeds, the Arabs promote their primitive Arabic culture as *Islam*. They have built stone idols which they serve with great pomp and ceremony on the Arab soil and thereby continue their ancestors' idol-worshipping practices. Many of the non-Arab Muslims around the world are happy to be part of it.

Although the Jews were – and many would argue *still are* – a most rebellious people, they never went to the extremes the Arab religionists did. The Jews idolised the golden calf and their hearts were filled with the adoration of the calf and they rejected the *Al Masih*,[81] Jesus the son of Mary, whose duty it was to demolish the Jewish religion.

There is no reason for us not to believe that the modern Arabs and the Arab religionists fit the passages in this early *surah* of the Qur'an. They are lying about God and they have a disease in their hearts. They introduced the greatest wickedness in corrupting God's prescribed submission while claiming to believe in God and the Hereafter. Only a race with such characteristics could commit all such wickedness and perpetuate it to this day. The Jews – whatever their failings – have stiff competition when it comes to rebellion against God.

---

[81] i.e. the Messiah

253

PART TEN

'Submission' becomes 'mosque'

We have seen that words are formed in the Arabic language on the basis of roots. Non Arabic-speaking Muslims have been made to believe that the Arabs and the non-Arab religionists were the masters of the Arabic of the Qur'an. We must not forget one important fact: God did not borrow the language from the Arabs when He revealed the Scripture to an Arab prophet. Modern Arabs and religionists are still struggling to understand many words and verses in the Qur'an. Moreover, having Arabic as one's mother tongue is no safeguard from believing some quite fantastical and ludicrous things. Some examples follow of what the leaders of the Arab religion – based on traditions as opposed to the Qur'an – preach:

- The Qur'an describes the earth as elongated – something like an egg (which it is) – but the religionists say the earth is flat and it is standing on the two horns of a bull. According to their experts, each time the bull shakes its head there is an earthquake somewhere in the world.

- The Qur'an talks about sub-atomic particles, but the Arab linguist say the size of a sub-atomic particle is equivalent to a mustard seed.

- The Qur'an contains a metaphorical description about the splitting of the moon, but the religionists say during the time of the Last Prophet half of the moon fell from the sky and landed behind the Prophet's son-in-law's house and the other half fell behind a mountain.

- The Qur'an says the sun is moving through specific orbits. The religionists say that at sunset, the sun prostrates itself underneath the throne and asks permission to rise again, and it is permitted; and then a time will come when it will be about to prostrate and it will ask permission to go on its course. It will be ordered to return whence it has come so it will rise from the west. Not many people can grasp the meaning of the religionists' explanation on this subject as written in the *sahih* book of Bukhari.

- The Qur'an speaks in favourable terms about the dog as a companion of the believer and also as a domestic animal that can be trained to hunt, but the Arabic linguist and scholars say it is forbidden for Muslims to keep dogs.

- The Qur'an says there is no intercessor between a person and God in the Hereafter, but the Arabic linguists and scholars say the Last Prophet and the priests will be their intercessors.

- The religionists and their Arabic scholars go on to claim that the suffering of the hell-fire for the followers of the Arab religion is only for a few days, but the simple Arabic in the Qur'an clearly states that the punishment of hell-fire is forever. Is it not time for the followers to study the Qur'an in a language that they understand?

- The Qur'an categorically says that it is an incumbent duty for a true Muslim to write a will for the benefit of his parents and relatives. But the religionists and the Arab scholars say it is forbidden to write a will.

256

- The Qur'an says people must use their common sense and not to accept anything blindly and verify everything before following a theory. The Arabic linguists and scholars say those who use their common sense will go to Hell and that the people must follow the priests blindly.

It is a fact that the majority of modern Arabs are still struggling with the meaning of many words in the Qur'an. Billions of Muslims believe they are the natural authority on the meaning of the Book. This simple misunderstanding allows the Arab religious elite to take advantage of the innocent people around the world by manipulating their understanding of simple Qur'anic concepts. The Arabic linguists and scholars cannot even give the exact number of verses in the Qur'an. The followers of the Arab religion have been misled to the extent that the majority of them will today insist that there are 6666 verses in the Qur'an. The fact is that there are only 6348 verses in the Qur'an.

Thus, a word connected to the concept of a continuous state of action enjoined upon mankind has been deliberately distorted to become physical places of 'prayer'. The purpose of the distortion was to create houses of worship for the growing Arab religion so that it, too, could have its own houses of worship like other 'religions'.

A word derived from the root word s*ajada* (which means *submit*) has been twisted to become *mosque*. In the Qur'an, the forms s*ajadu, yas-judun, usjud, sujud, sajid* and *masjid* are derived from the same root word.

A simple comparison with associated words in other verses will show the violation of linguistic norms by the religionists regarding the usage of the prefixes and suffixes.

257

For example, we see the following words:

- The root word *sahara* means *to cast a spell* or *to bewitch*. When somebody is bewitched, the prefix *ma* is appended to the root which becomes the ground form of the verb *mashur*. *Mashur* is not a place or a physical building, but the state of being bewitched.

  In 15:14 it says if God were to open up a gate to the sky through which we could climb we would say our eyes had been bewitched.

- The root word *satara* means *to inscribe* or *to write*. When God's Scripture is prescribed with His permanent decrees a prefix of *ma* is appended to the root to become the ground form of *mastur*. The Book is not the *mastur* but what was prescribed or what was inspired is the *mastur*.

  52:2 says, *'And a book inscribed'*. This means God's commands are prescribed in the Book.

- The root word *shahid* means *to witness*. When it is intended to show that the people are in the state of witnessing, a prefix *ma* is appended to the root and it becomes the ground form of the verb *mashud*. The place where the event took place is not the *mashud* but the state of witnessing is *mashud*.

  In 11:103 it says, *Indeed, these are signs for those who fear the punishment in the Hereafter. That will be the day the people will be assembled and they will be witnessing/mashud.*

- The root word *sajana* means *to imprison*. *Masjuni* signifies the serving of the term of imprisonment. *Masjuni* is not the *prison*.

- The root word s*akana* means to *inhabit or to dwell*. The act of dwelling is *maskun*. The building where one is dwells is called *buyut* or *house* and not *maskun*.

  You commit not error if you enter the houses (*buyutan*) which are uninhabited *(ghoiro maskun)*.[82] (24:29)

Similarly, the word *sajada* in the Qur'an means submit. The word *masjid* found in 9:107, 17:1 and 17:7 is simply a derivative from the root. It does not represent *a place where people go for prostrating*. The plural of *masjid – masaajid* – simply means the people who are observing the *submission*.

These are only the few comparisons from the long list of examples in the Qur'an. The words *mashur, mastur, maskun, masjid, mashud* and *masjun* are verbs with the prefix of *ma* before their respective root words. They refer to the continuous state of being of the active participles or 'doers' of the act. An honest examination of the text of the Qur'an can easily expose the mischievous distortion perpetuated by the religionists to change the meaning of simple words.

We find the word *masjid* in 2:187, for example. In this verse, a person who observes self-discipline[83] is required to

---

[82] *ghoiro* literally means *not*
[83] The word *Siyam* is traditionally translated as *fasting*. The concept of rituals and religious obligations found in all the translations of the Qur'an is due to the influence of religious elements found in the Old and New Testaments. The

observe certain rules. If he strongly adheres to the instruction, it means that he is in a state of submission. The Qur'an refers to such action as *'holding strongly'* or *'cleave in the submission'*.

> *a-kulu washrobu hat-ta yat-tabaiyana lakumul khoithu abyathu minal qhoithi aswadi minal-fajri som-maa atimul siam-ma ilal-laili walatubashiru hun-naa <u>wan antum a'kiffun-na fil-masaajid</u>. Tilka hududul-lah.* (2nd part of 2:187)

> Savour until it is clear to you the white thread and the black thread from dawn. Then, observe the discipline until the night and they are not happy when <u>you are devoted in the submissions</u>. Those are the limits of God *(hudu-dul-lah)*. (2nd part of 2:187)

The breakdown of this part of the verse is as follows:

wa-antum	and you
a'kifun-na	cleave
fi	in
masaajid	the submissions

The above instruction (which appears in the second part of 2:187) simply says *when the person is devoting himself in the submissions* he should refrain from having intimate relations with his wife.

But the religionists assigned non-existent meanings to the words making (1) *a'kiffun* which means to *devote or cleave* become *retreat* and (2) *fil-masajid* which means *in the submission* become *in the mosque*.

Qur'an speaks about disciplining oneself from extremism, sex, hunting, communication, war, etc.

Putting the sentence together, they say its meaning becomes: *while you retreat in the mosque*. They have ignored the message in the first part of the verse that says you must maintain the cordial relationship with your wife during the nights when you are devoted in the submission.

> *Uhil-la-lakum lailata-siam-mil rofash ila-nisaa-ikum hun-na li-bashal lakum wa-antun li-bashan lahun-na a'limal-lah ain-nakum kun-tun tah-tanu an-fusakum* (first part of 2:187)

> Permitted for you in the nights of discipline to maintain the cordial relationship with your wife. They are garments for you and you are garments for them. God knows that you would have wronged yourselves..... Thus give them the good news. (first part of 2:187)

This verse is about self-discipline when a person receives the knowledge of the Qur'an. He must maintain the cordial relationship even if his spouse differs - they are not happy when you are devoted to the newly discovered knowledge. While devoting himself in the submission (*a'kifuna fi ma-sajid*) he should not frown at even the closest person to him. That is all. It is a simple instruction.

The *deen* is prescribed

The concept of submission according to the Qur'an does not allow for the establishment of a house of worship, neither is it part of God's prescribed way (*deen-nil-lah*). It is simply not part of God's decrees (or the *sha'iral-lah*.)[84] The observation of submission is manifested through

---

[84] Or the *sha'irah of Allah*; this is in stark contrast to the catalogue of intolerant and often bizarre rulings created by the religionists known as the *shar'iah*. Please note the similarity of the vocalic sound - but they are not the same.

human values: by translating the general decrees of the Qur'an into personal actions and deeds – that is, by finding an appropriate application for them in life based on intelligence and reason.

That the *deen* is not an institution accessible through houses of worship should be evident by now. The ploy of making a sanctioned life possible only through access to 'company' premises is common to all *religions*, and religion is not what the Qur'an advocates.

The instruction to discipline oneself upon receiving the knowledge of the Qur'an in 2:185-187 was nothing new. It had been decreed to people long before the Qur'an was revealed. Surely, these people did not know what a mosque was. They could not, since the instruction *a'kiffuna-fil-ma-sajid* had not been interpreted by them (against the constructs of their language) as indicating a mosque. When the same instruction was given after the Qur'an was revealed to the Arabs, they introduced a new concept of rituals of fasting for one month to encourage their followers to retreat to a physical building. Then, on top of this, they are in the ridiculous position of having to insist the verse means '*you must refrain from sexual intercourse with your wives when you retreat to the mosque*'. There is simply no logic in the instruction.

2:183 gives a reason why self-discipline is enjoined on Muslims:

> O you who believe, discipline is decreed for you, as it was decreed for the people before you, so that you might be observant for a certain number of days. (2:183 and part of 2:184)

So, the disciplining of oneself was not a recent introduction. Rather, it is God's decree and has been practised by the previous people who received God's revelations. The religionists twisted the meaning of the word "*Som-huu*" to impose fasting on innocent people. All that is required for mankind is to discipline themselves when they acquire the knowledge about God after the Qur'an is revealed to them (2:185-186) by Gabriel (2:97)[85].

Each time the religionists distort a word from one verse they are forced to distort other words to cover their backs. As soon as we make a comparison to examine the rationality of a concept within the structure and integrity of the Qur'an as whole, we notice the divergence of the meaning in the message arising from the distortion by the religionists.

Masjid is submission

The religionists and their priests are not aware that the word *masjid* is used in the Qur'an to refer to the people who existed long before the time of the Last Prophet and that it does not refer to mosques or buildings of any kind. They totally ignore the significance of the history of Abraham, Ishmael, Isaac, Jacob, Moses, and Jesus in the Qur'an (all of whom submitted to God) as though these people were not worthy of recognition in *Islam*. Before the Arabs became Muslims, there were many others who submitted themselves to God. However, similarly there were many who abused the submissions.

---

[85] 2:97: Muhammad was made to say, 'Anyone who opposes Gabriel should know that he revealed this scripture into your heart with God's permission, confirming previous scriptures, and providing guidance and good news for the believers". The Quran can be transmitted to anyone's heart and it can happen at anytime of the year. The *Hijrah* Calendar was not invented 13 years after Muhammad became a prophet. Thus, the month of *Ramadhan* was not there.

wallazi taqqozu masjidan dhiro-ror wakuf-ran
watab-riqan bainal mu'minin-na wa-irsodan liman
ha-robal-lah wa-rosulahu min-qoblu (9:107)

And there are those who take the submissions to
create detriment and disbelief, and they created
dissent among those who believed, while
accommodating those who fought God and His
messengers from before. (9:107)

The phrase *min-qobla* indicates an event that took place
in the past (literally: *from before*). In other words, before
the time of the Last Prophet the *masjidan*[86] or *'submission'*
was already being corrupted to create problems and
disbelief.

The word *masjid* is a common term used in the Qur'an
to refer to the submissions and it was used long before the
time of Muhammad.

Furthermore, there is no historical evidence to support
the existence of any physical mosque patronised by
Muslims before the Qur'an was revealed. The Jews and the
Christians call their houses of worship synagogues and
churches. According to the religionists, *Islam* was
introduced to the world only after the Qur'an was revealed
to the Last Prophet (when in fact the Qur'an states that the
true *Islam* was initiated by Abraham, i.e. long before
Moses).

The Arab masters further boast that the first mosque is
one built – allegedly by the Prophet – at a special site
chosen by his pet camel in Medina twelve years after he

---

[86] *masjidan*: a singular masculine noun in the accusative

received the revelation. On the other hand, they render 2:144 of the Qur'an to mean that the Last Prophet was commanded by God to change the direction of the ritual prayers from Jerusalem to the sacred mosque in Mecca when in fact by their own admission there was no physical mosque in Mecca at that time. Perhaps, only the religionists are able to explain such contradictions.

In the Arab religion they do not cite any history of any physical building called a mosque, or the mosques of God or the 'sacred mosque' during the time of Noah, Abraham, Moses or Jesus.

Let us quote the remaining portion of the passage in 9:107:

> *Wala-yahlifun-na ain-arodna il-laa husna. Wal-lah-yashadu, in-nahum la-kazibun.*

> And they swear, "It is not our intention except to do good." And God bears witness that indeed they are liars.

Whilst it would be illogical to assume that the people were lying about the mosques we can safely say that they were lying about their belief. Whatever they practised in the submissions – or the *masaajid* – is not from God and His messengers.

The people in the verse claim that their intentions are honourable. But God says He bears witness that they were lying about their intentions. It is hard to imagine how someone could abuse a physical mosque. The section continues:

> *La-taqum fihi abadan, lamasjidan usisa 'ala-taqwa min-aw-wali yau-mi ahaq-qu an-taqum-ma fihi. Fihi*

rijalun   yuhib-bun   aiya-tha-thoh-haru.   Wal-lah
yuhib-bul mu-dhoh-hirin (9:108)

Do not set foot in it ever. Indeed, submission
established upon righteousness from the first day of
the truth is secure for you to partake in it. There are
men who wish to cleanse themselves. And God is
pleased with those who cleanse themselves. (9:108)

The objective of the submission or the *masjid* in 9:108
becomes clear. It is to cleanse people. If the religionists
insist their mosques can cleanse people, what is wrong in
saying the temples, synagogues and churches can do the
same thing?

It is also important to look at 9:108 which says, *la*
masjidan usisa ala taqwa minal-aw-wali yaumi aHaqu:

la masjidan	the submission
usisa	established
alataqwa	upon righteousness
minal	from
aw-wali	the first
yaumi	day
aHaqu	of the truth

The word *'minal aw-wali yau-mi aHaqu'* means *'from*
the first day of the truth'. This is something even the
religionists cannot explain. Does the word from the *'first*
day of the truth' refer to the engagement of the architects
and the contractors to put up a building correctly or does it
mean to establish the righteousness with the truth from the
first day? Do we find the truth in the houses of worship? Or
do we find plundering caretakers in them?

The fact is these verses stress the importance of not abusing God's prescribed submission after it was established with the truth. The submissions encompass personal commitments in the doing of the good deeds in our routine life in society, to parents, families, relatives, close associates, orphans, the poor, the needy and to fulfil the promises we make, and to continue to maintain our obligations and keep them pure. We must remain steadfast in the face of adversity, hardship and war.

The fundamentals of God's prescribed submissions are:

- belief in the One unseen God
- belief with certainty in the Day of Judgement and the Hereafter
- to work righteousness in doing the good deeds while living in this world

Obviously, these can be observed without any mosques or houses of worship.

There is no need for anyone to go to a physical building to search for religious 'experts' to learn the methodology on how to believe in the One God, the Hereafter or how he should conduct his life as a righteous person in this temporal world. He needs to understand God's Scripture, since that is where he will find the source of the truth. Having acquired knowledge from the Scripture, he can then establish his submissions or the *masjid* in making the distinction between the truth and falsehood.

The submission is prescribed

In their grand plan, the religionists first twisted the word *masjid* – which means *the submission* to become physical *mosque*.

They then twisted the same word appended with a suffix *lah* (meaning God). The word *masa-jidil-lah* in the Qur'an simply means God's prescribed submissions. Similarly, when the Qur'an says *deen-nil-lah* it means the deen prescribed by God. There, the religionists twisted it to become *God's religion*.

The innovators of the Arab religion impress upon the world that the Lord of the Universe assigned the religionists the job of breaking up bits off a mountain to create blocks and build a 'house' in Mecca, then a *mosque* and then, finally, to declare them sacred. Furthermore, since the 'holy water' didn't flow the way it was meant to, God had the modern-day Arabs install a water pump beneath these 'holy' places and declare the water sacred too.

According to 9:97: *the Arabs are staunchest in disbelief and hypocrisy*. The religionists cannot erase this statement from the Qur'an. It has been prophesised in the Qur'an that whatever they do, they will claim their intentions are good, but the truth is they are wicked people who are preventing others from following God's prescribed submission or the *masa-jidil-lah*.

The Qur'an has proclaimed in 6:38 that the Book is fully detailed and God did not leave anything out of the Scripture. Distorting God's Scripture is an act of wickedness. We have seen how the religionists abused the Qur'an and their wickedness is exposed:

> *Waman adhlamu mim-man mana'a masajidal-lah aiyaz-karor fihas muhu wasa'a fi-qoror-biha. Ulaa-ika makana lahm aiyad-khulu-ha ilaa-qor-iffin lahum fid-dunya khizyun walahum fil-akhirati a'zabun a'zim.* (2:114)

Who is more wicked than those who forbid the submission prescribed by God (*masa-jidil-lah*) by mentioning His name and persist in destroying it? It is they, who should not be allowed therein (*submission*), except those who fear humiliation in this world and severe punishment in the Hereafter. (2:114)

The conspiracy is uncovered. The wicked people in this verse are preventing others from God's prescribed system of submissions in the name of God. The religionists have corrupted God's word – or His *kalimah* in the Qur'an – to create the fake Arab religion. And they use God's name too.

The wicked people in this verse are the idol-worshippers who are active in *worship* and *ritual*. They mention God's name in their idolatry to destroy God's prescribed submission or *masa-jidil-lah*. The religionists did not promote the true submissions enjoined upon mankind, but they deceived the people around the world with their invented Arab religion to make them worship stone idols. They used God's name to support the claim that their intention were honourable.

According to the Qur'an, these idol-worshippers do not deserve to prosper or give life to God's prescribed submission.

> *Makana lil-musyirikin ai-ya'maru masa-jidal-lah shahidin-na a'la-anfusihim bil-kufri. Ulaa-ika habithod a'ma-luhum wafin-nar hum qorlidun.* (9:17)

It is not proper for the idol-worshippers to promote the submissions prescribed by God (*masa-jidal-lah*).

269

> They witness their own disbelief. They are wasting their deeds and they will abide in the hell-fire forever. (9:17)

The word *ai-ya'maru* means to give life or to promote.[87] Surely, we cannot give life to a physical building. The word *masa-jidal-lah* means the submissions prescribed by God. But people can promote or give life to God's prescribed submissions wherever and whosoever they are as long as they focus on the sanctioned submission, which the Qur'an calls *masjidil-Harami*.

The only people who deserve to give life to God's prescribed submissions are those who *truly* believe in God and the Last Day and those who uphold their commitments and keep them pure.

> *In-nama ya'muru masajidal-lah man amana bil-lah wal-yaumil akhiri wa-aqor-mas Solaa-ta wa-ataz zakaa-ta* (9:18)

> Indeed the people who deserve to promote the submission prescribed by God (*masa-jidal-lah*) are those who believe in God and the Last Day and those who uphold their commitments and keep them pure. (9:18)

It is apparent that the *'masajidal-lah'* is not a building. Rather, it is the submissions prescribed by God. The true believers are the right people to give life to – or promote – the prescribed submissions. The prescribed *deen* does not demand they perform any worship or ritual prayer at a specified location or in a house of worship. The true believers can promote God's prescribed submissions by

---

[87] see chapter 12.

calling the people to observe God and serve the Lord of the Universe by doing deeds for the benefit of society, parents, families, relatives, associates, orphans, and the poor etc.

According to the Qur'an, God created everything in the heavens and the earth, and all His creations are submitting to His *deen* willingly or unwillingly in peace. So there is no need for God to wait for humans whom He created to start building mosques from rocks, wood, cement or stone and then say, "These buildings are God's house." God is already the owner of all the minerals, metals, wood and stone in the world.

The message in the revelations

God revealed His Scriptures to mankind as a guide. Obviously, the clear guidelines in His Book are meant only for those who are observant, believe in the Unseen, observe their covenant with Him and are certain about life after death. But for those who disbelieve, He seals their hearts and their hearing, and He places a veil upon their eyes so that they cannot understand His Book. That is why He says the Messenger cannot guide those he loves. God guides whomever He wills and He is fully aware of those who deserve the guidance. The fortunate believers are committed to doing deeds to show their appreciation to the Creator. That is all. The Creator assures those who conduct their lives in accordance with the prescribed submissions that they will not be subject to fear or grief in this world and the Hereafter.

Men and women follow different paths. They have different cultures and ways of life through observing different systems. Although they were created with different colours and languages, their unifying factor is God who gives them life and death. The best among them, however, are those who work righteousness.

> Among His signs is the creation of the heavens and the earth, and the variations in your language and colours. These are signs for all mankind. (30:22)

> O mankind! We created all of you from the same male and female, and We made you into nations and tribes in order that you recognise each other. But the best among you is the most righteous. God is omniscient, cognisant. (49:13)

The Qur'an does not envisage a religion of '*holiness*' or a '*divine*' life. The Qur'an is a Book of guidance and good news for sincere people who wish to lead a righteous life by doing good deeds, by sacrificing their egos, greed and selfishness. A manual of life, if you like.

> Indeed this Qur'an is a guidance for the upright and good news for those who believe through performing good deeds. They have deserved the great recompense. (17:9)

We would live a better world today if the religionists were to follow the example of the Last Prophet and deliver the good news to the world. Instead, they choose to duplicate Stone Age barbaric laws denying the faithful basic human rights and freedom of speech.

During the author's brief visit to Mecca, Medina and Jeddah, he was surprised to see that all shops and businesses are forced to close each time the mosque's loudspeaker summons the people to prayer. Crowds of worshippers – men in ankle-length white robes and chequered headgear, women covered in black – hurry towards the mosque. On the street, squads of mutawwa (the feared religious police) trawl for slackers. The rules of behaviour and dress are draconian and enforced with barbaric cruelty. This is not what the Qur'an teaches.

Submissions during pre-Qur'anic period

Verse 9:107 describes the *masjid* (or the submission) which was corrupted during the time of the previous messengers. By corrupting it, the people were directly abusing God's prescribed submissions, which the Qur'an calls *masa-jidil-lah*.

- When the Torah was revealed to Moses, his people were enjoined to uphold the same *deen* revealed to Noah and Abraham. But they abused the submission (*masajid*) to keep others from God's prescribed submission (*masa-jidil-lah*). They introduced Judaism, an entity unknown to Moses.

- Jesus, the son of Mary, was sent to the Children of Israel to confirm what was given to Moses. They plotted against him and abused the submission (*masajid*) keeping the people from God's prescribed submissions (*masa-jidil-lah*). Jesus did not call any of his followers Christians, Catholic or Protestants.

- Similarly, the religionists abused the submission or the *masjid* and replaced it with the Arab religion. They abandoned the Scripture revealed to the Last Prophet which confirmed the Scripture revealed to Moses and Jesus. They, too, have kept people around the world from God's prescribed submissions (*masa-jidil-lah*). The Last Prophet never called his followers Sunni, Shiite or Wahabi.

This is how the submission was abused. Their common intention was to destroy God's prescribed submissions (*masa-jidil-lah*) as stated in 2:114.

One can hardly overlook the historical references to the Children of Israel, which are found throughout the Qur'an. For example, when they first received the Scripture they were warned that they would transgress on earth twice. When the first instance took place, God punished them through His servants who possessed great strength to invade their homeland. When the tide was turned in their favour, it was accompanied by another warning which said that if they worked righteousness, it would be for their own good, but if they worked evil they would suffer the consequences.

When the second transgression takes place, their opponents will neutralise them and they will enter the *masjid* the way they entered it the first time. Here we see the word *masjid* is attributed to the Children of Israel and it clearly does not refer to a physical building called a mosque. It simply means that long before the time of Muhammad, the Children of Israel were already in the *masjid* (or in *submission*). Thus, we can positively say that the Children of Israel were not inside any physical *mosque*.

The Children of Israel transgressed God's laws. They distorted the Scripture and rebelled. Out of His Mercy, God sent Jesus to confirm what was revealed to Moses:

> We gave Moses the Scripture, and subsequent to him We sent messengers, and We gave Jesus the son of Mary profound signs and supported him with the Holy Spirit[88] (*ruHul qudus)*. Whenever a messenger

---

[88] In spite of the unique quality in Jesus it didn't work wih the Children of Israel. Later, people who believed Jesus started to think he was God. They cannot imagine it is God's will he was created with God's words and the Holy Spirit.

came to you with commandments contrary to your wishes you became arrogant, you rejected some, and you killed some. (2:87)

They rejected Jesus the son of Mary and transgressed. God says if they worked righteousness it would be for their own good, but if they worked evil they would suffer.

Many years later, God revealed Scripture to a man who was not from among them. Nevertheless, the message of the Qur'an is the same as that given to Moses. The Qur'an gives special attention to the Children of Israel in the early part of the Qur'an (from 2:40 through to 2:123) telling them they should not be the first to reject the Book. They are assured that the Book confirms what was given to them. If the Children of Israel would read the Qur'an they would discover the truth – even about their own race.

The first portion of the second *surah* of the Qur'an is can be summarised thus:

1.	2:1-5	People who accept God's Scripture
2.	2:6-7	Those who disbelieve
3.	2:8-20	The hypocrites
4.	2:21-29	The message is addressed to the whole human race
5.	2:30-39	The history of a man who lived by God's guidance
6.	2:40-123	The message to the Children of Israel
7.	2:124-134	The history of a monotheist
8.	2:135-141	Resistance by the old guard

9. 2:142   Q: Why the Qur'an is sent to the
                   non–Israelite?

10. 2:143   A: As a test for those who want to
                   follow His messenger

11. 2:144-147   They knew it was the truth; they
                   recognised it

12. 2:148-152   Focus on the sanctions in the
                   submission revealed to the Prophet or
                   the revelation of the *masjidil-
                   Harami*. Everyone should focus their
                   attention on it.

Although the Qur'an was revealed to a non-Israelite,
the message in the first major *surah* is predominantly
addressed to the Children of Israel. 2:124-131 reminds the
Children of Israel about the history of Abraham who was
committed to God's system, and the manner in which he
and Ishmael established their commitments from God's
system. The choice was given to the people who received
the previous Scripture either to accept or to reject the
revelation.

Many people were oblivious to the essence of the
message about the Children of Israel in the Qur'an. The
details of the sanctioned submission were already in the
Torah, but the Israelites had distorted and abused that. They
had already entered the *masjid* or the submission the first
time around and they abused it. History does not record any
Israelites entering any mosques.

If we read 17:7 with care we see that:

> *in-naa ahsan-tum*   if you do good

ahsan-tum	it is good for you
li-anfusikum	for yourselves
wa-ain asa'tum	and if you do bad
falaha	it is bad for you
faiza	therefore, when
ja'a wa'dul	the promise comes
akhirah	finally
li-yasuu'u	they will disgrace
wuju-hakum	your faces
wali-yad-khulu	and they will enter/ inherit
masjida	the submission
mama	the same way
da-qolu	you entered
au-wala mar-rotin	the first time
wali-yutab-biru	and they control
ma	what
a'lu tat-bi-ror	they will get a full control of

They are reminded that they had entered the *masjid* earlier. This was when they received the Torah. *Da-qolu auwala mar-rotin* means *which you entered the first time*. It implies that they submitted to God after making a covenant with Him. That is the period when they entered the submission (or *masjid*). Obviously, the Children of Israel did not built any mosque.

Sanctions during pre-Qur'anic period

In *surah* 17, we find many historical facts about the Children of Israel including a list of the Ten Commandments. The first seven verses describe the fundamental tenets given to the Children of Israel. It should come as no surprise that the message here, too, was twisted by the religionists.

Those without preconceived ideas will be able to grasp the meaning and the intended purpose of 17:1-2:

> Glory be to the One who captivated His servant during one night from the sanctioned submission to the fringes of submission which were blessed, in order to manifest to him from Our signs. Indeed He is Hearer and Seer. And We gave Moses the Scripture and We set it as the Guidance for the Children of Israel. You shall not take other than Me as an advocate.

Briefly, the story in 17:1 talks about Moses being captivated by God to make him go to a certain location to witness God's signs. It must be read together with the subsequent verse 17:2 that starts with a diphthong *wa* which means *and* to indicate the continuity from the previous verse 17:1: *And We gave Moses the Scripture and We set it as the guidance.* When the two verses are read together we see that there were two events. First the manifestation of the signs, the second was the revelation of the Scripture. The words *masjidil-Harami* and *masjidil-aqsa* at hand were used at the time of Moses. What are they?

Literally the meaning of *masjid* is submission, the word *Harami* means *restrictions* or *sanctions* while the word *aqsa* means *fringes* or *within the surrounding area*. In some contexts it means convenience.

From the sanctioned submission (*minal-masjidil-Harami*) to the fringes of submission (*ilaa-masjidil-aqsa*) is not from one physical *mosque* to another physical *mosque* located far away. This is the Arab corruption. We need to realise that the word *aqsa* does not mean *far* but *the nearby fringes* as will be explained shortly.

17:1 says the event happened at night. According to the Qur'an, Moses was the only man to have an audience with God. No other messenger was given such a privilege. Moses had two audiences during his tenure and both took place at night.

If we read 17:1 together with the subsequent verses we see that it is telling us about the history of the Children of Israel at the time Moses witnessed God's signs before the revelation proper was revealed to him at a different location. Contrary to the fairy tales invented by the so-called experts (who manipulated this verse to say that the Last Prophet flew up to the seven heavens on a half-human horse that they called *buraq*) the Qur'an does not indicate nor advocate such absurdity.

Significant events such as witnessing God's signs are normally corroborated and expanded upon in other verses spread throughout the Book. As for the fairy tales concerning the 'heavenly journey', there is not a single verse in the Qur'an to substantiate the story. The source of miracles is a pagan remnant that lingered on within the vehicle of the Arab religion. They did this by manipulating the word '*Asra*' in 17:1 to make it to mean 'night journey'. This word in found in many places in the Qur'an to refer to captive when it is used as *Usara*. *Asra* simply means *captivated*.

On the other hand, the history of Moses' witnessing God's signs during the night is clearly written in the Book. Therefore, the event in this verse cannot be attributed to any other prophet than Moses.

The first audience:

> Has the history of Moses[89] come to you? When he
> saw the fire he said to his family, "Wait here, I saw
> a fire, maybe I can bring some of it or find some
> guidance at the fire." When he came he was called,
> "O Moses, I am your Lord, so take off your shoes.
> You are in the sacred valley of Tuwa. And I have
> chosen you, so listen to what is revealed. I am the
> One God, there is no god but Me. You shall serve
> Me and uphold your undertaking to remember Me.
> The hour is sure to come, I keep it almost hidden, to
> repay each soul for whatever it did. Therefore, do
> not be distracted by those who disbelieve therein
> and follow their opinions, lest you perish." (20:9-16)

- In 20:17-21, God refers Moses to the stick in his hands
  and turned it into a serpent – the first '**sign**'
  demonstrated to Moses.

- In 20:22 Moses hands are brightened and God says
  another 'Great **sign**' (*ayaa-tin-kubror*).

- In 20:23 God says He demonstrated from His **Great
  Sign** (or *min-ayaa-tina-kubror*). (The same word from
  'his Lord's **Great sign**' (*min-ayaa-ti-rob-bi-kubror*) is
  mentioned again in 53:18).

- In 20 24-25 God tells Moses to go to Pharaoh.

- In 20:26-37 the conversation continues, but strictly
  about his assignments.

---

[89] The history of Moses occupies a prominent place in the Quran. He was set as
a good example for those who wish to take a challenge in the cause of God. He
did not promote extremism, but persevered with his trust in the unseen God.

- In 20:38-40 God tells Moses about his personal history
  and in the last part of .verse 40 and the following verse
  God says, *'You have lived in Midyan for many years
  and now you have come according to the plan. Moses, I
  have made you just for Me'*. (The big assignment was
  for him to meet Pharaoh as seen in 20:24.)

If we link up 20:21-23 with 17:1 we see clearly that the
event was for the purpose of 'manifesting to him from Our
Signs' (*li-nuriyahu min ayatina*). The crux of the message is
to '*manifest the signs*'. It appears that God has only
manifested His signs to Moses by turning a stick into a
serpent and miraculously brightening his hand. This is the
only evidence from the Qur'an about the manifestation of
God's signs at night. The intention was obvious: the man
who saw the sign was to undertake an assignment. Moses'
first encounter with the Supreme God indicates the
beginning of his office as a messenger to free the Children
of Israel from the oppressive Pharaoh. During the first
audience, only the signs were manifested accompanied by
some instructions. That is all. The Scripture was not
revealed to him.

Therefore 17:1 refers to the history of Moses and it is
consistent with the passages in 20:9-48. But the religionists
created a long story about Muhammad's journey from a
non-existent mosque in Mecca to another non-existent
mosque in Jerusalem, and then expanded it by saying
Muhammad was taken up to the 'seventh heaven' to
negotiate with God about the 'ritual prayers'.

There is no evidence in the Qur'an that the Last
Prophet witnessed any sign from God during the day or
night other than receiving the Qur'an and recited it to the
people (29:51)

The *masjidil-Harami* and the *masjidil-aqsa* (which are associated with the submissions) existed as part of God's system long before the time of the Last Prophet. When the Qur'an was revealed, the story of the manifestation of God's signs was obvious to him in that it referred to a previous event of someone who saw them during the night.

There is nothing mysterious about Moses being captivated to witness God's signs during the night once we check with other verses in the Qur'an to identify the persons who actually saw them. Moreover, at the time when the Qur'an was revealed there was no such thing as a sacred mosque anywhere – either in Jerusalem or in Mecca.

Let us examine the verse and read it in conjunction with the transliterated rendition:

minal masjidil-Harami	from the sanctioned submission
ilaa Masjidil-aqsa	to the fringes of submission
al-lazi barak-na	which We have blessed
haw-lahu	around it
linuri-yahu	to manifest to him
min-ayaa-tina	from Our signs

The verse unambiguously talks about a premeditated event with no intention other than to witness a manifestation of God's Signs. We must read the complete verse to realise the objective of the event before examining the circumstances surrounding it. Here we see that the event was not meant for praying or worship, but to witness God's signs. We see that Moses was the only person who was made to see what he was supposed to see so that it strengthens his heart to do a job. During the audience, God told him, "O Moses, I have made you just for me" 20:41. He could have decided at that time whether to submit or not to submit to God after witnessing the signs. Whatever he was about to do were only the fringes of his submission to God and the Qur'an uses the word *masjidil-aqsa*. It was only a small part of his duty within the whole concept of submission that he had to observe. The word *masjidil-Harami* is used in the Qur'an to refer to the sanctions encompassing the whole concept of submission.

When Moses saw the fire, he was attracted to it and decided to leave his wife on the roadside not far from the valley of *Tuwa*. The distance was short and the meeting was very brief. The religionists did not try to relate the concurrence of Moses experience of this event in 20:9-47 with 17:1.   Instead, they manipulate the passage to propagate the famous *Isra'* and *Mi'raj*[90] fairy tales to dupe people into performing the five daily ritual prayers.

Before explaining the misunderstanding about the meaning of the word *aqsa'*, let us not overlook the history of the previous people. During the time of Moses – or even after his office – there was no such thing as the physical '*sacred mosque*' or the physical '*faraway mosque*' or any physical mosque at all.   There were submissions (or the *masjid, ma-sajid, masajidal-lah, masjidil-Harami,* and the *masjidil-aqsa*) as the parameters of submission to the One God.

Traditionally, *aqsa* has been understood to mean *far* or *faraway*. If we look at other passages in the Qur'an we see that it means *around the same area*. Let us see how the Qur'an is written when the word *far* is applied in some verses. Each time the word *far* is mentioned it uses the word

---

[90] These fantastical and somewhat ludicrous episodes have been described above. They will be known to anybody from a 'Muslim' background.

ba'id from the verb *ba'uda* to denote a distance, for example:

> *lau-kana a'rothon qoriban wa-safaran khor-sidon la-taba'uka walakin <u>ba'udat</u> alaihim shu-qortu wa-sayah-lif* (9:42)

> If there is a quick gain, or a short journey, surely they will follow you. And if it is *far* upon them the distance they will swear. (9:42)

In 9:42 the word *ba'uda* is used to describe a *far distance*. For other similar meanings of *far* the Qur'an uses the word *ba'id* to describe something very far.

> *fa-in tawal-lau fa-qul aa-zantukum a'la-sawa-e wa-ain-adri aqor-ribun am-ba'idan ma-tu'adun* (21:109)

> If they turn away, then say, "I have announced to you the same. And I have no idea whether it is near or far that which you are threatened." (21:109)

The word *aqsa* is derived from the root word *qasa* to mean nearby or the *fringes of a certain location*. This word is also used for imperatives or 'mood'.

Let us see how this word is applied to other subjects:

> *Iz-antum bil-u'dwan donya wahum bil-u'dwan <u>qus-wa</u> war-rokbu asfala min kum* (8:42)

> When you were at the valley area and they were at the valley's fringe, and the base was down from you. (8:42)

8:42 describes the presence of two groups of people in the same area. *Bil u'dwan* means *in the valley* and the word *qus-wa* (a derivative generated from the same root word *qasa*) means *around the same area*. Hence the verse implies that the enemies were in the nearby area and they were not far.

Let us take another example:

> *wajaa-a rojulon min-aqsal madinatu yash'a, qorla ya-musaa in-nal mala-aa ya-tamiru na-bika liyak-tuluka* (28:20)

> And a man came from the <u>fringe</u> of the city rushing, he said, "O Moses! Surely the rulers are planning to prosecute you." (28:20)

The word *aqsal madinah* is not '*a city that is far*'. The man who came rushing to warn Moses did not come from another city. He came running around the same area. According to the history from the Qur'an, Moses had killed a man and he was wanted by the authorities to face trial. The news became known to a man who came rushing from within the nearby area within the city to tell Moses that the authorities were planning to prosecute him.

Therefore, the word *masjidil-aqsa* does not refer to a physical building located somewhere very far. The term *masjid* used in the Qur'an is not a new word to refer to a physical building but it is always used to refer to the submission; besides, from Abraham onwards there had been no such thing as a house of worship called a mosque. Moses did not call his people to build any houses of worship. It was the later Jews who put up synagogues. They did not call them mosques. Jesus, the son of Mary, went to Jerusalem to demolish the religious system practised in the synagogues. The high priest ordered his crucifixion. Then his followers put up churches. Moses did not know anything about synagogues. Jesus did not know anything about churches. Similarly, Muhammad did not know anything about mosques. *Masjidil-aqsa* simply means the *'fringes of submission'*.

The second audience:

> *Wa-iz wa'adna Musaa Arba'eina lai-latan* (2:51)

> And when We appointed Moses forty nights. (2:51)

> *Wa-wa'adna Musaa salasina lai-lata waatmum-naha bi-a'sri fatama miqorta rob-bihi ar-ba'ina lai-lata* (7:142)

> And We summoned Moses for thirty nights and We fulfilled it with ten. Therefore, the appointment of his Lord is forty nights. (7:142)

The history of Moses occupies a prominent place in the Qur'an. Besides witnessing the signs during the first audience, his second meeting with God is repeated in two verses and then it is again mentioned in 53:1-18 to confirm that what he saw was from the Great signs of his Lord (*min-ayaa-ti-rob-bi-kubror* the same wording in 20:23). Many people have mistaken 53:1-18 for an event pertaining to the Last Prophet. He did not have any sign manifested to him throughout his life other than the Qur'an.

Anyone reading the Qur'an for the first time is confronted with a statement that will surprise him. Given to the religionists, in the Arab tongue, it is surprising now that the Qur'an gives such eminence to the people of another race – the Jews. Muhammad was a gentile, and in all probability wondered why so much of the book was addressed to another race. Early on we read:

Ya Bani-Israel, laz-kuru ni'amatal-lati an-amtu alaikum wa-u-qu bi-'ahdi ufi-bi'adikum-wa-iya-ya-farhabun (2:40)

O Children of Israel, remember the blessing I have bestowed upon you. And fulfil the covenant to Me. I will fulfil My covenant to you. And be apprehensive towards Me. (2:40)

Wa-aminu bima anzalta musod-dikhon lima ma'akum wala takunu aw-wala kafiri bihi wala tash-taru bi-ayaati samanan qorlilan wa-iya-ya fat-taqun. (2:41)

And believe what I have revealed confirming with what you have, and do not be the first to reject it, and do not trade My revelations for a small price and prepare for your meeting with Me. Do not confound the truth with falsehood nor shall you conceal the truth knowingly. And observe your commitment and maintain it pure and humble yourselves with those who are humble. (2:41-43)

This is amazing: the Children of Israel do not belong to the Arab race, yet they are addressed as the intended recipients of this Scripture.

According to the Qur'an, the Last Prophet and those around him belonged to a gentile race, which means they had no knowledge of God's Scripture. The religionists, however, came up with a ridiculous interpretation of the word *ummyin*. It is used to describe the Prophet and the Arabs. They said that it meant that he and they were illiterate. The Qur'an clearly says that the Prophet was able to write since in 25:5, the pagans accused him of writing tales of the past which they said were dictated to him day and night. In 25:6, he was commanded to declare to the non-believing Arabs that whatever he wrote was revealed by the One who knows the secrets of the heavens and earth. The religionists have conveniently ignored this simple fact.

> *Huwal-lazi ba'a-sha fil-ummi-yin rosulan min-hum yatlu alaihim ayaatihi wayuzak-kihim wayu'alimuhumul kitaba walhikmata wa-inkaanu minqoblu lafithola-lin mubin (62:2)*

> He, who sent in the midst of the gentiles (ummyin), a messenger from among themselves to recite to them the revelations and to purify them and to teach them the Scripture and wisdom. And, indeed, from before there were in total loss. (62:2)

The above verse confirms that the revelation was give to a gentile prophet. As far as the Jews and the Christians around the same area were concerned this was something out of the ordinary.

It is not inconceivable that at the time when the Prophet tried to talk to them, their immediate reaction was to question the relevance of the Qur'an being given to the Arab race.

The people of the previous Scripture (the Jews and the Christians) raised their objection about God's revelation being revealed to an Arab. They asserted that to be guided by God one had to be a Jew or a Christian.

> They say, "You have to be Jewish or Nazarene to be guided." (1st part of 2:135)

The Qur'an retorts:

Tell them, "We follow the principle of Abraham the sincere, he never was an idol-worshipper." (2nd part of 2:135)

True servants of God only follow the example of Abraham. From this reply we can positively say the Jews and the Christians are amongst the idol-worshippers until and unless they follow the principle of Abraham the monotheist. The fundamental belief of God's servant will testify the following statement to their faith:

> Tell them, "We believe in God and what was revealed to us and what was revealed to Abraham and Ishmael and Isaac and Jacob and the patriarchs, and what was revealed to Moses and Jesus and what was given to the prophets from their Lord. We do not make any distinction between any of them. To Him we are at peace *(Muslims)*." (2:136)

This is the perfect concept of a person who is at peace as far as the teaching of the Qur'an is concerned. He must believe in God, His revelations, and what was revealed to Abraham, Ishmael, Isaac, Jacob, the patriarchs, and what was revealed to Moses and Jesus and what was given to the prophets from their Lord. Nobody should make any distinction between any of them. Therefore, anyone who truly believes the above is considered a Muslim or those who are peace with God.

Unfortunately, all the 'monotheistic' religions today pick one prophet and disregard the rest. The Jews concentrate on Moses. The Christians can relate to Abraham, Isaac, Ishmael, Jacob, Moses and the other prophets only insofar as they have a bearing on Jesus. And the religionists, it has been demonstrated, have formulated their own religion around a tribally-biased illusory historical depiction of Muhammad, and it is this invention which is the source of the fanaticism, terrorism, extremism and ignorance in the Arab religion.

According to the Qur'an, the true rejecters are those who make a distinction between the messengers of God – and that is exactly what we find in all religions:

> Those who disbelieve in God and His messengers, and make a distinction among God and His messengers, and say, "We believe in some, and reject some," and try to follow an in-between path. These are the true disbelievers, and We have prepared for the disbelievers a humiliating retribution. (4:150-151)

> As for those who believe in God and His messengers, they make no distinction among any of them. God will recompense them. God is Forgiver and Merciful. (4:152)

The people of the previous Scriptures were told that the Qur'an was revealed in Arabic as a test for them to distinguish between those who would sincerely follow God's Messenger from those who would turn on their heels. Here we see God's Scripture does not necessarily need to be revealed to a specific community. The racial origin of God's prophet is not important; the message *is*. When mankind refuses to submit to God's message it is not the prophets or the messengers that they reject, but rather God's revelations.

> We realise that you are saddened by what they say. However, it is not you that they reject, but it is God's revelations that the wicked disregard. The messengers before you have been similarly rejected,

but they steadfastly persevered in the face of their rejection, and they were persecuted until our victory came to them. And this will always be the case; God's tradition is unchangeable. (6:33-34)

Focus on the sanctions of the submission

Before the Qur'an was revealed there were people who submitted to the *deen* and declared themselves Muslims. For example, Abraham specifically used the word Muslims when he prayed to God:

Our Lord, make us at peace (Muslims) to you, and from our progeny nations who are at peace to you. (2:128)

Then the followers of Jesus declared themselves Muslims:

And recall that I inspired the disciples, "Believe in Me and My messenger." They said, "We believe, and bear witness that we are at peace *(Muslims)*." (5:111)

The word Muslims simply indicates those who are at peace with God. According to 2:140, Abraham, Ishmael, Isaac, Jacob, and all the patriarchs were not Jewish, nor were they Nazarenes.[91]

They served God and fulfilled their commitments. They considered themselves to be at peace because they were able to fulfil certain requirements sincerely, and in this case, it is obvious they were required to focus on certain set of rules or sanctions ordained by God.

The suffix *-lah* in the Qur'an relates the key idea back to God. For example, when the submission is categorically

---

[91] *Nazarenes*, literally means those who support. This word is used in the Qur'an to refer to one who professes to follow Jesus of Nazareth the son of Mary and the supporters of the last prophet and the believers.

implied to have been prescribed by God it is called the *masajidal-lah*. When it talks about God's prescribed limits it is called the *hududul-lah*, God's decrees are known as *sh'iaral-lah* and the path of God is called the *sabi-lil-lah*. When these words appear in the Qur'an they indicate the specifics and they are taken as the guidelines in the sanctions. None of these words has a physical connotation but they are to be taken as the specific orders. Before the Qur'an was revealed those who were at peace were observing their commitments by focusing towards these specific sanctions.

The Last Prophet was similarly committed to the same system. Those who wish to submit themselves to the *deen* should focus on the sanctioned submission or the *masjidil-Harami*. Whoever they are and wherever they may be, they must focus their attention on it.

Although each individual is responsible for his personal deeds, each should race towards righteousness by focusing his submission within the limits of the sanctioned submission. The *masjidil-Harami* is nothing other than the details of the guidelines to be observed as prescribed in the Scripture.

Masjidil-Harami does not refer to a physical structure geographically located anywhere on the Arab soil. Had it referred to such a building, it would mean that the Arabs had received knowledge of the teachings of God at some prior point in history – which they had not – and thus could not have been *ummyin* – i.e. ignorant of revelation.

According to 62:2, the Arabs had no prior knowledge about God's revelations:

Wainkanu min qoblu lafi dhola-lin mubin (62:2)

292

And indeed they were from before in total loss. (62:2)

Thus, the Arabs did not know anything about a sacred mosque nor did they have a sacred building standing in the desert for the performance of ritual prayers. According to Arabic legend, their own 'sacred mosque' started as a wooden hedge similar to a cowboy ranch and was slightly larger than a modern basketball court. Even according to their own version of events – which has nothing to do with the Qur'an – the first mosque was built in Medina only twelve years after Muhammad's call to prophethood.

Readers will be surprised to know that:

- Nowhere in the Qur'an does it say there was a building by the name of *Sacred Mosque* during the time of the Last Prophet.

- There is no instruction from the Qur'an for the Last Prophet to build a building called the *Sacred Mosque*.

- Nowhere in the Qur'an does it say the people must perform the *'ritual prayer'* facing Mecca.

The prescribed sanctions revealed

When the Last Prophet received the Scripture he was told to do the most important thing (like the rest of the Muslims before him). He was commanded to focus his attention on the sanctioned submission (which is the *masjidil-Harami*).

Falanuwa-liyan-naka qiblatan tar-dhoha fawal-li wajhaka sat-dhrol masjidil-Harami. Wahaisu ma-

kuntum fawal-lu uju-hakum sat-dhro-hu wa-inal-lazi
utul-kitab liya'lamun-na in-nahu hak-qu min ob-
bihim. (2:144)

Therefore, we set the direction that pleases you.
Thus, focus your self towards the sanctioned
submission (*masjidil-Harami*) wherever you may
be. Therefore, focus your self towards it. Surely,
those who were given the Scripture knew this is the
truth from your Lord. (2:144)

The religionists claim the Last Prophet was
commanded to change the direction of his five daily prayers
from Jerusalem to Mecca. An important point to remember
is, at the time the Qur'an was revealed there was no
physical mosque anywhere around the world – not even in
Jerusalem. To say the meaning of the word *masjidil-Harami*
is a reference to a physical sacred mosque is a lie because
there was no such thing as a *sacred mosque* referred to in
the Qur'an. The word *Harami* appended to the word *masjid*
was deliberately distorted by the religionists to become
sacred. No Arabic scholar can explain how the word
masjidil-Harami could be translated *sacred mosque*. *Haram*
literally means deprive or forbidden and the correct word
for *sacred* in Arabic is *qudus*.

The Arab race was following their forefathers' religion
and the Arabs did not comprehend either *Islam* or the
revelation. The Qur'an says they were very hostile towards
the revelation; a hostility which is common even among the
present-day Muslims who are shackled by the Arab
religion.

The Last Prophet was not concerned about the pagan
who rejected the Qur'an, but he had proof that the Jews and
the Christians knew about God's revelation. His duty was to

tell them God had revealed the Scripture to him confirming what was given to Moses.

In 17:7, it says the Children of Israel had entered the submission (*masjid*) a first time, which means they had entered into a covenant with God when the Torah was revealed to them. They were focusing themselves on the sanctioned submission (or the *masjidil-Harami*) and so they could recognise the true sanctions prescribed by God. However, after Moses, they distorted God's word and created a racial religion and called themselves Jews. God addresses them in the Qur'an as the people who received the previous Scripture. Part of the Last Prophet's duty was to invite them back to the same sanctions, but many of them refused.

> *Wala-in atai-tal lazi utul-kitaba bikul-li Ayaa-tin ma-tabi-'u qibla-taka wama-anta bita-bi'e qibla-tahum* (2:145)

> And surely, if you were to give to those who were given the Scripture every single sign, they would not follow your direction, and you shall not follow their direction. (2:145)

> *Al-lazi na-ataina humul-kitaba ya'rifunahu kama-ya'rifun abna-ahum wa-inna fariqan min-hum li-ya'tumunal haq-qor wahum ya'lamun* (2:146)

> Those who were given the Scripture, they recognised it just like they recognise their own children. Indeed, they concealed the truth and they knew. (2:146)

The verse does not say they recognised the Messenger or a physical building which the religionists claim to represent their 'sacred mosque'. In fact, they recognised what was sanctioned in the Quran defining it as *masjidil-Harami*. The Last Prophet was instructed to focus on these sanctions even if the people who were given the previous Scripture refused to accept them. They concealed the same sanctions they received previously, and they could recognise the truth like they recognise their own children.

In 2:146, God says that this is *'the truth from your Lord'*. In other words, the people who were given the previous Scripture knew that God had revealed the sanctioned submission or the *'masjidil-Harami'* to the Arab race! Surely 'the truth' cannot be represented by a mosque of any description!

> *Al-Haq-qu min-rob-bika fala-taku-nan-na mum-tarin* (2:147)

> The truth is from your Lord, therefore do not harbour any doubts. (2:147)

The subsequent verses repeat almost word for word that the Last Prophet and those who follow him should continue to focus themselves towards the sanctions of the submission *masjidil-Harami* wherever they may be. The focus is towards the revelation and not a physical building. The religionists changed the meaning of this word to become a temple-like building since it was their forefathers' belief that their gods reside in stones and rocks.

> *Wamin haisu khoroj-ta fawal-li waj-haka sath-rol masjidil-Harami wa-in-nahu lal-haq-qu min-rob-bika wamal-lah bi-ghor-filin am-maa ta'malun* (2:149)

And from wherever you may be, you shall focus yourself towards the sanctioned submission (*masjidil-Harami*). Indeed, it is the truth from your Lord. And God is never unaware of whatever you do. (2:149)

Wamin haisu khoroj-ta fawal-li haj-haka sath-rol masjidil-Harami, wa-haisuma kuntum fawal-lu huju-hakum satroh-hu li-al-laa laku-nan-nas alai-kum huj-jatun il-laal lazi dhul-luma min-hum (2:150)

And from wherever you may be, you shall focus yourself towards the sanctioned submission (*masjidil-Harami*). And wherever you may be, you shall focus yourself to it so that nobody challenge you except the wicked from them. (2:150)

There is not even a hint of '*ritual prayer*' or mosques in 2:142-150. But the religionists – after fooling the people to make them pray ritually – deceived them further by saying that everyone must face a physical building in Mecca which they call the *Sacred Mosque*. Ironically, by their own testimony, they said the first mosque was built twelve years after Muhammad became a prophet.

2:142-152 – the wider context

Let us recap:

- (2:142): The fools among them ask: '*What makes them change their focus?*' Tell them: '*To God belongs the East and the West. He directs whoever He will to the right path*'.

The people who received the previous Scripture asked what had made the Arabs change their focus of belief from paganism to God's *deen*.

- (2:143): God says: *'We changed the direction as a test to distinguish those who would follow the Messenger from those who turned back. It is a difficult test, but not for those who are guided by God'*.

The revelation was now given to the Arabs as opposed to the recipients of the previous Scriptures (e.g. the Children of Israel).

- (2:144): God says: *'We have seen your face turning about the sky. Now we appoint for you a direction that pleases you. From now on, you shall focus yourself to the sanctioned submission* (masjidil-Harami) *wherever you may be. You shall focus your direction to it. Those who received the previous Scripture recognise this is the truth from their Lord'*.

Those who received the previous Scripture recognised the *masajidil-Harami* (or the sanctioned submissions revealed to the Last Prophet) is the truth from their Lord. A mosque cannot be a 'truth' of any kind.

- (2:145): God told the Last Prophet: *'Even if you show the followers of the previous Scripture any kind of sign they will not follow your direction. And you must not follow their direction. In fact, they do not follow each other's direction* (qiblah)'.

- (2:146): *The people who were given the Book recognised it just as they recognise their own children. Many of them conceal the truth.*

That is, they recognised the *mas-jidil-Haram* (or the sanctioned submissions in the Qur'an) just as they recognised their own children. Why? Because they had received a similar Scripture. The fact that they largely chose to ignore its contents is a different matter.

- (2:147): *'The truth is from your Lord. Do not harbour any doubt'*.

God assures us that the sanctioned submission (*masjidil-Harami*) is the truth.

- (2:148): *'To each is their own focus Therefore, you shall race towards righteousness. Wherever you are God will bring all of you together'*.

- (2:149): *'Wherever you may go, you shall focus towards the sanctioned submission* (mas-jidil-Harami). *This is the truth from your Lord'*.

- (2:150): *'Therefore, wherever you go, you shall focus towards the sanctioned submission* (masjidil-Harami) *Wherever you may be, you shall focus on it. The people will have no argument with you except the wicked among them. Do not fear them, but fear Me instead so that I may complete My blessing upon you, that you may be guided'*.

2:142-150 describes the changing recipients of the revelation from the people who received the previous Scripture (the Children of Israel) to the people of the Arab prophet. The *masjidil-Harami* is prescribed in the Scripture because in verse 2:151 it says the *masjidil-Harami* (or the sanctioned submissions) were recited by the Messenger:

> Such blessing as the sending of a messenger from
> among you to recite from our revelations, and to
> cleanse you, to teach you the Scripture and wisdom,
> and to teach you what you never knew. Therefore,
> you shall remember Me so that I may remember
> you, and be thankful to Me. And be appreciative.
> (2:151-152)

The Children of Israel received God's Scripture with the details of the sanctions in the submission. This became the focus of their submission to the One God, which the Qur'an calls *masajidil-Harami*.

Despite God's blessing and mercy they distorted the Scripture. They were the first to conspire against God and His messengers. They perverted God's way to create a religion and gave themselves a new name: the *Jews*. Moses knew nothing about the Jewish religion.

According to the testimony of the Jews when Jesus came to the Israelites he had a big problem with the Jews, some of whom tried to stone him. Later, the Talmudic rabbis and the Pharisees of the synagogue feared the truth he brought could end the religion of Judaism. To prevent this, they stirred up the people and falsely accused the man of blasphemy and conspired to have him put to death.

But the Arabs outstripped even the Jews. They were able to reintroduce their primitive Arab religion under the guise of the religion of *Islam* and found a way to perpetuate their forefathers' religion of nurturing the black stone. People around the world are now elevating the Arabs' grandfathers' deity in the centre of their invented 'Sacred Mosque'. They have replaced the sanctioned submission prescribed by God with a physical building and abused the word *masjidil-Harami* so that people accept it as meaning a sanctuary or *station* for their stone idol.

We concede that perhaps it may not be the direct intention of all translators to give the wrong meaning when interpreting the Qur'an. Many are simply duped by a culture and literature which they assume has a better knowledge of the Book than themselves. However, this does not remove the obligation of any scholar to verify interpretations for himself in a way which is in keeping with common sense and logic.

A key point for those sincere people who are looking for the grace and the pleasure of their Lord is to remember is that God in His glory cannot be associated with any human or anything tangible like mosque or stone outcropping or stone pillars. That includes (one almost wants to say *especially*) when they have been declared 'sacred' by humans.

PART ELEVEN

Wildlife conservation sabotaged

It is not surprising to find a chapter about wildlife conservation in a book such as this. Again, a sensible and nurturing injunction in the Qur'an has been twisted out of all recognition in order to fit the requirements of a pagan cult. This will be of particular interest to those who have undertaken the ritual known as *Haj* or 'pilgrimage'.

I stumbled upon this important subject while compiling verses about food. After reading 5:1 several times over in conjunction with the subsequent verses, I was confronted with a serious problem when I tried to understand how the word 'restricted' could be rendered as 'religious dress'. All the twelve translations in my possession, the lexicons and the concordance say that *Hurumun* is either the pilgrimage garb, or the state of sanctity during the pilgrimage (*ihram*).

The non-Arab Muslims depend on the religionists to explain the religious rituals and other aspects of 'worship'. For many years I had been aware that there was not a single Arabic ritual that came from the Qur'an, and that the source for of all these rituals was the so-called *Hadith* – a vast collation of hearsay and old wives tales falsely attributed to the Prophet. Whilst re-marketing their Arab religion, it seems that the religionists determined to maintain the characteristic of the Arabs' previous pilgrimage, and they distorted the sense of two verses in the fifth *surah* of the Qur'an to support their claims.

Before looking at the verses in question, we should remind ourselves that – according to the Qur'an – no other sources are needed in order to understand the important

303

points that it wants to make. No *tafsiir*, no *Hadith*[92] are necessary. In 39:23, God proclaims the Qur'an the best *Hadith* and a consistent Scripture. The Book also states that it is self-explanatory. This, of course, is directly contradicted by the entire Arab religion community of whatever flavour. If we are to take the Qur'an at its word, we can investigate further.

> God revealed the best narration (*Hadith*), a Scripture that is consistent. (39:23)

> They never come to you with any example, except We provide you with the truth and the best interpretation *(aHsana tafsir)*. (25:33)

Hurumun appears in the Qur'an four times. This word was twisted to mean the silly habit of wearing two pieces of seamless white cloth (for males) as the mandatory garb of pilgrims that the religionists say is the *ihram*. The two pieces of white cloth are actually remnants of a pagan heritage from the times preceding Rome and Greece when priests and nobles wore pieces of white cloth to signify 'holiness' or their station in society (such as the Roman toga).

The subject in verses 5:1-5 is food. There is absolutely nothing about pilgrimage here.

The translators do justice to the first part of 5:1. This is generally the case when their personal beliefs are not at stake:

> *Ya-aiyu-hal lazi na-amanu aufu-bil 'uqadi*
> O you who believe, you shall fulfil your covenant

---

[92] *Hadith*: are tales about the Prophet from various unverifiable sources.

Uhil-lat lakum bahi-matul an-aam
Permitted for you is the meat of all livestock

il-laa ma-utla alai-kum
Except those recited to you

This is the first part of 5:1 and the subject is about God's covenant, and the covenant is about food. The rest of the verse says:

Ghoi-ro mu-hil-lis soii-di
Do not permit the hunting of game

Wa-antum-Hurumun
(usually translated) While you are in pilgrim garb / *ihram.*

Herein lays the corruption. Such flagrant misreading of this verse requires an abrupt change of topic within a short space. Such anomalies do not happen anywhere in the Qur'an.

The first part of the verse gives us total freedom to consume the meat of all livestock, except those recited to us. The second part specifies consumption of the meats of wildlife under a specific condition: *wa-antum Hurumun.*

The words *wa-antum* mean 'and when you' or 'and that which you' or 'while you are'.

Wa-antum-hurumun means *that which you are restricted.*

Hurumun is a derivative of the root *H-r-m* or *Harama.* All derivatives generated from this root word can have different shades, but the essence of the meaning of the word is the same.

305

They can mean *forbidden, restricted, sanctioned, limited, controlled or constrained* but each time different and distinct derivatives are used for them such as *Haram, Hurum, Hurumat, Harrama, yuHarrimu, Hurima* and *muHarram.*

We can discover the meaning of these derivatives by making comparative reference to the contexts in which they appear. This is a simple yet important procedure and we don't need any long commentaries outside the Qur'anic injunction to understand or provide long commentaries or *tafsir*[93] the meaning of certain words.

For example, in 3:93 all food was permitted (*Halal*) to the Children of Israel except what they forbade or constrained (*Harrama*) themselves before the Torah was revealed.

> *Kulluu tha-ami kaana <u>hillan</u> li bani israiila*
> All food was permitted for the Israelites
>
> *Illa maa Harrama israa iilu alaa nafsihi*
> except what Israel forbade for itself
>
> *min qabli an tunazzila tauraatu*
> from before the Torah was revealed

The Children of Israel forbade/constrained (*Harrama*) certain foods before the Torah was revealed.

Therefore, in 5:1 the phrase *wa antum Hurumun* means *while you are restricted.*

---

[93] *Tafsir* is long commentaries to explain the Qur'an based on tradition and tales found in the various hadith books written by so-called learned people. It is equivalent to the Jewish *Tosefta* a compilation of traditions and sayings closely related to the *Misnah,* deriving from many authorities represented in it.

In other words, in 5:1 it is we, who must restrict ourselves from hunting. In 5:94 it is said Game hunting is a test for us (the verse will be quoted later). The subject of wild life conservation is now sanctioned by God within the passages of His decrees on matters of food.

The Qur'an does not say how long we ought to make the hunting of wild game restricted, but the Qur'an says it is part of God's decrees. Therefore it is up to us to decide. If the mountain goats in Afghanistan need five months to breed, then we must refrain from hunting the goats for those five months.

If the great leatherback turtles carry their eggs for two months and then lay their eggs on one particular night of the full moon in a year in Nicaragua, we must restrict the hunting for, say, three months before that particular full moon. If the deer is almost extinct and needs years to increase its population, then we must not hunt *ghoi-ro-soi-di* the deer for that number of years. *'Wa antum Hurumun'* means 'and that which you are restricted'.

5:1 stresses strongly not to allow hunting:

ghoi-ro	do not
mu-hil-li	make permissible
soi-di	game hunting

The prohibitions of hunting should be enshrined in state law to protect different species of animal. The law of the land must impose the restrictions on hunting at the right time.

To grasp the meaning of this message, we should pay a visit to the wildlife department in any country to find out why they impose different types of restrictions on hunting

307

various animals during specific months. The deer-hunting season in India may differ from the goat-hunting season in Yemen. There are seasons for different animals. It is we who must decide when to restrict hunting, and we must respect these laws if we fear God.

This is the true meaning of the message in 5:1. It has nothing to do with wearing a two-piece white cloth dress known as *ihram* and walking in circles around a cube-shaped stone idol in the centre of a mosque crying out for God to hear us.

We do not make any of the wildlife meat forbidden (or *Haram*), but we are *not allowed* to hunt them during a specific periods.

If we wish to observe the will of the Lord of the Universe, we are not to violate His decrees on the hunting of wildlife during the restricted months:

> Do not violate God's decrees (*sha'iral-lah*), or the restricted months (on hunting), and the guidance (about hunting), or the indicators (of hunting) or the harmony that is sanctioned in the system (*aminal-bai-tal-Harama*) when seeking the grace and pleasure of God. But when you are permitted (*Halal-tum*) (after the ban is lifted), you may hunt. Do not be provoked by the enmity of those who prevent you in observing the sanctioned submission (*anil-mas-jidil-Harami*) that you may transgress. And co-operate with each other in righteous deeds and piety, and do not co-operate with those committing sins and aggression. (5:2)

We are to co-operate with the lawmakers to protect the wildlife and by doing so we demonstrate our observation to the sanctions prescribed by God in His system. We must not co-operate with illegal hunters. However, if we kill wildlife during the restricted months (*shahrul-Harrama*) on purpose, the food is still permitted for us to eat, but we pay a fine.

O you who believe, do not kill wildlife when you are restricted (*Hurumun*). If anyone kills on purpose, he shall expatiate with an equivalent livestock to be judged by two equitable persons from among you to point out the maturity of the 'ankles' (*ka'bati*). Or expiation by feeding the poor or imposing self-abstinence[94] (*siyaman*) so that he regrets the consequences of his actions. God has pardoned his previous offences. Whoever reverts to his offence, God will avenge it from him. God is Almighty, Avenger. (5:95).

The right meaning of the word *Hurumun* can be verified from other verses of the Qur'an. For example, in 9:36 it is impossible to change the meaning of this word to none other than *restricted*.

> Surely the count of months according to God is twelve months in God's reckoning (*fil-kitaabi-llaah*) since they day He created the heavens and the earth. Of these, four are restricted (*ar ba'atun Hurumun*). That is the upright way of life (*deen-nul qayyimu*). (9:36)

The word *arba'atum Hurumun* means that there are *restrictions* on four of the months.

---

[94] The Arabic word *Siyaman* is traditionally translated as *fasting*. There is no mention about the duration period for the fast. Hence, it is logical to say the meaning is to discipline oneself from hunting until the animals are matured. It is not about fasting from eating or drinking.

The four restricted months refer to the cooling-off period after a declaration is announced to the idol-worshippers that God and His messenger disown them for their idol-worshipping practices. The day the announcement is made is known as the day of the Big Challenge or *Haji akbar*. In 9:1-4, the idol-worshippers and the non-believers are given four months to *'roam the earth'* to decide their position on the *deen*.

Today, more than a billion people on earth believe they must make themselves 'holy' for a few days. Each year, several million of them don indecent two-piece suits which they have named *ihram* and walk in circles around a cubical stone idol. And this when all God wanted them to do was to observe the sanctions in the system of not hunting the wildlife during restricted periods.

Just a slight twist to one simple word like this can cause disaster to a person's life in this world and the Hereafter.

The majority of 'Muslims' could not care less about observing the sanctions protecting wildlife, however. The religionists have generally succeeded in deflecting them from beneficial actions related to wildlife conservation and misled them towards jumping up and down in front of an empty stone box. Somebody, somewhere, must be having a really good laugh.

God created all living creatures on earth, and mankind is expected to co-exist with them in perfect harmony:

> *Wa-mamin dab-batin fil-ardi wala-thor 'iri yathi-ru bijana-haihi il-laa um-matin amshalakum* (6:38)

Any creature on earth including the birds that fly
with their wings are nations like you. (6:38)

Humans are not allowed to kill at random. Killing is
allowed only when justified:

Wala-taq-tulu nafsal-lati Haramal-lah il-la-bil-haq
(17:33)

You shall not kill the life, it is forbidden by God
except in truth. (17:33)

The presence of other living creatures is part of God's
creation. Humans cannot simply go around killing and
destroying anything they like.

God has created livestock as a provision for mankind.
Killing livestock for food is justified according to need.
God also allows mankind to enjoy the meat of wildlife.
Therefore killing animals is justified subject to certain
conditions.

There are two kinds of wildlife: that in water and that
on land. We do not have to impose any restrictions to
protect the water game but we must impose some
restrictions to protect the wildlife on land. For as long as we
observe the restrictions that, for us, is the state of *Hurumun*.
5:96 says:

uhil-laa lakum soi-dul bah-ri
Permitted for you (*uhil-la-lakum*) is the hunting of
water game (*soi-dul bah-ri*)

wathor-'amuhu mata-'al-lakum walis-syai-roti
Eat from them as provision, for you and those who
are travelling

Wa-hur-rima alaikum soi-dul bar-ri ma'dumtum huruman

And prohibited (*Hurrima*) upon you is the hunting of game on land for as long as (*mu'dumtum*) you restrict them (*Huruman*).

wat-taqul-lah hal-lazi ilaihi taq-syarun.

You shall observe God, to Whom you will be gathered.

In 5:96, we are permitted to eat game from the sea (*baHri*) but as for the game from the land (*baRri*) hunting is forbidden for as long as (*mu'dumtum*) we make their hunting restricted (*Huruman*).

We can see that the corruption by the innovators of the Arab religion is exposed again. Here, both the words *Hurrima* and *Hurumun* are found. Both come from the same root *H-r-m* or *Haram*.

They say that *Hurrima* in the first part of the sentence means *prohibited* but *Hurumun* in the latter part of the same sentence means a state of *sacredness*. They claim it means the *ihram* – the two piece white cloth worn during the act of walking around a cubical stone idol at the centre of their mosque. As we have seen, these verses have nothing to do with a pilgrimage of any kind.

The killing of wildlife is done everywhere. Such activity is called game-hunting. The Qur'an calls upon hunters to exercise self discipline by not killing wildlife out of season:

Ya-aiyuhal-lazi na-amanu la-yub-luwa-nakumul-lah bi-shai'ain minal-soi-di tana-luhu ai-diyakum wa-rimahukum li-yak-lamal-lah man-yu-ghor-fuhu bil-

312

ghaib. Fa-manikh-tada ba'da zalika falahu azaban alim (5:94)

O you who believe, <u>God may test you through game-hunting</u> within the reach of your hands and means. God wants to ensure those among you who fear Him (while He is) unseen. Anyone who transgresses after this has deserved painful retribution. (5:94)

The majority of civilised governments impose laws to protect wildlife. They do not know they are preserving the harmony of the sanctions in God's system (or the *baytil-Harama*). For them, it is simply a matter of good sense. They have studied the environment and life patterns in the animal kingdom and have realised that it is their obligation to protect living creatures – if only out of self-interest. As far as the Qur'an is concerned, such a perception is an act of righteousness.

Without doubt, *wa-antum Hurumun* does not mean *during pilgrimage*, neither does it signify the two piece pilgrim's clothes which they call the *ihram*[95]. Moreover, the word *ihram* is nowhere found in the Qur'an.

We must realise the beauty of the composition of the Qur'an. In most cases, a subject is detailed in sequential verses and then it is mentioned elsewhere. The prohibitions on food detailed in the Qur'an are part of the *sanctions* in the system (*baytal-Harami*) to be observed by those who submit to God.

The details of the prohibition are expanded in 5:1-5. In 5:3 in the midst of detailing the food God says:

---

[95] A man's pilgrimage is nullified if he wears anything under the *ihram* clothing. Imagine the heat and I have to struggle applying creams in between my thighs.

> Today, I have perfected the *deen* for you, and completed My favour upon you. And decreed *Islam* as the *deen*. (5:3)

God's prescribed way of life is perfected by the revelation pertaining to details of the restriction on food. A true person who is at peace must not submit to any restrictions beyond the limits set by God. The verse, however, ends with an exception:

> However, if one is forced to eat any of these without malice, then God is Forgiver, Merciful.

The same topic continues in the next two verses before a new subject is dealt with. The subject of food is repeated in eight straight verses (6:141-150) to corroborate the restrictions mentioned in the earlier chapters. The final part is mentioned again in eight straight verses (16:112-119).

As a matter of interest, the composition of the Qur'an is such that any isolated subject is always revealed in a verse of its own. Never are two unrelated subjects touched upon in the same verse.

Wildlife conservation becomes pilgrim's garb

A brief examination of 5:1-5 concludes the following:

- We are to fulfil our covenant with God so that we do not prohibit any food except that enjoined on us. We are not to permit the hunting of game during the restricted period.

- We are not to violate God's decrees (*sha'iral-lah*) or the restricted months (on hunting), or the guidance (about hunting), or the indicator (on hunting) or the harmony of the sanctions in the system when seeking the grace and pleasure of God. When we are permitted, we may hunt. We are not to be provoked by the enmity of those who would prevent us from upholding the submission sanctioned by God, and we are not to aggress. We are to co-operate with each other in righteous deeds and piety and not to co-operate with those committing sins and aggression.

- The people asked what was permissible. We are to tell them, "Everything that is good including that which is caught by trained dogs."

- Prohibited to us are animals that die by themselves, blood, the decaying meat, and food dedicated to other than God. The prohibition includes animals strangled to death, animals struck dead by an object, animals that have met their death by falling from a height, animals gored to death by predators, food dedicated to idols and food distributed by lots. These are the only restrictions about food sanctioned by God. Those who follow strictly to the limits without imposing more than what He had sanctioned, they will enjoy peacefulness, and He has called it *Islam*.

- Lastly, all good food is permitted, including that served by the people of the previous Scripture.

All these five verses are about food, including the meat of wildlife. Performing the pilgrimage or wearing of the pilgrim's clothing (*ihram*) is not a food item or related to food. That subject is simply not there at all. How the religionists could squeeze out pilgrimage and a non-existence state of sanctity of wearing a religious garb from these same five verses is an exercise in religious stuntmanship surpassing almost all other religious fakery.

The word *ihram* not found in Qur'an

It is important to note that the word *ihram* is not a derivative from the word *Haram* and this it is not found anywhere in the Qur'an.

If we pretend for a moment that *Hurumun* means what the religionists would have us believe it means pilgrimage or pilgrim's clothes, we end up with the following ludicrous situation if we apply this rule across the board. *Arba'atun Hurumun* in 9:36 will thus read:

- The count of months at the sight of God are twelve, four of them are pilgrimages.

or:

- The count of months at the sight of God are twelve, four of them are *in pilgrim's clothes*.

Either rendition is patently untenable.

The full text of 9:36 says:

> *Inna 'inda-tul shuh-ri 'indal-lah hisna 'a-sharor shah-ran fi-kitabil-lah yauma qorlaqas samawa-til ardht min-ha* <u>arba'atun Hurumun</u>. *Zalikal deen nul-qoyim. Fala tudht-limu fi-hin-na anfusakum wa-qorlitu musyrikin-na kaf-fatan kama yu-qotilunakum kaf-fatan. Wa'-lamu an-nal-lah ma'al mut-taqin.*

The count of months according to God are twelve, as decreed in God's Scripture since the day He

316

created the Heavens and the Earth, <u>four of them are restricted</u>. This is the perfect deen. Therefore you must not wrong yourself in them, and you may fight the idol-worshippers (*mushrikeen*) each time they fight you. And you should know God is with the righteous.

By virtue of 9:36 where the word *Hurumun* appears it is said that it means *pilgrimage* or *in the pilgrim's garb* and that the pilgrimage has to be performed for four months and in pilgrim garb. This is where we see the absurdity.

The preposterous move by the religionists to corrupt 5:2 will astound many readers:

Ya-aiyuhal-lazi ana-amanu la-tuhilu sha-a'iril-lah
O you who believe do not violate God's decrees

wala-shahrul-harom
and the Restricted months

wal – <u>hadya</u>
and the guidelines

walal-qolaida
and the indicators (of restrictions)

wala-aman-nal baitil-Harama
and the harmony of the restrictions in the system

yab-taghru fad-lan min rob-bihim warid-wa-nan
in seeking the grace and pleasure of your Lord

<u>*Wa-iza-Halal-tum*</u> *fas-dho-dhu*
<u>And when they are permitted for you</u>, then you may hunt

wala-yaj-riman-nakum shai-an qau-m

317

Do not be provoked by the enmity of any race

an-yasud-dukum anil-mas-jidil-Harami
who prevent you in observing the sanctioned submission

*an-taq-tadu wa-ta'awanu alal-bir-ri   wal-taq-wa
wala-ta 'awanu alal-ismi wal-udwan-ni wat-taqul-
lah ha-in-nal-lah sadi-dul-'iqob*
that you may transgress. And co-operate with each other in righteous deeds and piety, and do not co-operate with those committing sin and aggression.

The message in 5:2 is a continuation of the subject in the previous verse. It is about livestock and the hunting of wildlife. The word *hunting* (*fas-tho-dhu*) in this verse is a repeat from 5:1 where two verses complement each other on the same subject.

People's comprehension of many words in 5:2 was distorted (as usual, through the priestly application of the concocted *Hadith*) to indicate a *ritual observation* of the so-called *Haj* pilgrimage in Mecca.

The manipulators of the Arab religion gave a new meaning to the word *hadya* and the Qur'an exposes their scheme. The word means *guidance*. They changed this word to mean *an offering*, or *the sacrificial offering of an animal*. The Qur'an says that assigning food offerings to God is evil:

They even assigned God a share of the crops and the livestock He has provided for them, by saying, "This is for God." According to their claim they also say, "This is for our idols." However, what was assigned to their idols will never reach God, while that

318

assigned to God invariably ended up with their idols. Evil indeed is their Judgement. (6:136)

Please pay particular attention to this verse. God did not ask them to make the offering or to assign anything to Him. It was they who assigned portions of food and livestock to God and to their idols. God says their Judgement is *evil*, a very strong word in the Qur'an.

It is worth repeating this thought as it concerns the pilgrims who visit their stone idol in Mecca and *sacrifice* a goat, camel, or other livestock to God during the *Haj* pilgrimage – the Book of God says:

> The animal sacrifice will never reach Him and they ultimately end up with their (stone) idol. (6:136)

Animal sacrifice to deities was an Arab practice long before the time of the Last Prophet. The religionists have falsely attributed the origin of animal sacrifice to the prophet Abraham, but their justification thereof is another story.

Guidance becomes animal offerings'

The word *hadya* in 5:2 refers to guide, show, lead or point out. The root word *hada* means *guide*, and *hudan* is *the guidance*. The religionists did not expect that their mutilation of simple Arabic words in the Qur'an would eventually be uncovered. The word *Hadya* appears in the Qur'an many times. The word *hadiiya* in 7:186 and 25:31 shows that its meaning is *guide*.

> *Man-yud-lilil-lah fala hadi-ya lahu wayazaru-hum fi-dhog-yanihim ya'mahun* (7:186)

Whoever goes astray, God will not guide him (*hadi-ya lahu*). And He will allow him to wander aimlessly. (7:186)

Wakazalika ja'alna likul-linabiayan 'aduwon minal-mujrimin wakafabirob-bika hadiiyan mahjur'. (25:31)

We thus appoint for every prophet enemies from among the criminals. Your Lord suffices as guide (*hadiiyan*) and helper. (25:31)

But when this same word – hadya – appears in 5:2 and other verses, the religionists twist the word to mean sacrificial offering of animals as a religious rite in their Arab religion.

More corruption

Besides the corruption of the word *Hurumun* in 5:1, the enemies of God and the enemies of the Messenger corrupted a further six words in 5:2 to deceive the Muslims into joining them in visiting and worshipping their idols.

They have twisted the following words:

- *hadya* has become sacrificial offerings. The Muslims are actually carrying the torch of the Arab pagans in assigning food to the stone idols.

- *qola-ida* has become *the garlands marking the animals*. There is no logical purpose in God telling His servants '*Do not violate the garlands marking the animals*'. Yet the religionists are not even true to their own corruptions, for until today none of the animals sacrificed in Mina every year is garlanded!

The verse simply says do not violate the guideline *hadya* and the *qola-ida* (indicators) laying out the restrictions imposed on the hunting of wild game. If the law of the land says do not hunt the mountain goats during the breeding season and notices (indicators) are put up to that effect, don't do it. It is that simple.

According to 5:94, even the hunting of game can be a test for mankind. Surely, it does not mean putting garlands around the necks of cows and goats. Putting a wreath or garland around a goat, camel, cow, or any livestock to signify its holiness is a characteristic of certain 'religions', but it has no place in the *Islam* revealed by God.

- They twisted *wala-aminal baytal-Harama* to become *do not violate those who are visiting the sacred house*. Both counts are pure blasphemy as far as the Qur'an is concerned: both garlanding the animals and making a rock structure sacred. The religionists have truly fooled everyone into worshipping the stone idol in Mecca.

The message in the verse is very clear *do not violate the harmony of the sanctions in the system when seeking God's grace and pleasure.*

- The word *waiza-Halal-tum fas-tho-du* has also been manipulated.

Perhaps in the whole of the Qur'an , this is the easiest word to understand, even for the non-Arabs.

waiza	and when
Halal-tum	it is permitted (*Halal*) for you
fas-tho-du	then you may hunt

Any ten year old Muslim child will understand the word *Halal*. Their parents train them to eat only *Halal* food. The opposite of *Halal* is *Haram*. One is permitted and the other is not. This straightforward sentence is deliberately translated as: *and when you have completed your pilgrimage, then you may hunt.* How they reached such a mischievous misrepresentation is left to the imagination of the reader.

Wildlife conservation has no place in the Arab religion. The religionists invented the Arabic calendar, which cannot even determine the four seasons in a year. Although they kept the twelve months, winter can happen in any of the twelve months because their calendar moves and is not fixed to the seasons. Their calendar cannot permanently assign accurately a specific time period in every twelve months to restrict hunting as decreed by God. By the same token, their spurious pilgrimage season varies from year to year.

To aggravate the matter they distort the word *masjidil-Harami*. They deceived the people by their rendition of 5:2 as *'Do not be provoked by the enmity of those who prevent you from going to the sacred mosque'*. According to the Qur'an, there was no such thing as a sacred mosque. The fairy tales in the Arab religion also do not talk about a sacred mosque before the time of the Last Prophet. There was none – period. The religionists were not concerned about any mosque before the Qur'an was revealed. All their history centres on how they should preserve and promote the Black Stone.

The word *masjidil-Harami* can easily be understood by reading the context of the message about God's decrees sanctioned in the system. It says, *'Do not be provoked by the enmity of those who prevent you from observing the sanctioned submission'*. The early part of the message simply tells us not to violate God's decrees regarding the restricted months, the guidelines, and the indicators of hunting restrictions. These are sanctioned in the harmonious system. We are simply to ignore the enemies who refuse to observe the restrictions.

The sanctions on food[96]

The restrictions on the consumption of food are prescribed in the following verse:

> *Hur-rimat alaikumul mai-tahu wal dam-maa walah-mul khin-ziri wa-ma-uhil-la li-ghyoi-ril-lah bihi. Wal-mun-'haani-qotu wal mutarad-diyatu wal-nathee-hatu wamaa-akalas sa-buhu il-la ma-zakai-tum wa-ma-zubiha 'alan nusubi wa-antas-taksimu bil-azlam (5:3)*

> Prohibited to you the carrion, blood, the decaying[97] meat, and that over which any name other than God's has been pronounced. The animal that was strangled to death, and the animal that was struck dead by an object, and the animal that died by falling from a height, the animal that was gored to death, and animals partially eaten by beasts unless you rescued them alive. And those sacrificed to idols and those distributed by lots. All these are wicked. (5:3)

---

[96] Food is the common prohibitions imposed by all religions

[97] There is no mention of any specific type of animals sanctioned as unlawful in the Quran. In 5: 88 it says: *'You shall eat from God's provisions to you, that which is good and lawful, and observe God, in whom you believe'*. Swine is livestock – thus, it is God's provision.

This subject (about food) follows on from 5:1 that allows the conditional consumption of wildlife meat.

In 5:2, the emphasis is on the need for strict observation of God's decrees sanctioned in the system followed by the prescription of the limits or the parameters of those restrictions sanctioned in the submission with regard to food.

However, in the middle of 5:3 it says:

> Today, the disbelievers have despaired regarding your way of life (*deen-nakum*). Do not fear them, but fear Me instead. Today, I have perfected your way of life (*deen-nakum*) for you and completed My favours upon you decreed *Islam* as the way of life (*deen-nan*).

In other words, with the limitations on food, the system is complete. His servants must not impose any other restrictions to complicate matters.

People are reminded to be careful. The Devil will try to mislead us with additional prohibitions. All food (apart from that specifically prohibited) is allowed as long as it is good: The easiest way for the Devil recruits to deceive a man or woman is to make them obey a simple dietary restriction. For example, God designed some animals to be domesticated as provisions to mankind – this is His mercy and blessing. The same species of animals are also found in the wild. But the *u'lemas* and priests of certain religion tell their followers not to kill all living creatures including livestock. Hence, we see vegetarians all over the place.

Those who submit to these invented restrictions are termed as idol worshipers simply because; they reject God's blessings, His creations and the good things that He has provided for them. Some would say - vegetarians are defying the law of nature.

> *Fakulu mim-ma roza-qor-kumul-lah hala-lan thoyiban waskuru ni'matal-lah ainkuntum aiyahu ta'budun* (16:114)

> Therefore eat what was provided by God, permissible and good. Be appreciative of God's blessing upon you if you are serving Him. (16:114)

If someone says there are more categories of prohibited food other than which has been detailed in the Qur'an, then they have attributed lies to God and are destined to be doomed:

> *Wala-taqulu lima tasifu al-sinatukumul kaziba haza Halalun wa-haza Haramun litaftaru alal-lahi kaziba in-nal-lazi yaftaruna alal-lahil kaziba la-yuf-lihun* (16:116)

> And do not say lies, "This is *Halal* (permitted) and this is *Haram* (forbidden)," inventing lies about God. Surely those who invent lies about God will not succeed. (16:116)

This verse clearly says that those who impose restrictions beyond that which God has decreed are lying.

Animals caught by dogs are permitted

God allows believing men and women to enjoy the meat of wild animals caught by their dogs. This means a Muslim can keep dogs. The history of some young believers who took refuge in a cave in *surah* 18:18 says there was a dog as their friend in the cave. '*We turned them to the right*

325

*side and the left side, while their dog stretched his arms in
their midst'.* But in the Arab religion it is forbidden to keep
dogs. The author did not realise the benefits of having a
dog[98] until he got a German shepherd a few years ago.

> *Yas-alunaka ma-zaa uhil-la lahum. Qul uhil-la
> lakumul thor-ibatu wama 'al-lamtum minal jawarihi
> mukalibina   tu'al-limu-nahun-na   mim-ma   'al-
> lamakumul-lah fa-kulu-mim-ma am-sakna alaikum
> waz-kurus mal-lah alai-hi. Wat-taqul-lah in-nal-lah
> sari-ul hisab* (5:4)

> They ask you what is permitted for them. Tell them,
> "Permitted for you are all the good things that the
> dogs you trained catch for you according to what
> was taught by God to you." You may eat what they
> catch for you. And mention God's name over it.
> You shall observe God, God is most strict in
> reckoning. (5:4)

Not many translators were willing to translate the word
mukalibin as dogs because the majority of the so-called
Muslims believe it is forbidden (*Haram*) to keep a dog. The
Arabic word for *dog* is *kalb* and this word also appears in
18:22 where it states that there was a dog accompanying the
believing youth in the cave. The Qur'an compares people
who receive God's revelations – but who disregard them –
to dogs.

> *Walau shik-na la-rofaknahu biha wala-kin-nahu aq-
> lada ilal-ardhi wat-taba'a-huwa- hu kama-salil
> kalbi ain-tahmil alai-hi yal-hash ay-tat-rukhu yal-*

---

[98] This will strike someone without a 'Muslim' background as mad and weird
thing. 'Muslims' have convinced themselves that dogs are unclean. It is
believed that should a dog's spittle touch a man he becomes spiritually unclean.

hash. Zalika masalul qaumil lazi kaz-zabu bi-ayaatina. Fa qu-su-sil qoru-sorsa la-al-lahum yad-tafakarun (7:176)

Had We willed, We could have elevated him with the Scripture, but he insisted on sticking to the ground and following his own opinions. His example is that of a dog (*kalbi*). If you give him attention he pants, and when you ignore him he pants. Such is the example of those who reject our revelations. You shall narrate these so that they may think carefully. (7:176)

Al-yauma uhil-la-lakumud thoi-iba-tu wa-thor-'a-mul-lazi utul-kitab hil-lul lakum wa-tho-'a-mukum hil-lun lahum. Wah-musornatu minal-mukminati wal-muh-sornatu minal-lazi utul-kitab min qob-likum (5:5)

Today, all good things are permitted for you and the food of those who were given the previous Scripture is permitted for you. And your food is also permitted for them. (5:5)

NOTE: In each verse, the subject is always related. Unrelated subjects do not jump out in the same verse.

In 2:62 and 5:69, the food of the true believers of the previous Scriptures is also endorsed. Then in 5:5, we are told the food served by either of these parties is permitted for the other. Thereupon, He adds another point about the people of the former revelation. Such addition is done at the end of a verse about a particular subject but never in the middle of the subject matter.

The invented *pilgrimage* and *pilgrim's garb* (*ihram*) is sandwiched haphazardly by the religionists within a verse where it simply does not belong thematically. The clumsiness of this attempt to violate the perfect composition of the Qur'an is enough to alert the suspicions of the careful reader.

The religionists fulfil the Devil's promise

The enormous corruption of God's words in the Qur'an by the religionists only confirms that they have fulfilled the Devil's wishes. According to the Qur'an the Devil made a promise to God:

> *Qola fabima a'waitani la-aq'udan-na lahum siro-thokal mustaqim* (7:16)

> He (the Devil) said, since You confirmed that I have strayed, I will try to mislead all of them from your straight path. (7:16)

9:97 says, *'the Arabs are staunchest in disbelief and hypocrisy'*. God has revealed the indisputable fact about the Arabs. What can I say? Who else can make an ankle into God's house and get millions of people to worship it?

They have now succumbed to the Devil's evil design, which is found in 7:16 where he says to God, *'Since you have confirmed that I have strayed, I will try to mislead all of them from your straight path'*.

> The Arabs are staunchest in disbelief and hypocrisy and more likely to be ignorant of God's limit as revealed to His messenger. (9:97) Among the Arabs around you there are hypocrites, they are from the

city-dwellers. And they are very staunch in their hypocrisy. (9:101)

We have no reason to believe otherwise. The Arabs[99] referred to here are not the Arab nomads or Arab Bedouin as the urban Arabs would have us believe when confronted with the uncomfortable fact of these verses. Bedouin Arabs have never lived in cities. But the Arabs in general have had tremendous impact on the affect of the Qur'an in the world. They have successfully misled billions of people from the path of God.

Ka'bata (ankles) become God's house

All Arabs know an ankle is called *ka'aba*, but religionists went ahead to change the perception of the word *Ka'aba* (*ankles* or *joints*) to become a proper name for 'God's house'. The dissimulation has been achieved to accommodate their earlier premeditated distortion of the word *Hurumun* in 5:2.

The word *Ka'aba* is mentioned at three different places in the Qur'an and they are all grouped in *surah* 5. The title of this *surah* is *Al Maaidah* which means *The Feast*.

Before exploring the true meaning of the word *ka'aba*, we will have a brief overview of this *surah*.

There are 120 verses, and the subject of food is spread throughout (including the famous verse about the consumption of intoxicants). The general focus of the

---

[99] Every shackled mind including the so-called scholars in the Arab religion refuse to believe this verse refers to the urban Arabs. All of them ignore the word in 33:20 *badunaa-fil-a'robi* which refers to *Bedouin Arabs* or the nomads.

message in this *surah* is the three prophets who received God's Scripture namely Moses, Jesus and Muhammad.

- 1-5 give the details of the sanctions on food. 6 reinforces the essence of 1-5, particularly on personal hygiene. 7-11 emphasise the significance of upholding God's decrees.

- 12-47 are related to the history of the Children of Israel who transgressed the laws given to Moses and Jesus.

- 48-89 are about the message of the Qur'an as revealed to the Last Prophet, reminding the readers about the violation of God's prescribed submission by the people of the previous Scripture.

- In 90-93, the subject is again food; also advice against intoxicants, gambling and dividing the meats by lots. 93 says that those who believe and lead a righteous life incur no sin by eating any food so long as they observe virtuousness, believe in God, and good moral conduct and continue to do good deeds.

- 94-98 are an extension of verses 1 and 2 and regard wildlife conservation[100] and the penalties imposed in respect of violations of hunting restrictions.

- 99-100 take a slight diversion to inform us of the limited role of the Last Prophet. However, food is again mentioned in verse 103. Some of the names in this verse are beyond comprehension to many people – even to the Arabs. There are names like '*Baheerah*' '*Saa'ibah*' and

---

[100] The subject of wildlife conservation is not found in any translations around the world and the Qur'anic statement about the subject is very clear when we uncover the interpolations about the word '*Hurumun*'.

'*Waseelah*'. They are not camels, goats or donkeys, which are common to the Arabs.

- Jesus is mentioned in 110-120. The disciples want reassurance and make a preposterous demand on Jesus asking that he ask his Lord to bring a feast from the sky as a sign of celebration. Their request is granted with the warning that they will be punished severely if they disbelieve thereafter.

This is the contextual essence of the *surah*. The subject is largely food. And this – inside the context of food – is the only chapter in the Qur'an where we find the word *ka'aba*. It is mentioned three times:

> O you who believe, when you uphold your commitments you shall wash your faces, your arms to the elbows, wipe your heads, and wash your legs to the <u>ankles</u> (*ka'baini*).[101] (5:6)

The word *ka'baini* in this verse means *ankles*. The same word is used in 5:95[102] to mean the ankles of animals.

> *Yaaiyuhallazi na-amanu la-taqtalu soida wa-antum* <u>*Hurumun*</u> *waman qotalahu minkum muqota'amidan fajaza-un misluma qotala-minalna'ami yah-kumu bihi zawa'adli minkum* <u>*hadyan balighor ka'bati*</u> *aukafarotun tho'amu masakina au'adlu zaalika siyaman liyazuqo wabala amrihi 'afal-lah 'am-ma salafa waman 'aada fayantaqimul-lah minhu wal-lahu 'azizun zuntiqam.* (5:95)

---

[101] This is the dual of the word *ka'aba*

[102] The religionists ignore the context of the subject in this verse that starts from 5:94 to 5:97. All these verses refer to hunting of wildlife on land and in the sea.

O you who believe, do not kill the wildlife which you are <u>restricted</u> (*Hurumun*). If anyone kills on purpose, he shall expatiate with an equivalent livestock to be judged by two equitable persons from among you <u>to point out the maturity</u> (*hadyan balighor*) of the ankles (*ka'bati*),[103]. Or expiate by feeding the poor or discipline himself (until the animals are matured), so that he feels the consequences of his actions. God has pardoned his previous offences. Whoever reverts to his offence, God will avenge from him. God is almighty, avenger. (5:95)

The word before *ka'bati* in the verse is *hadyan baligha*[104] that literally means to guide/lead or point out the maturity (in the determination of the maturity of the ankles).

The word *hadyan* comes from the root *hada*, which means *to guide* or *to lead* or *to direct* or *to point out*. This is simple and a common word found in many other verses in the Qur'an. *Hada, Hadi, Huda, Hudan, Hadya and Hadyan* has the same essence of meaning. I have already explained about this word in this chapter under '*Guidance becomes animal offerings*.

The word *baligha* comes from the root *balagh*, which means to *mature*, or to *advance/mature* towards an objective.

For example in 4:6, if we take care of the child orphan we must test their maturity (*balagh*) as soon as they reach

---

[103] This is the plural of *Ka'aba*.

[104] Translators say the word hadya means sacrificial offerings. God uses this word used all over the Quran to mean guide and they consistently translate it correctly in all other veres except in 2:196, 5:2 and 5:95. This is a simple distortion that can be detected easily.

marriageable age before we hand over their rightful property to them. The word *balagh* (that means *mature*) in 4:6 is the same word used in 5:95 referring to the *maturity of the ankles* of the animal.

> You shall test the orphans when they reach maturity for marriage (*balaghu nikaha*). If you see rationality in them, you shall hand over their property. And do not consume their property excessively before they grow up (*aiya'baru*). (4:6)

In 4:6, the word *balagh* (which means *mature*) is further underlined by the word *aiya'baru* which means *before they grow up*. In other words, the orphans must be matured before we hand over their property to them.

The Qur'an says mankind's advancement or maturity on the straight path is useless to some of them even after the great wisdom has reached them. The same root word is used:

> They have received enough knowledge to set them straight, great wisdom, but their maturity (*baligha-tun*) seems to be useless. Therefore, leave them alone. (54:4-6)

Wildlife conservation, then, is an integral part of God's creation. It is a decree that has to be observed by humans. In 5:95, the use of *ka'bati* is related to the violation of the restrictions and the penalty one has to pay if animals are killed on purpose during the restricted period. Hunting is only allowed when the maturity of the animals can be identified through their ankles' stride. As for the birds the Qur'an says, nobody can kill them except God which implies that hunters will not be able to catch the birds except with God's will.

Do you not notice the birds assigned to fly in the sky? Nobody can catch them except God. This should provide signs for those who believe (16:79).

In 5:2 people are advised not to violate God's decree about hunting the wildlife during the period of restrictions.

O you who believe, do not violate God's decrees (*sha'iral-lah*), and the restricted months (*shahrul-Harama*), and the guidance (*hadya*), and the indicators (*qo-laa-ida*) and the harmony of the restrictions in the system (*bay-tal-Harama*) when seeking the grace and pleasure of God. But when they are permitted (*Halal-tum*), you may hunt. Do not be provoked by the enmity of those who prevent you from observing the sanctioned submission (*anil-mas-jidil-Harami*) and do not aggress. Co-operate with each other in righteous deeds and piety, and do not co-operate with those committing sins and aggression. (5:2)

The message in 2 is repeated in 97 to emphasise the significance of the restrictions of hunting the wildlife. Once the ban is lifted, *you may hunt.*

The message in 5:95 is so easily understood. For example, when the restriction (*Hurumun*) on deer hunting is enforced, if someone kills a deer he must be fined to the tune of equivalent livestock. The offender shall be judged by two equitable people from among themselves to ensure the restriction is observed until the ban is lifted.

Hadyan baligha al ka'bati literally means *point out the maturity of the ankle,* which in turn means they must determine the maturity of the deer by its natural moving

334

pattern through the strength of the *ankles* or by reference to its ankles.

Also, it is important that the fine be such that the person who violated the indicators of the hunting restrictions (*qo-laa-ida*) and knowingly killed the animal when he was restricted (*Hurumun*), be made to feel the consequences of his actions for killing the animal.

Therefore, it is the duty of the equitable people (modern-day game wardens) to determine the maturity of the animal that was killed and levy a suitable fine equivalent value of mature livestock.

If a person kills a deer by mistake during the open season of wild fowls while being observant to God, then it is his duty to admit his mistake to the wildlife office and to allow them to judge him. If two equitable persons do not judge him then it is his duty to feed the poor voluntarily for an equivalent value in livestock or discipline himself from hunting until the animals are matured (if he truly believes in God).

The word *ka'aba* also appears in 5:97. The message is identical to 5:2:

> God has set the 'ankles' (*ka'bata*) the sanctioned system (*baytil-Harami*) to be upheld for mankind, and the restricted months (*shahrul Harama*), and guidelines (*hadya*), and the indicators (*qolaa-ida*). This is to let you know that God, He knows everything in the heavens and the earth and what is beneath the earth. And surely God is fully aware of everything. (5:97)

Some critics who refuse to unshackle their minds who insist the word *ka'aba* means the rock structure and *Bayta* as the house standing in Mecca might find the above verse illogical. They have overlooked the significance of the wildlife conservation – which is for the benefits of mankind - as being part of God's decree in 22:36. The word *al-budna* (same root word used for Bedouins) in this verse means wildlife - a very important subject ignored by all translators.

Translators differ in their understanding, and some of them have erroneously said it means the camel. They have already confused themselves with the words *Jamal, ibbil, ba'ir, rikab, heem, 'shar* as camel, but upon realising too many words became camel they make a slight change to the word *dhomir* in 22:27. This time they say '*skinny camels*'! It seems that each time the Arabs cannot understand God's Arabic in the Quran they will tell translators and their scholars – 'its a camel'. Thus, perhaps out of their ego or pre-conceived ideas, critics will insist a word can have many meanings not connected to each other - whilst the Arabs may insist many words can have one meaning. It is the Arabic dilemma of the Arab religion.

The word *ka'aba* in 5:95 and 5:97 is related to the ankles of wild animals, a topic which starts from 5:94. The word is mentioned again indicating that mankind must not hunt these animals until they are matured by distinguishing their ankles (the animals will not settle down in the same area once they are matured), this law is sanctioned in God's system; observe the guidelines, and the indicators restricting the hunting during specific months. Experts identify the animals' maturity by their strides or their moving pattern.

And the wildlife *(wal-Budna)* was set from God's decree *(sha'iril-lah)*, which is for your own good.

> Remember God's name over it while you set sight of
> it and when it falls at a distance. Therefore eat and
> give away from it voluntarily to the people and to
> those who ask. That is what We created for you, so
> that you may be appreciative. (22:36)

The crux of the subject is that wildlife must be
protected and managed according to its lifecycle. People are
not supposed to hunt wildlife during the restricted period
particularly those who believe in the Unseen. If, for
instance, they have violated the decree they must expiate
their wrongdoings voluntarily as prescribed in 5:95. Game
hunting is a test *de facto* for those who fear the *unseen God*.

> O you who believe, God may put you to the test
> through game hunting within the reach of your hand
> and your means. God wants to distinguish those
> among you who fear the Unseen. Anyone who
> transgresses after this has deserved a painful
> retribution. (5:94)

Wildlife should be protected and should be allowed to
live according to God's system. Animals must not be killed
unless they can survive on their own feet (ankles)
characterising maturity. That is all.

The religionists concealed the message in the Qur'an
regarding wildlife conservation and fooled the people to put
on the togas that they call *ihram*. The people were made to
believe the *ankle* of an animal is God's house and they call
a stone cube covered in a cloth with a small black stone
embedded at one corner of it as *baytul-lah* (a word not
found anywhere in the Qur'an). They have made 5:95 to
read:

> O you who believe, do not kill any game during
> pilgrimage. If anyone kills on purpose he shall
> expiate with equivalent livestock judged by two
> equitable people among you as offering to reach
> God's house.

At the risk of repetition, I would like to state again that
offering of animal sacrifices according to the Qur'an is *evil*.
Attributing such religious rites to God is a great blasphemy.
Somehow the enemies of God have successfully diverted
mankind into committing this wicked act by manipulating
God's words in the Qur'an. I have to highlight the verse
again to show the seriousness of this pagan primitive rite:

> They even assign for God a share of the crops and
> livestock He has provided for them, saying, "This is
> for God," according to their claims. And they also
> say, "This is for our idols." However, what was
> assigned to their idols never reach God while that is
> assigned to God will ultimately end up to their idols.
> *Evil* indeed is their Judgement. (6:136)

Food assigned to idols like the stone house can never
reach God. Manipulating a simple sentence *hadyan baligha
al ka'bati* arbitrarily in 9:95 has led millions of people to
perform with diligence a detestable act of needlessly
sacrificing thousands of livestock each year. This is exactly
what is condemned in the above verse. God calls sacrificial
offerings the deeds of the Devil. They are evil.

Each year about two million people slaughter livestock
during their pilgrimage in Mecca as offering to God. The
devotees of the Arab religion also do the same slaughtering

of livestock all over the world on the same day. They call the day of Eid il Adha.[105]

Livestock and wildlife are provisions from God. People should exercise self-sacrifice by donating some of God's provisions to other people. Those who have the privilege of eating the meat of wildlife must donate part of the bounty to other people.

> For every nation We have set their own way of self-sacrifice to remember God's name over the provisions from animals and livestock. Your God is the One God, therefore you must submit to Him and deliver the good news to the obedient whose hearts cringe upon remembering God. They remain steadfast in the face of adversity and they uphold their commitments and give to charity from My provisions to them. Wildlife was ordained as God's decree, which is good for you. Remember God's name over it while you set sights at it and when it falls at a distance. Therefore, eat and give away from it voluntarily to people, those who ask. That is what We created for you, so that you may be appreciative. (22:34-36)

Today's Saudi Arabia uses its oil wealth to build hotels, restaurants and shopping complexes to cater to the pilgrims' needs. Fifty years ago, how could the pilgrims embark on their 'pilgrimage' without depending on wild game for food?

The religionists, however, realised this problem and they provided a simple solution. They say you may not hunt

---

[105] The yearly celebration of the pilgrimage to the stone house in Mecca

only in the immediate vicinity of the so-called 'holy mosque' that stands in Mecca.

Since the skyscrapers around their 'holy mosque' extend a few kilometres away from the mosque proper, game animals perhaps will not even be found in the middle of the desert some fifty–odd kilometres away. Whatever suggestion they offer, no potential pilgrim will make contingencies for a hunting trip when he pays homage to their god or gods.

It is the caretakers of these idols who simply make it up as they go along.

PART TWELVE

U'mra and *Haj*: the invented pilgrimage[106]

The violent and ridiculous Arab religion masquerading as *Islam* today has deceived people into paying homage to a stone building in Mecca. They have manipulated two words in the Qur'an to create a ritual that is erroneously touted as an article of faith in *Islam*. The words *Haj* and *U'mra* were distorted to become *the annual pilgrimage* and *the lesser pilgrimage*[107], respectively. These rituals were not ordained. They are totally contrary to the teachings of the Last Prophet whose duty was to deliver the message of the Qur'an only.[108]

'amr means life

The word *u'mro-ata* that is commonly referred to as the *u'mra* is a derivative from the root word *'m-r* where the apostrophe represents the 'ayn consonant, a laryngeal without equivalent in any Western language.

The root word *'amr* arising from this root refers to the *life* of something. In the Qur'an, this word is used to refer to a continuous act or response carried out with a purpose. For example, if we want to give life to a barren land, we have to develop or cultivate it until we see the result. The Qur'an uses *a'maru* to denote this. When God created humans, He

---

[106] I was startled to discover about this subject. It didn't take me long to know the truth. I assembled all the words on *Haj* and *'amr* in the Quran, and finally discovered the serious distortions about these two words.

[107] The author had performed both these rites and could not forgive himself for his own ignorance. He could have used the money to help the poor and needy.

[108] As people from 'Muslim' backgrounds will know, there is a huge body of extra-Qur'anic literature that supports the non-Qur'anic concepts of pilgrimage. The assertion here is that this extra-Qur'anic literature contradicts rather than supports the initial Qur'anic premises.

ta'mara on them or *gave life to* what He had created. This is also to be found in the Qur'an.

God *U'mrah* to humans

When you tell Muslims God *U'mrah* to human, in all probabilities, they will get into a trance. They never heard such a thing in their life. That is exactly what was revealed in the Qur'an.

From the same root word *'amr* (life) we see that God is forever performing the act of *u'mrah* (giving life) to humans so that they remain alive or *m'amuri* for a certain period of time which, in turn, is the *'umur* or age when the life expires. Thus, the word *u'mrah* cannot be translated as holy *visit* because these words come from the same root.

However, should He decide to stop a life from prospering, He says at 35:11 *wama-yu-'am-maru min mu-'am-marin* which, literally, means 'will not continue to give life *(yu-'am-maru)* from the life *(min-mu'am-marin)*'.

To illustrate the point, here are two more examples:

> *Huwa ansha akum minal ard was* ta'mara-kum *fi-haa fas-taq-fi-ruhu som-ma tubu ilai-hi* (11:61)

> He is the One who created you from the earth and gives life *(ta'mara-kum)*[109] to you in it. Therefore, you shall ask for forgiveness and repent. (11:61)

> *La-'amru-ka*[110] *in-nahum lafi-shak-ro-bihem yak-mahun* (15:72)

---

[109] When you tell Muslims *'God gives life to humans'* in English they can accept it as a fact. When you tell them in *'God u'mrah the humans'* they say you are crazy. That is the power of mental slavery.

By your <u>life</u>, surely they are intoxicated in their wandering. (15:72)

Humans give life (*u'mra*) to the earth

In order to advance in life, humans are capable of giving life to the earth inherited by them. In 30:9, we see that vigorous communities will become successful once they develop what is at their disposal. The Qur'an says there were some previous communities which were strong and successful after they *'amaru* the earth, or gave life to the earth upon cultivating it.

> *Wa-asha-rul ard-tho wa-'amaru-ha ak-saror min-man 'amaru-ha wa-ja-athum rosuluhum bil-bai-ina-ti* (30:9)

> And they initiated on earth and (*'amaru-ha*) <u>gave life</u> to it more than these have (*'amaru-ha*) <u>given life</u> to it, and their messengers went to them with clear revelations (30:9)

The word *'amaru* in 30:9 and *ta'mara* in 11:72 have the same essence of meaning signifying the act of accomplishing a cause, and both words are derived from the same root: *'amr*. Literally, the two verses are making reference to the act of giving life or prospering.

We also find the word *m'amur* from the same root word that means *alive* or *living* in 52:4 to signify the continuous state of being alive.

> *Wal-baitil m'amuri* (52:4)

---

[110] This is where the root word *'Amr* is found. *'Amr* means life - *'Am-ru-ka* means *'your life'*. This word can generate many other derivatives including *U'mra* without losing the same essence of the meaning.

And the <u>living</u> system. (52:4)

A careful examination of the context shows that this passage was wrongly translated in the service of the Arab religion. The religionists insist that translators should (ridiculously) translate the word *baitil m'amuri* as the *frequented shrine* or *much-frequented house*. In the beginning, they said the word *bayta* meant *house*, but this time around, the house is elevated to the status of a shrine or temple. The word *ma'muri* that means *alive* was ridiculously translated to become *frequented*. This is another example how passages in the Qur'an were simply distorted by the enemies of God and His messenger to make nonsense of a statement in the Qur'an. The frequenting of a shrine may have been suitable to the pre Qur'anic Arabic pagan faith, but is not appropriate in the light of the Qur'anic revelation.

The word *baiti-ma'muri* in 52:4 is a continuation of the context from 5:1:

> *wat-thoori*[111] (52:1)
> *wa-kitaa-bin mas-thoo-ri* (52:2)
> *fi-rok-khi man-shoo-ri* (52:3)
> *wal baiti-<u>ma'muri</u>* (52:4)
> *was-sak-fil mar-fu-'e* (52:5)
> *wal-bar-ril mas-juri* (52:6)

By the article (52:1)
and the recorded article (52:2)
in exposed scrolls (52:3)

---

[111] The word *'Thoor'* was wrongly translated as Mountain in all translations. We cannot imagine how God raised the mountain and told the Children of Israel to uphold it strongly (2:63 and 2:93). Yet when the same word is appended as *Mas-Thoor* it becomes the recorded book.

and the <u>living</u> system (52:4)
and the sky raised high (52:5)
and the oceans that fills with waves (52:6)

There is only one *bayta* in the Qur'an. It is the same one pointed out to Abraham 2:125, and purified by him for those who are devoted (*a'kiffin*) and for those who humble themselves in submission (*wa-roka'is-sujud*).

In 52:4, we are told that at the time Moses received the Scripture, God's system was alive before he became a prophet. Muhammad appeared many thousand years after him. Besides, there is no historical record to show Moses went to Mecca.

The message revealed to Moses is an indication that God's system existed and was alive, and that it would continue to be in that state after the Scripture was revealed to him. The Qur'an merely states the same system and the same message were given to Moses and Abraham as were revealed to the Last Prophet:

This is the same as in the previous Scriptures, the Scripture of Abraham and Moses. (87:18-19)

The word *baitil-ma'muri* has nothing to do with an altar, house, tabernacle, shrine, temple, synagogue, church, mosque or any house of 'worship'. The Qur'an simply abhors all forms of worship, religious rites or ritual prayer. These are but man-made. It is humans who declare holy or sacred what they themselves have.

The religionists were competing with other religions and fooled people into worshipping what their own grandfathers had worshiped. They took advantage of the circumstances to attribute their pagan rites and formulas to

God because the Qur'an had been revealed in Arabic and they were the self-proclaimed keepers of the faith. That is all.

The word *u'mra* in the Qur'an does not refer to a special journey or religious visit to be performed at a particular place. *U'mra* simply means to *give life* or *propagate* or *promote* God's prescribed submissions or the *masa-jidil-lah*.

> *In-nama ya'muru masa-jidil-lah man-amana-bil-lah wal-yaumil akhirah al-ak-siru wa-aqor-mus-solaa ta-wa-ataz zaka-ta wa-lamyaksha il-lal-lah fa-'sha. Ulaa-ika aye-yaku-nu minal-muh-tadin (9:18)*
>
> The only people who deserve to <u>promote</u> (*ya'muru*) God's prescribed submissions (*masa-jidil-lah*) are those who believe in God and the Last Day. They observe their commitments and keep them pure. They fear no one except Allah. They are the ones who are guided. (9:18)

The word *masajidal-lah* itself has been translated as a plural to mean *mosques of God*. If what the religionists are saying were indeed true, then all the mosques around the world would need to be owned by God. Then again, they insist that the people must *ya'muru* (or *promote*) only one mosque, the one in Mecca. If anyone refers to any mosque outside his or her country as *masa-jidil-lah* they will accuse them of blasphemy and declare that they deserve to be stoned to death[112].

---

[112] In the Quran there is no death sentence for any offences. In 2:178 it says, 'if someone kills another person the next of kin may judge the offender according to the law of equivalence followed by 2:179, 'Equivalence shall be life-saving law. O you who posssess intelligence - that you may observe'.

How the *u'mra* in 9:19 was distorted

In their rendition of 9:18 the religionists declare firmly that the meaning of the word *ya'maru* is to <u>frequent</u> God's mosque.

Yet they claim the same word in 9:19 means *managing the holy mosque*. Both words are derived from the same root *'amr*. Some translators even say *inhabiting the holy mosque*. That is the extent of their twisting.

According to the Qur'an, a person who manages or administers something is called *'amil* (from the word *'amila*). The root for *'amil* is *'-m-l* and the root for *'umra* is *'-m-r*. They are not the same. The word *'amil* appears several times in the Qur'an:

> *In-namas sor-da-qortu lil fuqoror wal-masakin wal-'amilin alai-ha (9:60)*

> Indeed, the charity shall go to the poor and the needy and those <u>administering</u> it. (9:60)

It may be favourable for the religionists to mislead the Muslims about the meaning of the Arabic words in the Qur'an, but they are powerless to alter the original texts. Unlike other books, the Qur'an has never been reviewed or edited. If we pick up a Qur'an written, say, 800 years ago or more from any country and compare it with the most recent text printed from anywhere in the world, we will find the Arabic texts, word for word and sentence for sentence, to be exactly the same. The author strongly believes the statement in the Book is true in nature, form and effect when it says:

> *Indeed, it is We who revealed the reminder, and surely We will guard it. (15:9)*

347

The religionists' erroneous claim that the Qur'an was written on leaves, parchments, stones, and animal skins. It is inconceivable and ludicrous that a message as important as the Qur'an should be revealed to mankind and then be recorded on parchment, leaves, stones and the like.

Obviously, the only way left to deceive mankind was by tongue-twisting tactics: convince the people that the Qur'an is untranslatable (like the Jews said about the Torah) so that the religionists can continue to distort the meaning of the Scripture, and then proclaim that the basis of whatever they say is from God. The followers of the Arab religion around the world are caught in this web after placing their trust in the priests who learnt their craft from the corrupt Arab sages. The Qur'an did not forget to tell us about them:

> Indeed there are among them traitors who twist their tongues with the Scripture so that you may think it is from the Scripture when they are not from the Scripture. And they claim it is from God when it is not. They have ascribed lies to God while they knew. (3:78)

A chain reaction begins once one word is distorted in the Book. They have to distort other words too. There is no end to the distortions, and most of the time the distorted passage becomes absurd when read as a whole. Today, the Book is seen as an inward-looking archive, particularly the present-day translations and so-called exegesis (or *tafsir*) of the Qur'an. This is the terrible result of the wordplay and semantic twisting that the words of the Qur'an have undergone at the hands of those who – more than anyone – should have known better.

Haj is challenge NOT a pilgrimage

One may ask why the concept of *challenge* is relevant to the Qur'an. The fact is that men and women are expected to face many challenges in their life, including the pursuit of knowledge. Unless they sincerely strive to find the right path, they became blind followers and are subjected to mental bondage. God endows both sexes the same freedom. Both were expected to think by themselves for their own good and well being. Nobody has the right to take away that freedom - in the name of God or whatsoever. Both men and women are given the equality to think critically, weigh and consider everything and verify everything. They should think about consequences before they make their decision.

God assists them in the way they themselves wanted to go. If a man or woman decides to reject God's revelation, they will not harm the Supreme God. In fact, God will encourage them to do so.

> As for those who reject our revelations, We will lead them on without their ever realising it. In fact, I will encourage them. Indeed My scheming is formidable. (7:182-183)

The same applies in all of life. If we choose not to subdue our eyes and keep chaste, God will lead us on without even realising that we are committing what we are not supposed to commit. Whatever good happens to us is from God, and whatever bad happens to us is from our own wrong doings.

When someone instructs us to travel to Mecca to perform a pilgrimage for the sake of God, we have the right to ask why. After all, humans are expected to use the power of reason.

After looking at the Qur'anic texts, I cannot find any straightforward indication of a pilgrimage. 3:97 however does give an ambiguous hint of a possible journey. This verse when read in isolation raises more questions than it answers. To understand the message we need only to read the two preceding verses to realise that the verses are not describing what the religionists want us to think they are describing. The essence of these verses is that God's system was established for those with strong conviction. The verse actually gives us very important clue – '*In the system there are profound signs of Abraham*'. It is the duty of those with conviction to take the challenge to search for such a system as well.

Lin-nas	for mankind
Lal-lazi	of those
Bi	with
Bakata	conviction

This passage was discussed under the sub heading of '*What is in the Bayta*' in Part Eight.

After having corrupted the word '*umra* to become *visit*, the religionists twisted the meaning of *Haj* to become the *annual pilgrimage*.

The root of *Haj* is *H-j*. The key concept connected with this root is *challenge* or *confront*.

The inconsistency becomes apparent in the variety of applications. While traditional *Islam* teaches that *Haj* means *pilgrimage*, it applies the derivatives of this word for example *ta-hajaa* and *yu-hajuu* to mean *argue*. This is their confusion and contradiction. For them, the same words mean wholly different things in different verses of the Qur'an.

The Qur'an categorically uses the word *jadal*[113] to mean *argue* and it is used many times. In 11:32, the people of Noah accused Noah of 'arguing' too much with them. They say 'you argue' with 'too many arguments'.

> *Qolu ya-Nuhu qod jadal-tana fak-sharta jadala-na fa'tinabiha ta'eduna ainkonta minal sodiqeen.* (11:32)

> They say, "O Noah, you argue with too many arguments. Bring us the doom you are threatening, if you are truthful." (11:32)

Clearly the word *jadal* mentioned in this verse refers to the 'arguments' between Noah and his people.

During the time of the Last Prophet there was a woman who successfully 'argued' with him:

> *Qod sami' allah qaula lati <u>tu-jadil-ka</u> fi-zaujiha wa-tastaki il-lal-lah. Wal-lah yasma'hu taha-wurokuma. In-nal-lah sami'un basir* (58:1)

> God heard the woman who argues with you about her husband and complained to God. And God heard the discussions. God is Hearer and Seer. (58:1)

The woman did not complain to the Prophet about her husband. She argued with the Prophet and then complained to God. From these two verses we see 'argue' cannot be

---

[113] The religionists expect everyone to believe that the word *Jadal* and *Haj* are two different words sharing one meaning.

classified under the same category of challenge. Furthermore it has a root word by itself.

Let me take a slight diversion from the subject. In the Arab religion women are considered second-class citizens and the rest of people cannot question or argue with the mullahs. Mullahs expect women to worship them, whereas in the Qur'an we are told there was a woman who argued with the prophet. So, what is so great about the deceitful mullahs?

Now let us return to the subject proper. In 42:16, two derivatives from the root *Haj* or *H-j* are used. The first word is *Hajuu* and the second word is *Hujaa* which are more appropriately translated as *challenge* and *confrontation*.

Let us examine the verse:

wallazi	and those who
yuHajuuna	challenge
fillah	about God
min	from
ba'dimaa	after what
tuhiiba	they received
lahu	with it
Hujaatuhum	their confrontation
dahidhothan	are nullified
a'inda	according to
robbihim	their Lord
wa'alaihim	and upon them
ghadhabun	the wrath
walahum	and for them
'azabun	punishments
shadid	severe

352

The words *Hajuu* and *Hujaa* come from the same root word: *Haj*.

The verb form is derived from the *H-j* root and is third person imperfect signifying future. In the Hereafter, the followers will confront their priests or religious scholars asking them if they can spare them the hell-fire. In 40:47 it says:

Wa-izza-ya-ta-haa-ju fin-nar (40:47)
And when they dispute in the fire (40:47)

In 40:48 the religious priest and the scholars will say to their followers, '*We are in this together, God has judged the people*'. When the followers speak to their religious scholars in the Hereafter it shows that they do not argue or quarrel with their leaders. The word *yata-Hajuu* in 40:47 means *dispute*.

'*Hajii Akhbar*' means the 'Big challenge'

The point is that the key concepts connected with the root *H-j* is an intellectual challenge or confrontation based on reason, rational argument, debate or discourse that has nothing to do with going on a pilgrimage.

We find an interesting message in *surah* 9 about a temporary suspension of enmity between God and His messenger against the idol-worshippers:

Reprieve is herein granted from God and His messenger to those among the idol-worshippers who sign a peace treaty with you. Thus, you may roam the earth freely for four months, and know that you can never escape from God, and that God will inevitably defeat the rejecters. And a declaration is herein issued from God and His messenger on the Great Day of Challenge (*yau-mal-Hajii-akbar*), that God disowns the idol-worshippers, and so does His messenger. If you repent it is good for you. But if you turn away then know that you can never escape from God. (9:1-3)

The believers are encouraged to strive in the path of God against those who are corrupting the earth through idol-worship and religious practice. Humans are supposed to free themselves from any kind of religious bondage and to practice God's way of life in total freedom. Those who can find the way to God's system will discover that religion is part of idol-worship. It is the duty of anyone committed to God's system to strive against idol-worship.

The Great Day of Challenge is the time when a declaration is made to the idol-worshippers that the truth-bearers challenge them. The Qur'an in its infinite wisdom allows a four months peaceful agreement before any engagement in a confrontation. As long as the idol worshipers observe their commitments to the agreement, the truth bearers should not initiate a war against them. Contrary to the traditional understanding of physical war, the Qur'anic concept of war is fought solely for the purpose of cultivating the truth against falsehood.

Nowadays, it can be done in so many ways without anyone having to carry any destructive weapons. After all, the war is about idols. Abraham did not carry any weapon to wage war against his people when he told them to stop serving the idols. He used his common sense. Similarly, we do not need weapons to tell people to use their common senses and stop serving the stone idols carved by the Arabs. Although God encourages the believers to fight against those who fight them, He specifically commanded them not to aggress because He hates the aggressors. If we intend to challenge the disbelievers and the idol-worshippers we are to follow the guidelines the verse sets out.

The non-Muslims have always blamed the teachings of the Qur'an for propagating the killing of 'infidels'. This is an understandable misapprehension. We cannot blame people for associating the Book with the people who profess to believe in it. The war declared in this verse clearly says the enemies are expected *to repent to God and reform*. That is all. If they refuse then they should be told that *they can never escape from God.* In other words, God will deal with them for the falsehood they profess either in this world or in the Hereafter. There is no such thing as a physical war fought against anyone unless the enemies initiated it.

In 2:190-193, it says it is the duty of those who believe in God and the Last Day to strive in the cause of God against those who fight against them, but not to commit aggression. This is the true *jihad* according to the Qur'an. Killing is only allowed if enemies attack you with a view to killing you, and you may evict them only from whence they evicted you.

The Qur'an stipulates that oppression is worse than murder. If the enemies refrain, then there is no reason to fight with anyone. Fighting is encouraged only to prevent oppression so that people can practice God's prescribed submission in total freedom.

During the four restricted months the truth bearers must not fight against their enemies. In case they are attacked during these restricted months, then 2:194 applies.

If they attack you during the restricted months, then you may fight during the restricted months. And sacrilege (the violation of agreement) may be met by equivalent retributions. If they attack you, then you may attack them to inflict an equivalent retribution. However, you shall observe God and know that God is with those who observe Him. (2:194)

Once the restricted months are over, you may attack the idol worshipers wherever you encounter them, agitate them, provoke them and keep after them. However if they repent and observe their commitment and keep them pure, then you shall pardon them. God is forgiver and merciful. (9:5)

The concept of striving in the cause of God (or *jahadu-fi-sabi-lil-lah*) in the Qur'an is the opposite of the *jihad* of the Arab religion. The religionists are happy to kill people. They promise their followers heaven for killing 'infidels'. Such teachings are falsely attributed to God and not to be found anywhere in the Qur'an – a book they have sorely abused.

9:1-4 emphasises the significance of the declaration to disown the idol-worshippers, and that is the day of the Great Challenge or *Hajii Akbar* from the Messenger or those who follow the Messenger. It is *not* a great 'pilgrimage' of any kind.

Hajaa ibrohim

In 2:258 is the story of a man who challenged Abraham. The phrase used is *Hajaa ibrohim*. It should be clear that this does not mean that he sent Abraham on a pilgrimage to Mecca.

Many Muslims who have completed their pilgrimage to the stone idol in Mecca append the word *Haji* to their name (e.g. Haji Sulaiman or Haji Raheemudin) – a habit which Arabs find highly amusing.

> *Alam-tara-ilal-lazi* <u>*Hajaa   Ibrohim*</u> *fi-rob-bi-hi* (2:258)

> Have you not considered the man who <u>challenged Abraham</u> about his Lord with it? (2:258)

Hajaa ibrohim has the same fundamental root as *Haji i'mara-ta mas-jidil-Harami* in 9:19 which refers to the people who take the challenge to promote the sanctioned submission.

This study highlights how the semantic distortions against the Qur'an by the religionists have had a very damaging effect, and how – as soon as they twist one word – a chain reaction occurs because they then have to change the meanings of other words from the same root word to support the deception. *Haj* – as we have seen – has not been left unscathed in this regard.

The Arabic in the Qur'an is easy and perfect. Let us briefly remind ourselves how the Qur'anic Arabic renders nouns denoting people relating to the root-word concepts.

- The meaning of *Solaa* is *commitment* or *obligation*. A man who (singular) is committed is called a *muSollan* (2:125). If plural they are called *muSollin* (107:5).

- The meaning of *Islam* is *peacefulness*. A man who is at peace is said to be a *Muslim* (2:131). If plural, *muslimin* for men and *Muslimat* for women.

- The meaning of *ihtada* is *to be truly guided*. Many guided people are called *muh-tadin* (2:16)

- The meaning of *azan* is to *announce*. A man who makes the announcement is called a *muazzinun* (7:44).

Similarly the meaning of the word *Haj* is *challenge*. People who take the challenge are called *Hajii* (19:19). People who are involved in the challenge are called the *muHajiirin* (9:100).

The challenge is *Haj*. In 3:97 God says take the challenge (*Hajuu*) to His System if we can find our way there. In 2:196 Take the challenge (*Ha-jaa*) to promote (*u'mro-ta*) the guidance (*hadya*) to the people until it is made permissible (*mahilla*). They are the rightful people to promote (*ya'muru*) God's prescribed submission (*mas-jidil-lah*) (9:18) who take the challenge (*Hajii*) (9:19) by promoting (*i'marata*) the sanctioned submission (*masjidil-Harami*).

> It is the duty upon mankind towards God to take the challenge (*Hajuu*) to the system (*bayta*) for those who can find their way. (3:97)

For those who are convinced about God and want to observe His prescribed way of life, they must take the challenge *Hajuu* to His system *'if they can find the way'*. This is the *challenge* or *Haj* only for those who are willing to accept the responsibility to strive in the path of God with their money and lives in promoting the sanctioned submission. Otherwise they can be the ordinary person on the street whilst observing their commitments in doing the good deeds and good works without associating God with anything (or to profess a religion).

The religionists say *Haj* is a pilgrimage culminating in worshipping the stone house in Mecca. This is the extent of their distortion.

We are not to put on the Roman togas, shave our head, throw stones at some brick pillars, kiss a black granite stone, walk in semi-circles around another stone structure crying, "I have come God, I have come" and then walk away feeling satisfied that we have fulfilled our commitments. Rather, we are actively and consciously to take the challenge or the *Haj* to move ourselves closer to living a way of life (*deen*) that is sanctioned by God. That is *Haj* is about.

3:97 states: *'manis-tha-tha'a ilaihi sabiilaan'* which means 'whoever can find his way there'. If pilgrimage were indeed a religious ritual to the *Ka'aba* in today's Mecca in Saudi Arabia, or even the Mecca of 500 years ago, there would be no mystery in finding our way there. Even 500 years ago, people knew where Mecca was. One simply had to get on a camel or horse (or a jumbo jet today) in order to reach it. Where is the difficulty in finding it?

But we cannot get to God's system by jumping on a jumbo jet or riding on a camel. We must take the *challenge* to get there. It is a test of our commitment. We definitely cannot get there by shaving our head, wearing a toga, throwing some stones at a stone pillar like a child, kissing a piece of black granite or walking in circles around another stone pillar. If we insist on doing these things, we become religious morons doing something without using our common sense and without having any knowledge of the Qur'an. It is not difficult for humans to take the challenge *Hajuu* to God's system and be devoted to His System or to humble in submission to His system. His system is not a religion. Period.

Islam or *'peacefulness'* is the universal way of life that can be observed by any human on earth. It requires no institution. Each and every person is responsible for whatever he does during his lifetime. Each will be judged as an individual. We are expected to serve the Lord who created us, and it is our duty to submit to the Lord's prescribed way of life and to preserve its purity.

Haj means an intellectual *challenge* or a *response to a challenge* and it does not mean pilgrimage in any shape or form. Similarly, *hijr* does not mean what the religionists say. It is not primarily about emigration. Its core meanings are related to leaving (i.e. *shunning* or *leaving off*) and in this sense it is connected to the essence with that of the purpose of *Haj*.

> Indeed those who believe and take the challenge (*ha-jaa-ru*) to struggle with the money and lives in the path of God as well as those who shelter and lend support they are protector of each other. But those who believe but have not taken the challenge (*yu-ha-jee-ru*) you owe them no obligation to lend support to them from anything until they take the challenge (*yu-ha-jee-ru*). But if they seek your assistance in the way of life (deen) it is therefore your duty to support them unless there is among you made an agreement with them. God sees whatever you do. (8:72)

Here the word *ha-jaa-ru* and *yu-ha-jee-ru* refers to two types of believers. Both are staying in the same area. Both words were erroneously translated as emigrating by the religionists. A person who strives in the path of God is not required to emigrate from his hometown. The evidence can be found in 3:195.

> Their Lord responds to these by saying, "I never neglect to reward any worker among you, male or female; you are equal to each other. Those among you who take the challenge (*ha-jaa-ru*) and get banished from your homes, I will certainly redeem all their wrongdoings and admit them into gardens with flowing streams". Such is the reward from God. God possesses the best reward. (3:195)

If *ha-jaa-ru* means emigrating, then there is no way they can be banished from their home. Clearly this word refers to the activities of striving in the cause of God by taking the *challenge* which is the *ha-jaa-ru* or to take the challenge in the path of God *ha-jee-ru-fi-sa-bi-lil-lah*.

Abraham, for example, settled in a new place – implying that those who wished to follow him would have to establish their commitment to the sanctioned system. He did not emigrate to another town or country to strive in the path of God.

Moses remained in Egypt until he moved away because of oppression. Moses and his people were banished for striving in the path of God.

Shuaib remained in Midyan and Jacob remained in the desert until his son summoned him to the city. They never moved to a new town to promote God's *deen*.

Jonah tried to flee from his people but was severely dealt with.

In spite of rejection, Jesus did not move to another place. On the other hand, we have a key example (see 2:61) of the Children of Israel who – having physically forsaken Egypt – remained essentially steeped in the things which Egypt had to offer. Was theirs a state of migrating at this point? It would seem not.

Abraham and Ishmael were never in Mecca

There is hard evidence in the Qur'an that Abraham and Ishmael[114] had never stepped their foot in Mecca - unless the Muslims disbelieve what is written in their own Holy Scripture.

There is also no evidence from the Qur'an (including 2:125-129) that Abraham and Ishmael built a physical house. The truth is like Moses, Jesus and other messengers, Abraham and Ishmael were never in Mecca as prophets or messengers to warn the Arabs.

If Abraham had been inspired by God to go to Mecca to build and purify God's house, he would have been duty-bound to warn the Arabs in Mecca and the Arabs around it.

But the Qur'an says the Arabs were gentiles which mean they had no prior knowledge of God's Scripture or received any information about serving God. They had received no warner before Muhammad

> We did not give them the Scripture to study. And **We did not send messengers to them before you as warners.**[115] (34:44)

---

[114] After reading the Qur'an for many years I did not noticed the message in the Book pointing out that there were no messengers or prophets to the Arabs race before Muhammad. Without any Quranic evidence Muslim scholars are parroting their virtual idols that Muhammad was genealogically related to Ishmael through Shu'ib and Salleh. They cannot even show us where is Midyan on the world map.

[115] Warners are God's messengers who deliver the message from God.

This is the hard evidence and it is so easy to understand. *"We never sent to your race any messenger before you became a messenger"*.

Muhammad was the first messenger to the Arabs around him. Since the religionists believe that Muhammad was born in Mecca, there is no way Abraham could have been sent there previously.

The key of submissions to God is to uphold what He had sanctioned in the scripture. The sanctioned submission *(masjidil-harami)* was set for mankind as God's original system *(baytul ateeq)*. The detail of the sanctions was first revealed to Abraham when he was commissioned to become the leader for mankind. Then, Abraham was told to announce it to the people not to pollute these sanctions.

> Indeed those who disbelieve and they prevent others from the sanctioned submission *(masjidil-harami)* which was set for mankind to be devoted equally that is very apparent. And whosoever introduces in it any wickedness We will make him suffer the retribution. And when We settled for Abraham a place in the system (We said to him), *'You shall not associate Me with anything*, keep My system *(bayti-ya)* cleansed for the groups of people who are upright and humble in submission'. And announce to the people with the challenge that was given to you as a person and upon every responsible individuals that was given from every resource enormously so that they witness the benefits for them and that they will remember God's name during the days known to them over whatever provisions (We gave) to them from the animal livestock. Therefore eat from it and feed the needy

and the poor. And then they should remove their impurity and they should fulfil their covenants so that they get used with the original system *(baytil-ateeq)*. And whosoever honour God's restrictions it is therefore righteousness for him by His Lord. And permitted upon you the livestock except what has been recited to you and avoid the uncleanness of idol worship and stay away from false utterances. Be upright for God and do not associate anything with Him..... (22:25-30)

In 60:4 it says, *'A good example has been set for you by Abraham and those with him'*. Abraham and those who followed him kept the sanctioned submission *(masjidil-harami)* purified. They avoided false utterances or *something else* besides God's revelations. Abraham was given with the challenge *(bil-hajii)* as seen in 22:27 to lead the true Muslims to God's system. Abraham did not call anyone to go to Mecca to perform a pagan's rite, but to take the challenge to stay away from idol worship by observing the sanctioned submission *(masjidil-harami)* revealed by God.

If *Haj* meant what the religionists would have us believe it means - all the God-fearing people over the ages – from Abraham onwards – would have had to have made at least one journey to Mecca. There is no evidence in the Qur'an or anywhere else to indicate that Isaac, Jacob, Ishmael, Joseph, Zechariah, John, Moses, Aaron, David, Solomon, Jonah or Jesus travelled to Mecca for any reason whatsoever. And if they had, then the Arabs would have received a messenger before Muhammad which, by their own admission, they did not.

The Arabs were pagans

The religionists were ignorant of God's Scripture and they knew nothing about an orderly way of life or the *deen* adhered to by Abraham, Ishmael, Isaac, Jacob and the other prophets, and nothing about what was revealed to Moses and Jesus. Therefore they had no idea of God's prescribed way of life *(Deen-nil-lah)* encompassing His decrees *(shari'al-lah)*, His limits *(hududul-lah)*, the existence of a harmonious system sanctioned by Him *(aminal-baytal-Harami)*, His prescribed submission *(masa-jidil-lah)*, His sanctioned submission *(masjidil-Harami)* and the concept of 'in the path of God' *(fi-sabi-lil-lah)* which had been known to Abraham, Moses, Jesus and the previous messengers.

God says the Arab race was *ummyin*[116] referring to them as gentiles, a race who had no prior knowledge of God's Scriptures. 62:2 says:

huwal-lazi ba'asha	He is the One who sent
fil-ummyin	in the midst of the gentiles
rosulan min-hum	a messenger from them
yatlu a'laihem	to recite upon them
wa-yuzak-kihem	and to purify them
wa-yua'limuhumul	and the knowledge of
kitaba	the Scripture
wal-Hikmata	and the wisdom
wa-ainkanu	indeed, they were
min-qoblu	from before
lafi-thola-lin mubin	in total loss.

---

[116] The word ummyin was wrongly translated as illiterates by all the popular translations. Many qualified scholars still think this word refers to illiterates and their logic says the whole of Arab race were illiterates. Is there any thinking person who wish to agree with them?

Indeed, before Muhammad was sent to the Arabs, they were in total loss about the orderly way of life or the *deen*. Sadly, but not unexpectedly, they continue to be.

Obviously as pagans they refused to serve God alone. From day one - they rejected the messenger and the revelations. Muslim scholars boast about this man portraying him as the most popular figure among the Arabs but nothing about his disappointment and frustration. Let us read the untold stories about this man from the Qur'an.

First, let us find out about the people around him including those close to him. We see that the Qur'an gives a completely different picture. The u'lema says they have in their possession the sayings of the prophet outside the Qur'an. This is exactly what his close friends demanded from him when he was alive. They said, "Change the Qur'an with *something else*". Obviously Muhammad refused.

> When Our revelations are recited to them, those unmindful of meeting Us say, "Provide us with a Qur'an other than this or why don't you change it?" Tell them, "I cannot change it on my own. I simply follow what is revealed to me. I fear, if I disobey my Lord, of the retribution of a terrible day. It is completely up to God. Had I will, I would not have recited all these to you nor you would ever find out about it. I have lived among you for a long time and you know me well. Why can't you understand?" (10:15-16)

So, where do all the *hadiths* which the Muslim scholars called the sayings of the prophet come from? The Last Prophet told all his friends that he follows only what was revealed to him – and everyone knows the only thing revealed to him was the Qur'an and nothing but the Qur'an.

The *hadiths* of the prophet are actually the *'something else'* besides the Qur'an.

The Last Prophet almost conceded to the demand by his contemporaries in order to maintain the friendship. Out of mercy God strengthened his heart and admonished him in the strongest term that He will inflict the prophet with double punishment in this world and after death - if he had invented *something else* besides the Qur'an.

> They almost diverted you from Our revelations revealed to you because they pressured you to invent *'something else'*. Only with that condition they would have considered you as a friend. If it were not that We strengthened you, you almost leaned towards them a little bit. Had you done so We would have doubled the punishment for you in this life and after death. You would have found no one to help you against Us. (17:73-75)

Now, this is where we see Muslim scholars and the mullahs refused to believe what the Qur'an says. They insist the messenger gave them *'something else'* apart of the Qur'an. They call this *something else* the *Hadiths* of the prophet. In other words, they say the Qur'an is wrong.

Innocent Muslims around the world were deceived by their *u'lemas* that the Last Prophet had many friends. They say he had thousands of followers and supporters. In 9:40 it says he had only one man with him in the cave. What happened to all his other loyal followers?

All Muslim scholars ridiculed the prophet by saying that he was illiterate despite the proof from the Qur'an that this man was a learned person. In 44:14 the Arabs around the Last Prophet said he was a *mu-a'lamun* which means,

367

'he is a learned man', but somehow they also said he was a lunatic or *maj-nun*.

> *An-naa lahumus-zikro. Wa-qod-jaa-ahuum ro-suulon-mubin, som-maa tawal-lau a'nhaa, waqor-luu, **mu-a'lamun**-maj-nun.(44:13-14)*

> How did they respond to the reminder? And surely there came to them an obvious messenger, and then they ignored him and said, 'He is learned (*mu-a'lamun*) but a lunatic (*maj-nun*)'.

Today the religionists, ayatollahs, u'lemas, gurus, mullahs and the so-called Islamic scholars around the world promote the idea that the last prophet was illiterate whereas the Qur'an says the opposite. If they think whatever they utter about the prophet is a simple matter, perhaps they should think what the Qur'an says about slandering:-

> You reiterated the accusation with your tongues, thus uttering with your mouths what you did not know for sure. You also thought it was a simple matter, when it is a very serious offence at the sight of God. (24:15)

If the so-called 'Islamic scholars' can create a flagrant lie about the prophet's literacy – then, the rest is history.

They totally ignored all historical facts written within the pages of the Qur'an about the Arabs around the Last Prophet. The first thing his people said about him:

> This is nothing but a man who wishes to divert you from what your forefathers served. This is nothing except invented lies. This is nothing except magic. (34:43)

Lunatic, liar, magician, fabricator are the common terms used by the Arabs against the prophet. The Arabs around him refused to believe the revelations. To add salts to injury they said he made up the revelations, but God provided the answer:

> Do they say he made it up? Indeed, it is the truth from your Lord to warn a race (*qaum*) which did not receive any warner *before you* so that they may be guided. (32:3)

The Arabs around him were not only staunch disbelievers and hypocrites but they were also good as rumour mongers.

They knew the prophet was preoccupied with writing down the revelations, but they spread some stories to bring into disrepute whatever he wrote.

> The disbelievers (Arabs) said, "This is an invention that he has fabricated with the help of some people". Indeed, they have uttered a blasphemy and falsehood. In addition, they said, "**He is writing** the tales of the past which were dictated to him day and night". (25:4-5)

The prophet was told to inform the disbelieving Arabs:

> Tell them, "(what you were writing) was revealed by the one who knows the secrets of the heavens and the earth. He is forgiving, merciful". (25: 6)

This is another example how the Qur'an is composed. It returns to and reaffirms a single subject in many places. In this verse it says the Arabs were rumour mongers. The *something else* besides the Qur'an that the *u'lema* holds dearly for their salvation is the by-products from them.

369

Contrary to popular belief, the Last Prophet's mission failed to achieve any response from his own people. His disappointment is seen in the following verse:

> Perhaps you wish to kill yourself upon their rejection to believe this message. (18:6)

Some translators indicate that the Prophet wished to commit suicide because the Arabs refused to accept the Qur'an. We can empathise after reading about them in the Qur'an. The modern Arabs claim they are following the teachings of the Qur'an, but the Qur'an is saying the opposite.

As long as the Muslims around the world remain loyal to the Arab religion they will be shackled to a false belief – until the Day of Judgement. On that great day they will listen to the true sayings of the messenger:

> The Messenger will say, my Lord, my people have deserted this Qur'an. (25:30)

These are Qur'anic facts Muslims cannot reject. In the hereafter the messenger will not utter anything about the word *hadith* or *sunna* revered by the Arab priests, but only the Qur'an.

In 34:44 it says the Arabs did not get any warner before Muhammad. There is also no evidence from the Qur'an that Abraham was sent to the Arabs as a warner to teach them construction techniques for the building of a house for God in a place called Mecca. Abraham and Ishmael were not construction workers sent to the Arabs in Mecca.

Abraham was more of a demolition expert who destroyed idols. He did not construct a new idol in the form of a cubic house and then say, "This is God's house!" This is what the polytheists say. They build idols and say, "This is my God!"

The stone house claiming to be the *Ka'aba* in Mecca today is one of the greatest of the religionists' scams. It was the religionists who built it and they have managed to fool hundreds of millions of people into humbling themselves in submission in the direction of a stone house. What people see today is not the universal *peacefulness* sanctioned by God, it is an Arab religion packed with primitive Arab culture and Arab tribal laws.

The 'challenge' for Sunnis & Shiite

The practising Sunnis and Shiite reading this who have thus far believed there is a holy mosque, holy house, holy land, holy water, holy black stone, holy grave and holy footprints should make a choice.

They can either:

1.   Continue to devote and humble themselves to a stone *shrine* or a *stone house* which are entities related to idol-worship (and they should remember that whatever they conceal in their hearts does not escape God).

Or:

2.   Stop worshipping the stone idol in Mecca and serve the One God by devoting and humbling themselves in submission through God's system (*bait*) based on the teachings of the Qur'an alone, free from religious intention and invention.

Which would *you* rather answer for on the Last Day?

In spite of the fact you were born Muslims, that does not deprive you of your right to exercise your freedom to think, speak, and to express your opinions with the *truth*.

The mental bondage is inherited from your innocent parents who inherited it from their forefathers. They were the generations of the past – they await whatever they have earned – while you await what you earned. You will not be questioned about what they have been doing.

Thus, the final say is with *you alone*. You decide whether to remain shackled or to unshackle *yourself* from the chains that bind you. You cannot experience what you are unwilling to express.

Before we proceed to the concluding chapter let us embrace one of the most logical approaches by taking an intellectual challenge against clergy and scholars of the Arab religion - the group of people who claim they are carrying the Word of God to Muslims the world over.

A message to Arab religionists

This is a special message to the priests of the Arab religion who claim they are following the Qur'an. The primary challenge I wish to put to you revolves around five basic questions:

- Does Allah, the Lord of the Universe, reside in a house in Mecca?

- Are you sure the empty square rock structure in Mecca was fashioned on direct orders from God?

- Why do you bow and prostrate to the rock idol every day?

- Will you continue to fight God and destroy His measurable way of life or do you wish to preserve the *deen-nil-lah* as revealed to the Messenger?

- How can you 'serve' a rock structure carved by the Arabs? Was it not God who created the Arabs and the rocks? Why do you lead the people to worship it?

The crux and basis of the Arab religion resides in the rock hunk mistakenly called the *Ka'aba*. Without this stone house the 'religion' cannot exist. Think about it. Surely the eternal sufferings of your soul in the Hell fire will depend on your sense of reasoning. I would like to quote the words of the messenger Sallih[117] who said to his people: *'Thus, you shall seek clemency, and then repent to Him'*. (11: 61)

My challenge to the clergy, then, is to:

---

[117] A prophet mentioned in the Qur'an whose name and deeds are not known in the Christian or Jewish dispensations.

- Pick up a trade or profession for the benefit of society and uphold your commitments to obey God and His messengers and keep them pure.

- Serve God and submit to His prescribed Way – or the *deen-nil-lah* – on the basis of the Qur'an alone.

However, those of you with a point of view which differs from what is outlined here and who have pledged to lead the flocks on the true path and have any basis from the Qur'an to substantiate such 'vernacular' *Islam*, please bring evidence from the Qur'an.

The Qur'an maintains that: *'produce your evidence if you are truthful'* and it also says *'opinion is not the substitute for the truth'*. Those of you leading your flocks to the square rock house should perhaps ponder on another reference to rocks in the Hereafter:

*Beware of the hell-fire whose fuel is **people and rocks**. It is waiting for those who have rejected.* (2:24)

If that alone cannot make you to reflect, then wait - and I am waiting along with you.

For the faithful and the discerning, the days of rhetorical acrobatics and tongue twisting are over. If *'the prophet cannot guide anyone including those whom he loves'* (28:56), how are you going to guide the people when you yourselves need God to guide you?

There is no such thing as theology in God's Scriptures. In 6:59 it says 'At Him are the keys to all secrets; *nobody will know about Him except He'*, and in 6:103 it says *'No vision can encompass Him, while He encompasses all vision'*. How is it then, you claim you know what God is and what He wants?

374

The Qur'an says God is the <u>only one</u> Who guides[118] – He is the one who created us[119] - He teaches people by means of the pen – He teaches them what they never knew[120] – He is the only one who gives them the clear knowledge about His signs[121].

Perhaps Muslims could have been leaders in science, physics or biology if they have studied *God's signs* in the heavens and the earth – unfortunately their minds were shackled to a belief which promotes decadence. In 2:164 it says *'there are signs in the heavens and the earth for intelligent people'*...... The scientists studied the sun and moon, the space within the universe, water cycle, the manipulation of the wind, Electro magnetic force, radio waves, sailing, the clouds and the fruits including the grains. These are among the subjects mentioned in 2:164 and in many other verses of the Qur'an, and the Westerners are precursors in these fields today. They are the true servants of God who studied God's signs in the heavens and the earth for the benefit of mankind.

For example, at the time when the West was striving hard to fly - they studied God's sign about the manipulation of the wind – but the non-Arab *u'lemas* were busy finding ways how to master the medieval Arabian myth and culture. When the West advanced from solo gliding to supersonic speed breaking the sound barrier the *u'lemas* continued to ignore God's signs in the heavens and the earth, instead they were engrossed with pagan rituals and rites. Despite

---

[118] You can never guide anyone. God is <u>the only one</u> who guides in accordance with His will. (2:272)

[119] He is the one who created the Humans (55:3 & 96:1)

[120] He teaches them by the pen and He teaches them what they never knew. (96:4-5)

[121] He teaches mankind about His signs in the sky and the earth (55:1-4)

the comfort of travelling from one country to another in business class of Jumbos and Airbuses the *u'lemas* say the Western ideas and technologies are secular-based and they are infidels. Surely this is vicious and unjust. Without secularism, Muslim scholars all over the world will become parasites in their own village. The Muslims today cannot even think how invent, design or manufacture consumer products for global market. There are among them who cut some twigs from the trees to use as toothbrushes and then attribute the vapid acts to the messenger.

There is also no such thing as the 'knowledgeable' or '*u'lema*' in God's prescribed way of life or the *deen-nil-lah*. The sly *u'lemas* misled the people by quoting sura 35:28 out of context claiming that; it is they who reverence God, thus they qualify themselves by that name. If we read the verse properly it says:

> Do you not see that God sends down the water from the sky to produce fruits of various colours? The mountains show white and red streaks of different shades and shining black, also the people, the animal and the livestock are of different colours? That is why the servants of God who truly reverence Him are the knowledgeable *(u'lama)*. God is almighty and forgiving. (35:27-28)

The Arabic word *u'lama* is defined by the Qur'an as those who are knowledgeable about God's sign in the heavens and on earth – not about religion. This is the only verse the word *u'lama* appears in the Qur'an besides 26:197 (referring to the knowledgeable among the Children of Israel). This verse excludes the self-proclaimed experts in rituals and rites. Unfortunately it is the same experts who allege those well founded in knowledge in scientific fields are seculars and un-Islamic.

The pseudo-scholars have deviated despite having prime access to God's revelations, and continue to mislead the people from the path of God and defame the Qur'an by their actions while publicly bearing witness that it is the truth. This is no way to fulfil their covenants with God according to the Qur'an.

For those choosing to ignore the warnings so clearly stated in the Qur'an, it is appropriate to remember:

- Indeed, these revelations are clear in the chest of those who possess knowledge. Only the wicked disregard our revelations. (29:49)

- Some people argue about God without knowledge, without guidance and without an enlightening Scripture. (22:8)

- You cannot guide those you love. God is the one who guides whomever He wills. He is fully aware of those who deserve the guidance. (28:56)

- To Him belong the past and the future, and no one attains His knowledge except in accordance with His will. (2:255)

- Have you noticed those who claim for themselves to be pure? God is the only one who purifies whomever He wills without injustice. Look how they invent lies to attribute to God. (4:49-50)

Thus, my question to you; Have you taken a promise from God that He never breaks His promise; or do you declare yourself to be pure without basis?

Do you still want to guide the people when God categorically says that there is no provision for this?

Do you not know that God's prescribed way of life – the *deen-nil-lah* – does not depend on the Arabian culture, dress or language?

Many study the Arab religion, but ignore the *deen*. This *deen* is now full of rituals, incantations, liturgies, physical body movements and 'religion' all of which you give testimony to. You insist on 'worship'. God does not need worship. He wants every individual to serve Him through their personal commitments, by the doing of good deeds. All the messengers of God were sent to demolish religion, worship, pagan rituals, and rites; namely, to get rid of the self-same type of system you are upholding. In this, and thus in all things, you are fighting God and His messengers in order to promote a pagan way of life. Beware, for you have picked a formidable foe!

Defenders of the faith such as Noah, Abraham, Ishmael, Isaac, Jacob, Joseph, Moses, Aaron and Jesus pioneered God's prescribed way of life – the *deen-nil-lah*. They demolished religion. The Last Prophet's mission was no different.

All of them had one common objective. They sincerely believed that the revelation was the truth from their Lord and they fulfilled their vows by upholding the covenant. They then 'linked' (*ya-siluu*) whatever was commanded by God as the providence to bind (*ai-yu-Solaa*) the people to an orderly way of life in doing the good deeds and good works to serve their Lord who created them.

They never disseminated their own ideas nor abused God's revelations for personal interest. They never tried to manipulate God's word they way you do. None of them earned a living through the deen. They never substituted the truth with falsehood or concealed the truth knowingly whilst enjoining righteousness upon the people. Besides, none of them tried to impress the common folks with weird religious garbs or became priests or u'lemas.

Most importantly none of them promised heaven to anyone, including Muhammad.

The following verse is repeated four times in the Qur'an. The many examples of the faithful in history who lived according to the prescribed *deen* should be a lesson to us:

We have cited in this Qur'an every kind of example, that they may take heed. (39:27; 17:89; 18:54; 30:58)

The priests of the Arab religion are the fruit of the efforts of the pagan Arabs who sought to impose their brand of religion on the innocent and sincere people. The nature of their 'programming' brooks no dissent or non-conformity and has produced recruits the world over with pre-programmed behaviour guaranteed to uphold and advocate their values and their teachings. You have slandered Abraham, the chosen leader of mankind, who was totally committed to God's prescribed way of life. Moreover, you have created the tale that Abraham was the first person to worship the stone idol in Mecca. Even Muhammad has not been spared of your slander.

Therefore, the author maintains it is infinitely unwise for you to continue on this path. Such behaviour is self-destructive in this life and the next - not only yours but also the Muslims of today and tomorrow. As a man of peace, I appeal to you to come back to your sense and do not associate God with anything tangible. Last but not least, do not say about God other than the truth and He is much too glorious to be associated with your rock idol.

CONCLUSIONS

The message of the Qur'an

The basic message of the Qur'an is to observe God the Lord of Universe by submitting to the way of life prescribed by Him. It is to believe in the One God and the Last Day and to work righteousness; it is to fulfil one's obligations by upholding the covenants one commits oneself to.

In God's prescribed submission (*mas-jidil-lah*) there are also God's decrees and God's limits which are the *sha'iral-lah* and *hududul-lah* respectively. These are the sanctioned submissions (or *masjidil-Harami*). Whoever we are and wherever we may be, we as individuals must focus ourselves to the sanctioned submission.

For example, in 5:3 God prescribes the limits of restrictions about food. He says, prohibited for us is the consumption of:

1. blood
2. carrion
3. the decaying meat
4. food dedicated to other than God
5. animals that die through violent death.

The subject of food is among God's decrees. God sanctioned these prohibitions in the submission. Those who submit to the *deen* are required to focus on these sanctions.

> You shall focus towards the sanctioned submission (*masjidil-Harami*). Wherever you may be, you shall focus on it. Even those who received the previous Scripture recognise that this is the truth from their Lord. God is never unaware of what you do. (2:144)

381

God says He is aware of everything we do. He is not concerned with where we live or where we go. But wherever we are we must focus on the sanctioned submission revealed by Him.

Each time God instructs His servants to observe a certain set of commitments He indicates this by saying, *'these are the limits of God'*. For example:

> Divorce may be retracted twice. Thereafter, you shall allow them to stay in your home amicably if they so desire, or allow them to go amicably. You shall not take anything back you have given to them, unless the couple fears the violation of God's limit (*hududul-lah*). If they fear the violations of God's limit (*hududul-lah*) then they incur no sin if the wife forfeits anything voluntarily. These are God's limits. You shall not transgress them. If anyone transgresses God's limits (*hududul-lah*), then they are wicked. (2:229)

These are God's prescribed limits for individuals to uphold in this domestic institution. The prescribed limits (or *hududul-lah*) are mentioned 14 times and they are confined to domestic issues. The religionists have abused the word *hudud* by introducing a set of barbaric laws of their own contrivance which they have named the *hudud* law. Naturally, it has nothing in common with sane and balanced Qur'anic injunctions.

This is how they abuse God's name. In the *hudud* law they invented – which goes by the same name God chose for His limits – they can stone people to death, annul marriages arbitrarily without hearing the parties involved, declare you an apostate measured against their Arab religion, incarcerate you for not professing the Arab religion, banish you from the state and confiscate your property. And this they do in the name of God!

Here is another challenge to the *u'lema* priests. There is not a single *hudud* law in the Arab religion implemented by the so-called Islamic countries which is derived from the Qur'an. Not one. Can you prove otherwise? If not then hang up your robes and do something more useful with your lives before it is too late.

The Arabic tribal laws (which they call *hudud* laws) were not prescribed by God in the Qur'an. The true prescribed limits or *hudud* in the Qur'an are fair principles which are meant to be interpreted and applied by individuals without any religious elements. These are the facts.

Serve God as individuals

Since the time of Adam God has dealt with His servants as individuals. He created every person on the face of the earth, and each will come before Him as an individual on the Day of Judgement. He does not share His kingship with anyone and He has *never* allowed any of His servants – not even prophets – to forcibly impose any of His prescribed limits on anyone.

The religionists were not requested by God to build a building called 'God's house'. They built a cubical stone structure which began life as a temple and is now an idol in the middle of another temple – one which is no different from the temples the 'Muslims' regard as pagan.

No matter what we want to believe, we cannot go against the truth from God when He says the Arabs are the worst community. Translators are forced to exonerate the

Arabs by saying the word *a'robi* mentioned in the Qur'an refers to the Bedouins or a special brand of the Arab race. God is explicit in everything. The word *a'robi* has nothing to do with the Bedouins. The Bedouins are called *Baduu-na-fil-A'robi* – a term which is also found in the Qur'an. The word *a'robi* means the Arabs in general including the city-dwellers.

> And those who are around you from the Arabs are hypocrites and from the people of the City. They persist in hypocrisy and whilst you may not know them, We know them. (9:101)

The Qur'an was good on the day it was revealed; it is good at present and it will remain good until the Day of Judgement. When it refers to the Arabs it means just that: *Arabs*. The Arabs must solve the problem among themselves of identifying the guilty ones. Meanwhile nobody can change the truth in the Qur'an and none can abrogate the verses to say something nice about the non-believing Arabs. Unless they repent and believe in the Qur'an, God condemns these people forever. The question is: *will they admit their wrongdoings and will they repent?*

Perhaps the innocent Arabs may find the answer if they ask themselves the significance of an orderly way of life towards peacefulness with the following:

- Is there a concept of *the house of God* for peacefulness?

- Can they attain global peace by cherishing a rock structure and called it God's house?

- What has the stone house and a little black granite, two outcropping rocks, a copper block, and stone pillars got to do with God?

- What kind of peacefulness towards mankind can they achieved when they perform the religious rites around a rock structure built by their own hands?

These ideas are not found in the Qur'an.

From being a reconstructed cubical house surrounded by sand forty years ago, the 'Ka'aba' is now a lavish building with Italian marble floor fitted with water pumps to channel the refrigerated 'reverse-osmosis' water from beneath the cube house (which they claim to be holy). On the Arab soil everything and anything is possible with a little bit of imagination. The rocks can be made divine and the desalinated seawater can be made sacred.

The religionists pronounced only two magic words – 'Zam-Zam' – without having to Houdinise the process to turn the sea water to become 'Holy'. Today Muslims all over the world will include 20-50 litres of Zam-Zam water in their excess baggage to take home.

Only the religionists could come up with an idea as ridiculous as placing God's house in Mecca and then making the Devil His neighbour in nearby Mina.

As far as the poor visitors are concerned, they are not interested in the true meaning of the word *u'mro-ata* or *Haj* because these words are in Arabic. They leave the language to the religionists. Their main concern is to perform the *u'mrah* and the *Haj* even if they have to bow and prostrate to the local mountain rocks.

Dialectical Acrobatics

Some of the idol-worshippers *(mushrikin)* say the stone house in Mecca represents the *glory* of God; others say that it is only God's house *symbolically*. Such are their dialectical acrobatics. Similarly, they say the pillar in Mina is not the Devil but it *symbolises* the Devil. Why on earth do they need to symbolise God when God is omnipresent and omnipotent and why in God's name do they give dignity and recognition to the Devil by 'symbolising' him at all?

Symbol means something that represents something else by association, resemblance, or convention, especially a material object used to represent something invisible. Now, this is exactly what the Muslims are associating with the Supreme God.

The fundamental teaching of Qur'an propagates the belief of the unseen God and it clearly says, "*This scripture is infallible; a guide for those who are observant and believe with the **unseen**"* (2:2-3) and the most important commandment brought by Moses, Jesus and Muhammad was, "***You shall NOT serve except God***" (17:23).

When people make it a duty upon themselves to visit a symbol - they are actually associating and serving the symbol with the Supreme God. But the Qur'an says, "*God will NOT forgive the association of anything besides Him... Anyone who sets any idol besides God has forged a great blasphemy*"(4:48). And the Qur'an also says, the human being tends to believe only what he sees in front of him (75:5).

Yet some idol-worshippers claim they need the square rock structure in Mecca as the direction to focus their ritual prayers. Unfortunately there are no instructions in the Qur'an that people should face a specific direction when they pray - but there is a clear injunction that they should focus their direction to God's prescribed sanctions as revealed in the Qur'an.

After considering all the evidence from the Qur'an, there is no doubt that the meaning of *u'mra-ata* (commonly known as the *'umra*) is *to give life to* or *promote* God's prescribed submission (*mas-jidil-lah*). It does not talk about promoting a stone structure built by the Arabs in Mecca.

It is the duty of those who subscribe to the *deen* to cleanse the system, keep it pure and respond to the challenge by striving in the path of God against the idol-worshippers and the disbelievers who are polluting (or have polluted) God's *deen*.

Humans need a paradigm shift to follow the *deen* ordained by God. It is our duty to take the challenge to God's system. It is a system of observing the moral conduct based upon universal values. It is a simple concept and easy to be observed by any man or woman.

Those who *submit* to the system are assured of safety. At the very least, they will be free from the shackles that bind them. God's system can be observed by anybody irrespective of gender, racial origin, culture or colour. All people are equal in the sight of God because He is the One who created them, therefore, they should observe Him the way He should be observed. I wish to remind the reader again that when I use the term He or Him, it does not mean God is being personified.

Mankind should respond to take the challenge *(Hajuu)* to God's system *(bayta)* and give life to it *(i'mara-ta)* so that they can enjoy the true peacefulness. Religion is the greatest enemy of *peacefulness* or *Islam*. Forget about the Arab religion, the religion of Christianity, and the religion of Judaism or any other religion. Leave it to God to deal with those who follow religion to disbelieve in Him.

How could anyone disbelieve in God, when they were nothing, and then He gave them life (to live in this world), and then He will put them to death, and then He will bring them back to the next life? Of course the most difficult part is to be very certain about the life in the hereafter. Perhaps less than one percent of the world population do not believe in such a thing. What does it cost to believe in it? Absolutely nothing! What IF there is there is such a thing as life after death? Perhaps at that time it would be too late to find out that no amount of money can buy us out, no one can avail another, no one can be helped, and no intercession will be accepted. Or, it is too late to even realise all ties among us are severed and we return to the One who granted us life and death - to be judged as individuals.

No matter who we are, surely none will escape from the One who granted us life and death. That Unseen Power will inevitably make us answerable for everything we do in this life. He has counted every single one of us and everything that is in the skies and on earth - male or female. Every single one of us is nothing except a slave of our Master who created us. Is it worth to follow masters beside that One Master?

God has made everything easy for mankind. He will not burden any soul beyond its mean. Thus, people can observe His way from their residences, offices or wherever they may be. Judged by the standards of the Qur'an the people who are dressed in weird 'religious' attire and involved in 'worship' are far from God's deen. They are bowing and prostrating to the direction of the rock cube - consciously or not – worshipping a stone idol. I have quoted

Sura 6:159 in the early chapter of this book, people who are following a way of life according to religion are not following any of God's prophets. God sent His prophets to promote peacefulness by observing good deeds and virtuousness - not 'religion'.

The corruptions

Here is a summary of the corruptions which have been practised against the sense of the Qur'an by Arab religionists to suit their own purposes:

1. *A'kiffin wa-roka'is-sujud* in 2:125 and 22:26 was made to mean *bowing and prostrating* physically when, in fact, it signifies *humble in submission to God's sanctioned system.*

2. *Solaa-ta wa-atu-zakaa* is not ritual prayer and wealth tax. It means we are to *uphold our commitments and keep them pure.*

3. *Solaa* does not refer to ritual prayers. Its meaning was corrupted to become *rituals*. The Qur'an encourages personal commitment through deeds.

4. *Thor-iffin* is not walking around or *Tawwaf* around the stone idol in Mecca but the meaning is *groups or throngs of people.*

5. *A'kif-fun* is not a retreat to a house or to a mosque, but *to hold strongly to God's system* or *bayta. Wa-antum a'kiffun fi-masaajid'* in 2:187 means *and when you are devoted in submission.*

6. *Bayta* is not a physical house belonging to God..

7. *Masaajid* are not buildings but *submissions.*

8.   *Masa-jidil-lah* are not God's mosques but the submissions *prescribed by God in His system.*

9.   *Masjidil-Harami* is not 'sacred mosque'. It is the *sanctioned submission* prescribed by God.

10. *Bayti-ya* is not *My house*, but it is *My system.* God does not own a house.

11. *Hurumun* is not a pilgrimage or the pilgrim's garb. The word in 5:1 was twisted to perpetuate the invented *Haj* pilgrimage of the Arab religion. The word *Hurumun* simply means *restricted* or *forbidden.*

12. *U'mrah* is not a visit to the Stone House, but is to *promote God's prescribed submissions* or the *mas-jidil-lah.*

13. *Haj* is not a yearly pilgrimage to the Stone House. It is to take the challenge: (1) to the system (2) to deliver the message until it is accepted in society (3) to promote the sanctioned submission and (4) in the path of God (see: 3:97, 2:196, 9:19 and 4:100).

14. The accepted sense of many words from the Qur'an has been severely mutilated to suit the rituals of the man-made Arab religion. The worst distortion of God's word is in 2:196. The perception of the meaning of almost all the words in that verse has been distorted. Animals, food crops or livestock sacrifices cannot be assigned to God. Such practice is evil.

For the Muslims who believe the Qur'an is the word of God, their duty is to:

1. Find the path to the System (*bayta*) and take up the challenge (*Haj*) to promote what has been sanctioned by God in the Qur'an to establish the peacefulness or the true Islam.

2. Uphold commitments (*Solaa*), keep them pure (*zakaa*) according to God's decrees (*sha'iral-lah*) and to promote (*ya'muru*) the prescribed submissions.

3. Take the challenge (*Haj*) and promote (or *i'mara-ta*) the sanctioned submission (*masjidil-Harami*) and strive (*jahidu*) against the idol-worshippers (*mushrikeen*) and the rejecters (*wal-kafireen*) who bow and prostrate to stones, rocks and wood (and in this case falsely attribute their practice to *Islam*).

4. Not violate decrees or upset the harmony in the sanctioned system (*baytal-Harami*).

5. Live according to the sanctions in the system and uphold their obligations.

Last but not least, God's deen is not a 'religion'. Religion is what's left over once men have taken full institutional control of God's revelations. God has revealed a way of life. As we look around us, religion serves the contrary purpose – it enslaves people's mind, cultivating disorder, separating people, bound in hatred, myth and superstition – a condition which is in the temporal interests of a small ruling elite.

To readers of translations

For those many who have rejected the *Hadith* books written by men, this book represents another step in their journey on the path of God.

But the Devil says: *'I am waiting for them on your Straight Path and I will mislead all of the without exception'*. It would be inefficient of him to waste his time waiting for people who are already on the wrong path.

Perhaps those who have read the Quran could recall the verse in 7:16-17:-

> *He (the devil) said, "Since You willed that I go astray, I will always skulk on Your right path to mislead all of them. Then I will come to them from their front, from behind them, from their right and from their left. You will find the majority of them are unappreciative".*

The verse is startling, but if such people are gratified with what they understand from the translations without any careful study or verification, they are likely to be frozen along with the translator's personal understanding and beliefs which – as a rule – are taken wholesale from the very *Hadith* books the reader has rejected.

So turn away from the religionists who claim to be the champions of the religion of Islam. The only way to know about the true Islam is to read the Qur'an in its purity and use it as the criterion to judge the religionist's teachings. Do your own research to discover the distortions and put your trust in God. He is our only protector.

Do not accept anything that you yourself cannot ascertain. Your hearing, eyesight, and your heart each of them will be questioned about it. (17: 36)

Thus, if you are unable to verify, stay away from organised religion. Live a full life. The moral rule to attain a peaceful life in this world (no amount of money can buy it) is to believe with the unseen God and be an upright person for your own good. To qualify, all one needs to do is to be observant to the natural laws, lead a virtuous life by doing good deeds in this world and do what is obvious as a normal human being. God created men and women with basic instinct to understand what is good or bad. When He says 'honour your parents', we don't need any rabbis, priests, monks, or mullahs to tell us how to honour our own parents.

Lastly, 'The God our Lord needs no one' – including the rabbis, pope, ayatollahs, priests, monks, mullahs, theologies, religious scholars, saints, and spiritual leaders. These are names that you invented - you and your parents - they follow nothing except conjecture and their own opinions about the one God. God never placed any power in them. It is people who make them what and who they are. If you exercise your right to put them in power – they will remove your right and freedom immediately - then say - "*if you speak against us you are an apostate*", or "*you are an infidel*", or "*you are doomed*", and render you to be stoned to death by a true believer. Thus, *Is God alone worthy to be followed or the one who needs the guidance himself*?

Think about this carefully. Why should you be a member of any organised religion when you can be what and who you want to be - by yourself? What if you a peaceful man or a peaceful woman, truthful, kind, caring, sincere, humble, compassionate, charitable, steadfast, and loving individual - does it matter to God if you are <u>NOT</u> a member any of these clubs? Must you call yourself a Muslim or a Jew, a Hindu or a Christian, a Buddhist or a Bahai?

When we reject these earthly lords - are we rejecting GOD? Not at all! We have made the best decision in our life to severe the relationship with earthly gods and return to the true God who created us. We have more reasons to believe in Him as it opens the possibility of His system playing a role in our life. He promised that if we believe in Him alone and be committed to do good deeds and uphold our obligations sincerely, He will liberate us (men and women) as independent leaders on earth and He will endow us the *'Peacefulness'*.

We have the freedom to
choose to live by our Ego
- or -
by our Wisdom

'What we are and
who we are'

Is rendered in the
language of either One.
'We are not given the freedom
to be Both'

Printed in the United States
By Bookmasters

Printed in the United States
By Bookmasters